Essentials of environmental management

Paul Hyde and Paul Reeve

First published 2001
Second edition 2004
Third edition 2011

© Paul Hyde and Paul Reeve 2011
Printed in England by the Lavenham Press Limited

ISBN 978 0 901357 48 9

Published by IOSH Services Ltd
The Grange
Highfield Drive
Wigston
Leicestershire
LE18 1NN
UK
t +44 (0)116 257 3100
f +44 (0)116 257 3101
www.iosh.co.uk

FSC

Mixed Sources
Product group from well-managed forests and other controlled sources
www.fsc.org Cert no. SGS-COC-004865
© 1996 Forest Stewardship Council

Contents

About the authors

Paul Hyde

Paul Hyde MIEMA MIEnvSc CEnv graduated in Geography (Nottingham, 1979) and subsequently obtained an MSc in Environmental Technology (Imperial College, 1981) and an MA in Heritage Studies (Salford, 2003). He is a full member of the Institute of Environmental Management and Assessment (MIEMA), a full member of the Institution of Environmental Sciences (MIEnvSc) and a Chartered Environmentalist (CEnv). He is also a Fellow the Institute of Place Management (FIPM).

Paul has substantial experience in environmental issues at both operational and strategic levels. Since 2002 he has diversified into the visitor economy and place management, including tourism impacts, sustainable tourism, heritage interpretation and green space management. Previously, he was an environmental consultant with CSR Network (now Two Tomorrows) – a strategic consultancy which helps organisations to address the wider corporate social responsibility agenda.

Between 1993 and 1998 he was senior environmental adviser at the Engineering Employers' Federation (now EEF – the manufacturers' organisation), where he co-produced and delivered the first IEMA associate membership training course in 1996. He was also environmental adviser with the US oil company Amerada Hess (1998–2000), where he was responsible for producing the 1998 environmental report for the corporation's UK operations. He also undertook a seven-month assignment in Brazil in 2000, working on environmental management, licence applications and emergency response for Amerada Hess's new offshore exploration and onshore supply facilities. Previous experience also includes environmental roles with British Gas (1990–1993) and operational positions with British Gas, Wiggins Teape Paper and Core Laboratories.

Since 2006, Paul has been a Green Flag judge for parks and other green spaces and, since 2009, a Green Heritage Site judge. In 2008, he was chair of the One Earth Festival, held in Grosvenor Park, Chester – an event developed to raise the general public's awareness of sustainability, including nature conservation, waste and energy, fair trade and local sourcing. He is also a member of the Cheshire Regionally Important Geodiversity Sites (RIGS) group. He is currently a freelance consultant on environmental and heritage matters, operating as In-Place.

Paul Reeve

Paul Reeve CFIOSH FIEMA CEnv graduated in Environmental Science from the University of Sussex in 1981. He is a Chartered Fellow of both the Institution of Occupational Safety and Health (IOSH) and the Institute of Environmental Management and Assessment (IEMA).

Paul has considerable experience of assisting companies with ISO 14001 and BS 8555 and integrating health, safety and environmental management systems. He has been actively involved in developing sustainability policy and practice in the engineering, public transport and, currently, construction sectors (including some early planning of aspects of the 2012 Olympics). Paul is also an experienced trainer on both IOSH and IEMA environmental courses, and he advises leading certification bodies on health, safety, environmental and sustainability issues.

Paul is head of safety and environment at the Electrical Contractors' Association, based in London, and an environmental adviser to the Specialist Engineering Contractors' Group. His current role includes supporting the implementation of 'low to no carbon' measures, particularly for use in existing buildings, and the adoption of more sustainable industry practice, notably in the areas of waste minimisation and carbon footprinting. Paul is a regular contributor to health, safety and environmental publications, including IOSH's *Safety and Health Practitioner* magazine and *The Environmentalist*, the IEMA journal.

Paul was head of safety and environment at the Engineering Employers' Federation until 2001, and in the mid-1990s he conceived and co-wrote the first course leading directly to associate membership of IEMA. Paul also chaired the British Standards Institution's pioneering group on environmental management systems in engineering and, as an adviser to the UK government's 'Envirowise' programme, he compiled the guidance on implementing environmental management systems for that sector. He has also chaired the Engineering Council's sustainability awards panel.

Paul's previous experience includes a period as executive director of the Chemical Industries Association's 'Responsible care' initiative, which promotes continual improvement in health, safety and environmental performance.

Paul is a Chartered Chemist, having obtained an MSc in surface chemistry in 1983 (University of Bristol). In recent years, he has had several articles published on the need for sufficient hazard information to support the responsible application of nanotechnology.

Introduction

The widespread development – and application – of environmental management is still only some two decades old. Most of the landmark developments – such as ISO 14001, the rise of sustainable development and corporate social responsibility, 'carbon footprinting' and, notably, a fully fledged environmental management profession – have occurred since the early 1990s.

Even so, environmental management is now a well-established activity in all types of organisation.

Many industries now realise that safety-related process accidents can lead to major environmental impacts, and that both safe and environmentally responsible products are vital for good corporate relations.

Some organisations are already applying environmental management as part of corporate risk management, improving stakeholder relations and the environmental performance of products and services. The vast majority find that environmental management delivers improved process efficiency and significant cost reductions, in addition to risk control and legal compliance.

The development of environmental management has led to a rapid expansion in the number of environmental management professionals. For example, the Institute of Environmental Management and Assessment (IEMA) currently has over 15,000 members, while the Institution of Occupational Safety and Health (IOSH) recognises that thousands of its members now cover health, safety *and* environment in their everyday remit. Increasingly, other professions also require access to environmental know-how and grounding in environmental management techniques.

To get the most out of environmental management, organisations need people who can understand, communicate and apply its essential and, in some cases, distinctive principles. To help provide these skills to individuals and their employers, there is a range of courses available from leading professional and academic bodies.

This book is designed to be an essential reference for environmental management course candidates. It provides a definitive text on the principles of environmental management, tailor-made for professional training to any level (notably IOSH and IEMA examinations), or as part of higher academic courses.

However, *Essentials* is also intended as a useful and ongoing resource for all safety, environmental and related professionals.

In summary, this book:
- considers the interaction between organisations (notably businesses) and the environment, including a comprehensive overview of key environmental issues and pressures
- explains the key management tools for both assessing an organisation's environmental aspects and impacts and checking on environmental performance
- maps out the key environmental management processes, including setting environmental objectives and targets and communicating with key stakeholders as part of the 'plan , do, check and act' management cycle
- provides support to any organisation seeking to model its environmental management system (EMS) on ISO 14001
- explores how organisations can build on environmental management address wider issues, especially sustainability, the supply chain, carbon management and the interface with corporate social responsibility, including health and safety.

The authors, Paul Hyde and Paul Reeve, combine extensive and wide-ranging practical experience of the application of environmental management with that of course training. *Essentials* provides a user-friendly framework which sets out the key principles and approaches underpinning this important professional discipline.

1: Business and the environment

1.1 The 'business–environment' interaction

The 'environment' is everything that surrounds us. Its physical, chemical and biological elements are crucial to life on earth. The environment can be subdivided into three main components – air, water and land. These components (also known as 'media') provide the conditions for the development and growth of communities of organisms – plants and animals (including humans). These communities depend on the complex and dynamic inter-relationships between physical, chemical and biological factors.

1.1.1 The environment – the ultimate resource
The natural environment is fundamental to human activity and wellbeing. It is the ultimate resource for human society, providing air and water, minerals and biological materials (including food). It is also a 'sink' for the unwanted by-products of society (wastes).

Businesses and other organisations, as a key feature of modern society, process the earth's resources to provide a vast, and increasingly sophisticated, range of goods and services. The use of the environment is summarised in Figure 1.1.1.

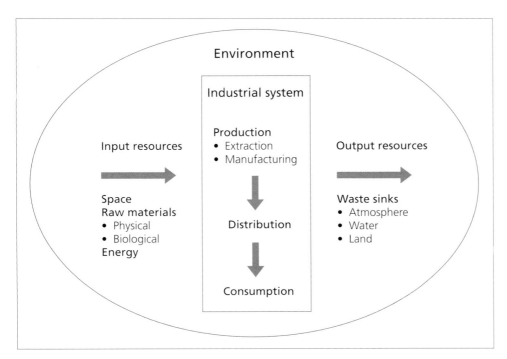

Figure 1.1.1
Environmental resources

This use of the environmental resources leads to changes in the environment – known as 'environmental impacts'. Environmental impacts can vary both in scale and in the type of impact. They can be immediate, from a single event (eg a dam project which floods a large valley), or gradual and from a multiplicity of sources (eg the build-up of CFCs and other gases from numerous sources, which damage the stratospheric ozone layer). The changes can be positive as well as adverse, eg measures that create habitats which help conserve wildlife. Specific environmental impacts are considered in Chapter 1.3.

The dominant role of humans in modifying the natural environment, particularly through agricultural practices, urbanisation and industrialisation, has given rise to terms such as the 'man-made environment' and the 'built environment'. These man-made environments can be considered to have cultural, heritage or other amenity or economic value. Protection of heritage and amenity can be as much of an environmental management issue for some organisations as ecological protection.

1.1.2 How organisations interact with the environment

Environmental management is the process by which an organisation identifies its important environmental interactions (known as environmental 'aspects') and acts in a way that seeks to minimise its negative environmental impacts (for definitions, see Table 1.1.1). The identification, assessment and management of these interactions and their resulting impacts are dealt with in more detail in subsequent chapters. In this chapter, however, the key concepts are briefly introduced.

ISO 14001, the international environmental management system (EMS) standard, defines 'environment' as the "surroundings in which an organisation operates, including air, water, land, natural resources, flora, fauna, humans and their inter-relation".

Table 1.1.1
ISO 14001
definitions –
aspects and
impacts

Term	Definition
Environmental aspect	Element of an organisation's activities, products or services which can interact with the environment.
Environmental impact	Any change to the environment, whether adverse or beneficial, wholly or partially resulting from an organisation's environmental aspects.

Different organisations have different environmental aspects (interactions) and impacts. The aspects and impacts will depend on factors such as:
- the activity, product and service mix of the organisation
- the location of its operations (proximity to sensitive environments, means of access to markets and distribution choices)
- the choice of its key suppliers (location, distance, nature of the materials/energy supplied, environmental sensitivities, and the environmental performance of the supplier).

An important distinction is that between 'direct' and 'indirect' aspects. Direct environmental aspects are those that arise directly from the organisation's operations. They are interactions over which the organisation has direct control and responsibility. For example, in a manufacturing company they would arise from manufacturing processes and activities taking place on site. Indirect aspects are those that arise from the activities of others with whom the organisation deals – typically along the supply chain. Indirect aspects will be subject to varying degrees of influence from the manufacturer. Indirect aspects can be extremely important to manufacturing operations, but they can have particular significance in service organisations, eg banking.

A useful approach to determining the environmental interactions of an organisation is to identify the various inputs and outputs of the key activities, products and services. Usually, these will fall into the main categories listed in Figure 1.1.2.

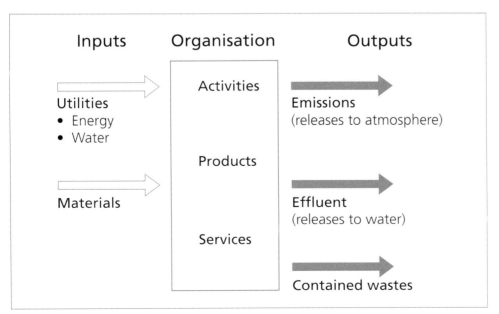

Figure 1.1.2
Typical generic environmental interactions (aspects)

The list of inputs and outputs can be expanded. For example, the land itself can be a key input, particularly for a new development, or an output if it is a decommissioned site. Noise and vibration might also be relevant outputs.

It is also useful to distinguish between planned (intended) events and unplanned events. Planned events are a part of normal operations while unplanned events are typically associated with incidents or unintended operating practices. Examples include those listed in Table 1.1.2.

Table 1.1.2
Planned and
unplanned aspects

Planned aspects	Unplanned aspects
• Outputs or inputs arising from normal operations, eg production wastes, fuel combustion emissions, use of energy, water and materials • Releases that are maintained below a regulatory requirement or internally set standard/target • Planned clearance of land	• Incidents such as leaks or spills, fires or explosions • Unintended situations where regulatory standards are not complied with/emission or discharge limits are exceeded, eg equipment malfunction, operator error • Accidental felling of protected trees

Waste oil, for example, should be contained until it is either reprocessed and recovered or responsibly disposed of. However, an incident leading to loss of containment (eg tank corrosion or vandalism) would lead to a spill (accidental release) of the waste oil that could reach the drains or a watercourse or seep into the ground. The prospect of an oil spill represents a *potential* environmental aspect rather than an actual aspect (unless, of course, the event actually happens).

An organisation can have a large number of actual (and potential) aspects and impacts, and it is essential to know which ones are 'significant'. There is no standard method for establishing which environmental aspects are significant. However, those organisations aiming for, or working to, an EMS standard (such as ISO 14001) are required to be systematic and logical in their approach to assessing significance. Generally, the significant environmental aspects of an organisation should be those that:
• are subject (or potentially subject) to regulatory control or a code of practice signed up to by the organisation
• are of particular concern to key stakeholders
• have (or potentially have) a demonstrable impact on the environment.

This key area is further considered in Chapter 2.2.

1.1.3 Environmental receptors

An organisation's environmental aspects can affect a wide range of environmental 'receptors'. Example releases (environmental aspects) and receptors are shown in Table 1.1.3.

Releases	Environmental medium	Final receptors

• Emissions from combustion
 • Evaporative losses
 • Dust
	• Atmosphere	• Humans
		   ○ Neighbours
		   ○ General population
		   ○ Sensitive individuals/ communities

• Effluent discharge
 • Leaks and spills
 • Dumped waste
 • Windblown waste
	• Water (rivers, lakes, sea, ocean, aquifers)
	
	 • Land (plus ground water)
		• Property
		   ○ Buildings and structures
		   ○ Crops and domestic livestock
		
		 • Wildlife (plants and animals)
		   ○ Conservation species and habitats
		   ○ Sensitive species and habitats

Table 1.1.3 Examples of releases and receptors

For construction activities and extractive industries (eg quarrying, oil and gas production) the use of physical space can also be an important aspect, affecting other land or sea users or disrupting natural habitats (as receptors).

1.1.4 Resource productivity – a key goal

Because the environment supplies resources such as materials and energy and provides disposal sinks for wastes (gaseous, liquid and solid), environmental management should put a high priority on 'resource productivity'. This is returned to again in Chapter 5.2, which deals with sustainability.

In simple terms, improving resource productivity means minimising the use of resource inputs and the generation of waste outputs for a given amount of goods and services provided. Within this overall environmental management framework, organisations will need to decide on priority issues for action, depending on specific regulatory, stakeholder or environmental risks.

1.2 Introduction to natural systems

The earth's natural systems are extensive and complex. To illustrate, in simple terms, how natural systems operate, this chapter provides a brief overview of the following:
- ecosystems and food chains
- energy flows and biochemical cycles
- the hydrological cycle
- the carbon cycle.

1.2.1 Ecosystems
The natural world is made up of ecological systems, often referred to as 'ecosystems'. It is possible to regard the entire earth as an ecosystem, but the planet can also be viewed as a complex series of ecosystems ranging from microscopic systems to extensive global systems such as oceans. These systems interlink and provide the basic processes that, ultimately, sustain life on earth.

'Habitat' is a similar term to ecosystem – definitions are given in Table 1.2.1.

Table 1.2.1 Definitions – ecosystem and habitat

Ecosystem	Habitat
A community of interdependent organisms and the physical and chemical environment they inhabit.	The specific environment in which an organism lives. This is shared with other organisms in a complex set of inter-relationships.

Examples of ecosystems (or habitats) include estuaries, coral reefs, lagoons, woodlands, forests, rivers, lakes, heath and moorlands. Cropland and grazing land (as well as towns and cities) can also be regarded as ecosystems.

Natural ecosystems are normally complex in terms of the number of species, inter-relationships between the different species, and the inter-relationships between the biological and non-living elements. Ecosystems require an energy source to enable them to function, and for the vast bulk of ecosystems, the initial energy source is the sun.

In simple terms, ecosystems have a set of basic components, as outlined in Table 1.2.2.

Component	Key processes
Energy source	For most systems this is light energy from the sun.
Mineral/nutrient source	This is obtained from the 'abiotic' substances in the environment – inorganic matter and non-living organic compounds. In terrestrial ecosystems this is largely concentrated in the soil.
Producers	For most systems this is mostly green plants. They utilise energy in the form of sunlight and take up simple inorganic substances from the physicochemical medium in which they live (typically soil for land-based systems, sediments or water for aqueous ecosystems). These energy and material inputs are transformed into complex organic materials in the cells of green plants.
Consumers	Consumers are mostly animals, including humans, which intake organic material as food. This is used for energy or rearranged biologically to create other complex organic materials. There are different types of consumer: • herbivores, which feed on plants • carnivores, which feed on animals • omnivores, which feed on plants and animals (humans fall into this category).
Decomposers	These are micro-organisms such as bacteria and fungi. They consume organic matter, breaking down the complex organic molecules into simpler forms. This process releases nutrients which can be used again for subsequent green plant growth. They are nature's recycling facility.

Table 1.2.2 The basic components of an ecosystem

From the table above it can be seen that ecosystems contain 'food chains'. Examples of food chains are given in Table 1.2.3.

Ecosystem	Producer	Primary consumer	Secondary consumer
Grassland	Grass	Mice	Hawks
Grassland	Grass	Cattle	Humans
Sea	Phytoplankton	Zooplankton	Large fish
Food chain ···→			

Table 1.2.3 Examples of food chains

The links in a food chain are interdependent. Disruption at one level will affect the entire chain. For example, if producers are reduced in number (eg through use of land for another purpose, disruption of water supply or pollution), the food supply for the primary consumers will be decreased. This is likely to reduce (or redistribute) the population of primary consumers, which in turn will affect the availability of food for secondary consumers.

Food chains also provide a pathway for the transfer of pollutant substances from air, land or water to organisms (receptors) higher up the food chain, including humans.

Figure 1.2.1
The basic elements of an ecosystem

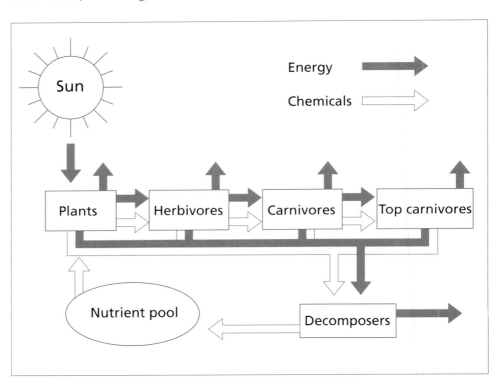

Ecosystems contain two fundamental processes – the flow of energy through the system and the cycling of chemicals (see Figure 1.2.1).

The cycling of chemicals occurs because of the key role of decomposers in the system. Decomposers convert complex organic substances into simpler ones that make mineral nutrients available to plants again. For land-based ecosystems, this tends to be via the soil nutrient pool and for aqueous-based ecosystems, it is either from sediment or minerals dissolved in the water.

Energy is required to drive ecosystems. However, energy is progressively lost from these systems – mostly as heat, which is dispersed in the earth's atmosphere. Each link in the food chain – whether green plant (using solar energy), herbivore, carnivore or decomposer (using energy contained in organic food, ie calories in carbohydrate matter) – uses a substantial amount of the energy available for biological functions such as digesting and absorbing the food, respiring, growing and (for animals) moving. This energy is released as heat. Because of this, only some 10 to 20 per cent of energy is normally transferred from one level to the next in the food chain.

This means that for only a few top carnivores to survive in natural systems there is a requirement for a much larger mass of animal prey below them in the food chain and below that, an even larger mass of green plant food to support the prey. This helps to explain why human land use and land management practices are affecting biodiversity, as agriculture and urbanisation compete with natural habitats.

1.2.3 The hydrological cycle

Water is vital to all life on earth. It is important to understand the hydrological cycle (see Figure 1.2.2) since it describes the various mechanisms and routes that allow water to circulate in the environment. Furthermore, the cycle provides a mechanism for the transport and transfer of pollutants in the environment, ie it provides pathways to receptors.

Since water is a fundamental resource for ecosystems and human society, any physical disturbance to the cycle can have profound environmental impacts. Such disruption is occurring directly through human activities such as water extraction, drainage of wetlands and damming of valleys to create reservoirs for water supply or hydroelectric schemes. Also, there is increased concern that the cycle is being disrupted, potentially profoundly, through global climate change associated with greenhouse gas emissions from human activities. This could lead to increased incidents of floods or droughts and changing rainfall patterns in different parts of the globe.

The main constituents of the water (hydrological) cycle are considered in Table 1.2.4.

Figure 1.2.2
The hydrological cycle

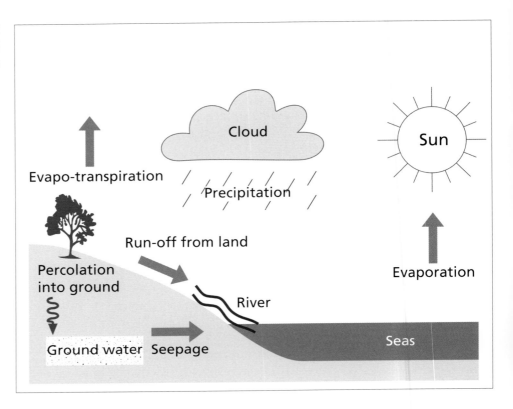

Constituent	Key processes
Atmosphere	Water vapour condenses and falls to the earth's surface (land or sea) as rain, sleet, snow or hail (precipitation).
Land surface	On reaching the land surface, some of the water: • runs off the surface to enter streams and rivers • is absorbed by the ground • is retained in soil and plants • evaporates or is transpired (respired or lost by plants) back to the atmosphere to complete the cycle.
Surface drainage	Streams and rivers flow towards the sea, and some of the water will be: • temporarily stored in lakes and ponds • evaporated back to the atmosphere to complete the cycle.
Ground water	Water will seep through the ground, and some will: • be stored in sediments and strata (aquifers) • be taken up by plant roots (and transpired to the atmosphere to complete the cycle) • seep back to the surface to flow into streams and rivers.
Seas/oceans	Seas and oceans receive: • the flow of water from river systems • some precipitation directly from the atmosphere. On reaching the marine environment, this water will be transported by currents and tides. Water evaporates from the seas into the atmosphere, to complete the cycle.

Table 1.2.4
The main constituents of the water cycle

1.2.4 Carbon cycle

The carbon cycle is another indispensable natural cycle. A simplified representation of this complex cycle is presented in Figure 1.2.3.

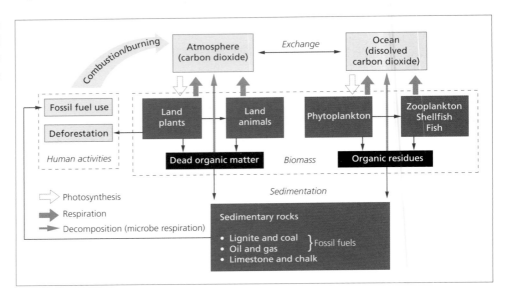

Figure 1.2.3 Simplified schematic of the carbon cycle

Gaseous carbon dioxide (CO_2) in the atmosphere is converted into organic compounds by the process of photosynthesis in plants. The carbon is then stored in the biomass of the plants during their life. Herbivores obtain organic carbon compounds by eating plants and carnivores obtain organic carbon by eating herbivores. When the plants or animals die, the dead organic matter is consumed by decomposer organisms, which return CO_2 to the atmosphere.

An equivalent cycle occurs in the ocean environment (and to a smaller extent in other aqueous environments). CO_2 is soluble in seawater and is used by phytoplankton (small and microscopic free-floating aquatic plants) in photosynthesis. Zooplankton and other marine animals consume the phytoplankton and carnivorous marine animals consume these marine herbivores. This marine life dies and is decomposed, returning CO_2 to the seawater.

In both systems, the respiration of plants, herbivores and carnivores also returns CO_2 to the atmosphere or ocean.

However, not all the carbon is returned to the atmosphere or seawater by decomposition/respiration. A proportion is laid down in sediments either as hydrocarbon matter or as calcium carbonate (from shells and other skeletal material). Over geological time the hydrocarbon matter is converted into coal, oil or natural gas (the fossil fuels) and the calcium carbonate forms limestone or chalk. This means that significant amounts of carbon are locked up in such geological deposits.

Human activities are altering the carbon cycle. The combustion of fossil fuels in power generation, industry, homes and vehicles is returning carbon (in the form of CO_2) to the atmosphere from the deposits built up over geological timescales. Deforestation is another activity leading to the return of CO_2 to the atmosphere through the burning of timber and undergrowth and the resultant degradation of soils. As will be seen in Chapter 1.3, the CO_2 released from what would otherwise be carbon 'stores' (geological formations and forest ecosystem biomass) is of major concern, since there is substantial evidence that the build-up of CO_2 is contributing to global climate change. As will be considered elsewhere in this book (in particular sections 1.3.4, 5.1.5 and 5.2.9), there other types of greenhouse gas (eg methane and refrigerants) that are also adding to the greenhouse effect and global climate change. Furthermore, these gases are powerful global warming agents (see Table 2.4.2). A molecule of methane, for example, has a global warming potential 21 times more powerful than a molecule of CO_2.

1.3 Overview of key environmental concerns

Environmental concerns range from local effects (such as the effect of noise on neighbours) to global issues (such as the generation of CO_2 from business and other sources, leading to global climate change). Fundamental to environmental management, however, is the growing concern that the earth does not have an unlimited capacity to supply resources or to assimilate wastes.

1.3.1 Sustainability and carrying capacity

Pressures on the earth's natural systems have led to concern about these systems' ability to maintain quality of life or even to support present and future human populations. There is concern that the 'carrying capacity' of the earth is at risk of being exceeded both by the sheer growth in demand for resources (including 'sinks' to dispose of wastes) and by the degradation of essential resources through the impact of human activities. This is summarised in Figure 1.3.1.

Figure 1.3.1
Interaction of the industrial system with the earth's carrying capacity

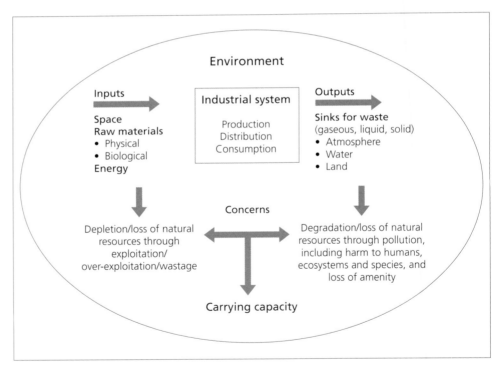

Carrying capacity is a key sustainability issue (for definitions, see Table 1.3.1). The link to environmental management at the level of the organisation is that *everyone* contributes in some way to local, regional or global environmental impacts. Organisations can identify whether they have significant environmental interactions that contribute to these concerns. By managing these interactions, they can help move society towards more sustainable production and consumption practices.

Sustainability, as an overarching issue, is returned to in Chapter 5.2.

Carrying capacity	Sustainability
Ecologically, this refers to the maximum number of organisms that can be supported by an environment's resource base or, on a global scale, the earth's natural systems. In human terms, quality of life issues are an integral part of the picture so that it considers population size but also levels of economic activity and of acceptable wellbeing.	A fundamental requirement of the sustainability agenda is to ensure that the needs of the world's future generations are not jeopardised by those of the current population. A key threat is that human activity on a 'business-as-usual' basis will significantly disrupt or damage natural systems so that the earth's carrying capacity is both exceeded and degraded.

Table 1.3.1
Carrying capacity and sustainability: definitions

1.3.2 The nature of resources

Resources are essentially those things that are of use to society – whether to provide water, food, shelter, heat or light – and other goods and services that offer required levels of human comfort and amenity. Resources can also include waste 'sinks'.

There is a fundamental distinction between those resources which can be considered as renewable and those as non-renewable. This is set out in Table 1.3.2.

Table 1.3.2
Renewable and
non-renewable
resources

Type	Characteristics	Examples	Concerns

Renewable (flow)	Resources that can be replaced in immediate or short timescales (and at least within the scale of a human lifetime) by natural processes that tend to be related to planetary cycles powered by solar radiation flow.	• Vegetation
		  ○ Forests (timber, amenity, new medicines)
		  ○ Crops (food, organic fuels, oils and fibres)
		• Animals
		  ○ Wildlife (amenity)
		  ○ Domestic livestock (food, fibres, fertiliser)
		  ○ Fish stocks (food, oil, fertiliser)
		• Water (drinking water, industrial fluid, amenity, disposal medium)
		• Wind, sunlight (energy)
			Availability depends on the balance between the rate of use and the rate of replacement. These resources can be over-exploited so that they are progressively degraded and depleted, causing availability problems in terms of both quality and quantity, eg over-harvesting of fish stocks.

Non-renewable (stock)	Resources that have been created (effectively stocked up) over a geological timespan and which can only be replaced over similar timescales. In terms of current population and for generations in the foreseeable future their supply is, therefore, finite.	• Fossil fuels
		  ○ Oil, gas, coal (energy, petrochemicals)
		• Mineral ores
		  ○ Iron, bauxite, platinum (metals)
		• Stone and aggregates (construction materials)
			In human terms, these are finite resources and therefore will ultimately be depleted. The depletion timescale is dependent on the amount of resource remaining and the rate of exploitation and use.

Understandably, resource depletion is a major concern. Environmental management practices should seek to:
- reduce wastage of resources (non-renewable and renewable)
- consider renewable alternatives to non-renewable energy and materials
- ensure renewable resources are replaced (eg plant new trees to offset cut timber) or regenerated (eg maintaining fish stocks at levels that allow them to breed and grow).

Note that for a specific resource base the better quality, more accessible reserves are normally used first, with the exploitation of poorer quality reserves in more remote areas occurring later. This increases environmental impacts as additional energy inputs and waste outputs are required to obtain useful amounts of the required resource. It also means that even before a resource is exhausted, overall resource productivity tends to decline.

1.3.3 Pollution

'Pollution' is the general term for a range of adverse environmental impacts. It results from the introduction of substances or energy into the environment that can be detrimental to human health or comfort, harm valuable species and ecosystems, interfere with the food chain, damage property or degrade amenity.

In the 2008 EU Directive on Integrated Pollution Prevention and Control, pollution is defined as: "… the direct or indirect introduction, as a result of human activity, of substances, vibrations, heat or noise into the air, water or land which may be harmful to human health or the quality of the environment, result in damage to material property, or impair or interfere with amenities and other legitimate uses of the environment."

Pollution is an increment added by humans to natural processes and cycles. In other words, it arises as a result of outputs from human activities such as releases of atmospheric emissions, effluent discharges and solid wastes into the environment. In addition to substances, these outputs include noise, vibration, heat and light as forms of waste energy. Once released, outputs can follow pathways provided by nature (eg wind, rain, flowing water, permeable ground, the food chain) to have an adverse impact on one or more parts of the environment (receptors) that are sensitive to them. These impacts can occur over the short or longer term, depending on the nature of the pollutant and the sensitivity of the receptor. The source–pathway–receptor relationship is summarised in Figure 1.3.2.

Natural inputs of similar substances (or energy) are not considered to be pollutants, although emissions (eg from volcanoes) can lead to major environmental effects. However, since such natural inputs are not under the control of organisations, they are usually excluded from the type of environmental management covered by this book.

Figure 1.3.2
The source–
pathway–receptor
relationship

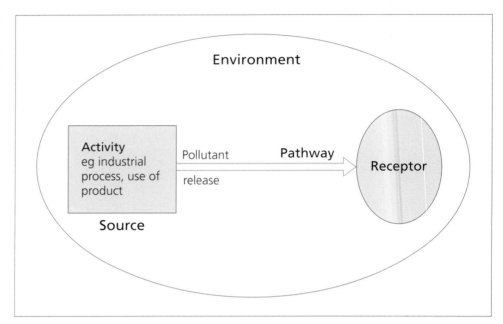

Because the environment is complex there can be multiple impacts from a given pollutant and the distinction between receptors and pathways can be blurred. For example, environmental media – air, water, land – can be both pathways *and* receptors, as can organisms in a food chain.

The environment has a certain capacity to deal with pollutants through natural processes. For example, some organic material introduced into a watercourse will eventually degrade through the action of micro-organisms, while gaseous emissions can be dispersed into low concentrations by the wind and atmospheric turbulence. However, this ability to cope with pollution is dependent on the type of pollutant, the volume released and the nature of the receiving environmental medium – air, water or land.

Certain substances, however, are persistent and do not readily degrade. Some substances with long environmental lifetimes – for example, hazardous substances which build up in the human food chain, CO_2 (associated with climate change) and CFCs (associated with ozone depletion) – are linked with major environmental concerns.

Furthermore, the total amount of pollutants released from multiple sources can mean that ambient concentrations reach critical levels even if individual emissions are small. For example, emissions from motor vehicles together with the contribution from domestic or small business sources can lead to serious local pollution. Pollution is not just a question of emissions from large industrial installations.

1.3.4 Major environmental issues
Table 1.3.3 provides a summary of key environmental concerns, all of which fall under the wider sustainability agenda introduced above. Many are inter-related.

Concern	Description of impact	Important aspects may include...
Climate change	There is substantial evidence that the accumulation of greenhouse gases such as CO_2 and methane (which absorb re-emitted infrared radiation from the earth's surface) is modifying the earth's energy balance, causing net global warming. If such emissions continue on a 'business as usual' basis, models suggest that CO_2 levels may double by the end of this century. Note: CO_2 molecules have a long atmospheric life span, typically more than 100 years. Also, the other greenhouse gases have higher global warming potentials than CO_2 (molecule for molecule) – for example, methane is 21 times more powerful (see Table 2.4.2). Temperature rises could lead to complex and profound impacts, including a rise in sea levels leading to flooding of low lying coasts, extreme weather events (droughts, storms) and a shift in vegetation zones and hydrological systems – with consequent impacts in biodiversity, agricultural productivity, famine, disease and human migration.	emissions of: • carbon dioxide • methane • nitrous oxide • perfluorocarbons • hydrofluorocarbons • sulphur hexafluoride.

Table 1.3.3
Key environmental concerns

Table 1.3.3
Key environmental
concerns
continued

Concern	Description of impact	Important aspects may include...
Stratospheric ozone depletion	Some man-made gases containing chlorine and bromine do not break down readily in the lower atmosphere and so persist for many years (some longer than 100 years). These gases spread throughout the atmosphere and eventually reach the stratosphere, where they are broken down by ultraviolet radiation, releasing free chlorine and bromine atoms. Chain reactions caused by these free atoms increase the conversion of ozone molecules (O_3) to oxygen (O_2). Such ozone depletion is a major concern because the high altitude ozone layer protects the earth's surface by filtering out excess ultraviolet (UV) radiation from the sun. As the layer is depleted, increased levels of UV radiation reach the surface, where it can damage genetic material, increase the risk of cancer and cataracts in humans and animals, damage plants and reduce crop yields.	emissions of: • chlorofluorocarbons • hydrochlorofluorocarbons • carbon tetrachloride • methyl chloroform • methyl bromide • halons • 1,1,1-trichloroethane. Note that key ozone-depleting substances are now banned.

Concern	Description of impact	Important aspects may include...
Acid deposition	Certain gases react in the atmosphere to become acids, increasing the acidity of atmospheric moisture. Gases such as sulphur dioxide and nitrogen oxides are oxidised, particularly in the presence of metals on airborne particulates and by ozone, hydrogen peroxide and ammonia, which act as catalysts. The acidified moisture returns to the earth's surface as acid rain, acid snow or acid fog. This can occur hundreds of miles from the source of the pollution. This deposition results in the acidification of receiving waters and soils, particularly in areas that are already acidic. Areas with alkaline geology normally neutralise the acidity. The acidification of soils mobilises aluminium ions that reach watercourses and, together with enhanced acidity, are toxic to fish. The acidification of soils has also been implicated in forest degradation and the accelerated weathering of building materials.	emissions of: • sulphur dioxide • nitrogen oxide • nitrogen dioxide • hydrogen fluoride • hydrogen chloride.

Table 1.3.3
Key environmental concerns
continued

Concern	Description of impact	Important aspects may include...
Tropospheric ozone creation	Oxides of nitrogen and volatile organics undergo a series of complex reactions in sunlight to form ozone at ground level. The photochemical reactions also produce peroxyacetyl nitrate (PAN) and aldehydes to give a complex mix of secondary pollutants referred to as photochemical smog. Ozone at ground level damages plants and certain materials, causes eye and lung irritation (it is implicated in increased levels of asthma and other respiratory disease) and contributes to acidification processes. Its formation is particularly prevalent in clear, stable atmospheric conditions and where the terrain constrains air movement, eg areas surrounded by high ground.	emissions of: • nitrogen oxide • nitrogen dioxide • volatile organic compounds/unburnt hydrocarbons, including alkanes, alkenes and methane.
General air quality	Deterioration in local air quality through the build-up of a range of pollutants, including a complex mixture of acid species, ozone and other photochemical pollutants but also others such as particulates, carbon monoxide and traces of various toxic substances such as benzene (which is carcinogenic). Still atmospheric conditions can trap pollutants to form smogs. There is a distinction between summertime smog where photochemical ozone, PAN and aldehydes predominate, and wintertime smog where acid species, particulates, carbon monoxide and traces of toxic substances build up. These have a variety of health and amenity impacts.	emissions of: • particulates (smoke and dusts) • carbon monoxide • nitrogen oxides • sulphur dioxide • volatile organics • benzene • lead.

Concern	Description of impact	Important aspects may include...
Water pollution	Contamination of water resources by a large range of pollutants. Depending on the pollutant, the body of water and other factors, a range of effects such as eutrophication (supply of excess nutrients), low oxygen levels (excess organic matter), presence of toxic substances, presence of unsightly or odorous matter or general degradation of water quality are possible. These can result in loss of amenity (eg fishing, water sports, nature reserves), inability to use water for drinking purposes and a general reduction in biodiversity. The water environment is also an important pathway to other receptors.	discharges of: • suspended solids • nitrates and phosphates • hazardous substances • oil • solvents • heavy metals • persistent organics • pesticides • organic matter • litter.
Contaminated land	Contamination of land by a large range of pollutants. Land is typically contaminated through historic practices such as the dumping of hazardous wastes. It can also occur through present day incidents such as spills and leaks of hazardous substances, or fires (hose water can spread contamination). The presence of contaminating substances poses a variety of risks to users of the land and can lead to the contamination of adjacent watercourses and ground water (the latter being particularly difficult to remediate).	accumulations of: • hazardous substances • hazardous wastes, eg. heavy metals, asbestos, combustible and explosive materials, toxic substances.

Table 1.3.3
Key environmental concerns
continued

Table 1.3.3
Key environmental
concerns
continued

Concern	Description of impact	Important aspects may include...
Biodiversity	Biodiversity concerns the variety of life on earth. It is reflected in the diversity of habitats, of species of plants and animals, and of genetic diversity. Biodiversity is a key part of the ecological balance that helps the planet to function. Also, biodiversity guarantees the supply of biological resources, including materials, food supplies and amenity value. It includes protection of habitats and species that are endangered. A wide range of interactions can affect biodiversity, eg pollutant releases, land clearance and physical alteration or human presence. It is strongly inter-related to other environmental concerns, eg climate change and water pollution.	• land take • land use changes • land management • polluting releases • pesticides • noise and vibration • major incidents • water extraction • drainage • disturbance.
Resource depletion	Renewable resources can be over-exploited when utilisation exceeds replacement. The demand for non-renewable resources is generally accelerating so that depletion timescales are shortening. Also, waste generation is not being minimised sufficiently and waste items and materials are not being used optimally as resources through reuse and recycling.	use of: • minerals • fossil fuels • water • biomass. generation of waste.
Waste containment and disposal	The mounting volume of waste (notably due to the 'throw-away society') is causing increasing difficulties. Available landfill volume is becoming scarce and the incineration of wastes can be subject to local community opposition because of concerns regarding atmospheric releases. Waste generation also contributes to resource depletion. The safe long-term disposal of hazardous wastes is another major concern (particularly for radioactive wastes).	generation of: • large volumes of contained solid and liquid wastes • hazardous wastes • radioactive wastes • wastes that could be used as material inputs.

Concern	Description of impact	Important aspects may include...
Nuisance	Interference with another's use and enjoyment of the environment (including loss of amenity) through something that bothers or causes distress or damage to that person or which degrades property, eg noise or light at night disturbing sleeping patterns of neighbours, or improperly contained food waste that encourages vermin.	• noise • vibration • light • smoke, dust and fumes • accumulations of waste • litter • visual appearance • odours.
Hazardous substances	Certain substances are of particular concern because of a range of hazardous properties – for example, toxicity or carcinogenicity. Certain compounds persist in the environment and bioaccumulate (build up in organisms, especially those near the top of the food chain) with a range of toxic effects. Radioactive materials are an important and distinct category of hazardous substances.	• heavy metals • organochlorine compounds • pesticides • dioxins • endocrine disruptors • radioactive substances • asbestos • certain nanomaterials, eg carbon nanotubes.
Major incidents	There is the potential for large-scale events which result in acute (short to medium term) damage to local environments. These can involve the loss of human life, the death of fauna and flora, and possibly longer-term effects to wider areas and populations – particularly where there are sensitive receptors.	• oil spills • chemical spills and fires • gas explosions • radioactive incidents.
Genetically modified organisms	There are concerns, not universally accepted, about the risk of genetically modified organisms (GMOs) disrupting natural populations leading to unexpected biological and ecological effects, including the possibility of new diseases and weeds.	genetically modified: • plants • animals • microbes.

Table 1.3.3
Key environmental concerns
continued

1.4 Pressures and instruments for change

Effective environmental management requires effective 'change management'. The pressures for change may come from a variety of organisations, groups or individuals that have an interest in the business or organisation in question. The collective term for these interested parties is 'stakeholders'.

1.4.1 Stakeholder pressure and an organisation's 'operating space'

Examples of key stakeholders affecting an organisation are shown in Figure 1.4.1.

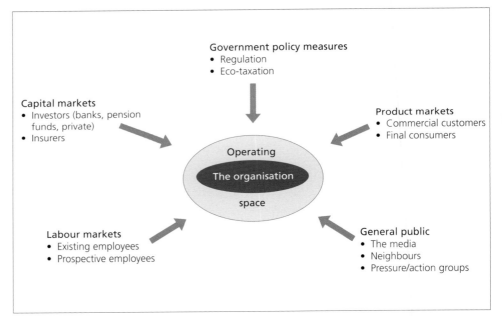

Figure 1.4.1
Sources of pressure on an organisation's 'operating space'

The views and requirements of stakeholders affect how the organisation can operate. Stakeholder pressures can be thought of as affecting the organisation's 'operating space'. This is what it can or cannot do without encountering difficulties in terms of:
- the law
- attracting capital
- keeping existing customers and gaining new business
- retaining staff and attracting new recruits
- being the focus of community or green group action
- receiving 'bad press'.

While legal requirements imposed by the statutory environmental protection authorities are of paramount importance, businesses are increasingly coming into contact with other stakeholders on environmental issues. Such contact can arise from environmental requirements in contracts, liaison with the local community or questions raised by investors, insurers and employees.

Addressing the issues raised by stakeholders is a key element of environmental management – it can include understanding what the issues are, assessing the implications for the organisation in terms of actions and constraints, and communicating on both progress and difficulties (including any conflicts of interest). Increasingly, environmental management is being integrated into various organisations' corporate social responsibility agendas.

The principal stakeholders and their interest in an organisation's environmental policies and practices are given in Table 1.4.1.

Table 1.4.1 Stakeholders and their interest in environmental issues

Stakeholder		Environmental interest
Government and its agencies	Government	Wants businesses to help achieve environmental policy objectives, comply with the spirit and certainly the letter of environmental law, and innovate to achieve social, economic and environmental progress.
	Regulatory authorities	Require that businesses under their jurisdiction comply with regulatory requirements, can readily demonstrate compliance and are capable of continually delivering compliance.
Product markets	Business customers	May be exerting pressure on suppliers and contractors to demonstrate responsible management of environmental issues. They may be establishing specific environmental performance requirements for products or services. If the requirements are not met this could result in loss of business.
	Consumers	Some, but not all, consumers are currently actively seeking green products. Many consumers are less inclined to buy from businesses associated with poor environmental records or related problems. Businesses that develop products showing beneficial features, which include improved environmental performance, should be able to improve their market opportunities.

Table 1.4.1
Stakeholders and
their interest in
environmental
issues
continued

Stakeholder		Environmental interest
Capital markets	Investors	There is a growing market for 'ethical investment' and this includes environmental factors. Increasingly, there are pressures on investment funds to explain their policies with respect to ethical and environmental issues. The developing environmental agenda is presenting new risks – and opportunities – for banks and institutional and private investors as providers of capital. Increasingly, investors want to know that organisations are identifying and managing environmental risks as part of their business plans.
	Insurers	Insurers often include conditions that constrain the ability to claim for many environmental problems. Businesses that can demonstrate sound environmental management practices are more likely to secure access to insurance – and at more competitive premiums.
Labour markets	Existing employees	Businesses with a poor environmental image may find it more difficult to retain employees, especially when work opportunities in more progressive firms arise. Good environmental practices and employee involvement in implementing environmental improvements present opportunities to enhance workforce morale, motivation and performance.
	Prospective employees	Businesses with a poor environmental image may find it more difficult to recruit employees, particularly if they are in competition with firms with a more progressive environmental approach. Good environmental practices and employee involvement in implementing environmental improvements can be seen as important attractions for applicants.

Stakeholder		Environmental interest
General public	The media	The media can actively pursue, persist with or even sensationalise an environmental incident or environmental problem experienced by an organisation. Media action will raise an organisation's profile so that other stakeholders can become concerned and involved. Significant management resources may then be needed to address the consequences. Environmental achievements (eg a new product, clean technology project or partnership initiative) may be taken up by the media. This can help to build or enhance a positive reputation.
	Neighbours	Neighbours may seek legal redress for environmental issues such as nuisance, health or planning concerns. Action can be taken through criminal or civil courts. Interactions with neighbours (notably when negative) can also provide a story for the media, particularly the local press. Good community relations can improve access to local labour markets and enable planning applications to be progressed more smoothly.
	Pressure groups, eg 'green groups'	These can exist for any single issue or set of issues and they include local and international organisations. Their relationship with the media and local or national governments may give these organisations substantial influence as public opinion-formers on an organisation's reputation. Pressure groups can initiate significant changes in the environmental behaviour of organisations.

Table 1.4.1
Stakeholders and their interest in environmental issues
continued

1.4.2 Instruments for change

Environmental laws that require specific environmental actions and controls are crucial instruments for improving the environmental performance of organisations. However, governments are increasingly turning to wider measures that encourage business to develop better environmental practices in response to economic and market forces.

In summary, there are two main approaches to ensuring or modifying an organisation's environmental performance – the use of regulatory controls and the use of economic instruments (see Figure 1.4.2 and Table 1.4.2).

Figure 1.4.2
Instruments of government environmental policy

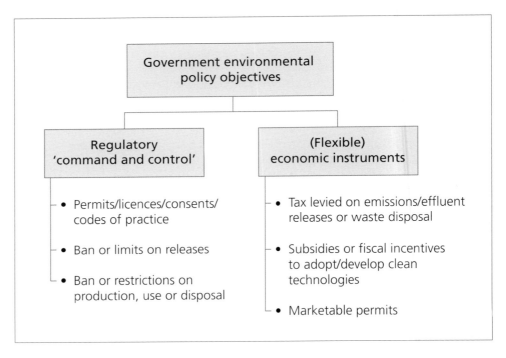

Economic instruments (though underpinned by legislation) attempt to offer business greater flexibility in managing environmental interactions. This is in contrast to the more prescriptive approach required by legislation enforced by regulators.

Policy approach		Examples	Management implications
Regulatory controls	Based on legal requirements to do (or not do) something. This is then enforced by a regulatory agency with legal penalties (eg fines or imprisonment) for non-compliance.	• Meeting conditions in discharge consent, air pollution emission licence, waste management licence • Working to the duty of care for waste handling, storage, transfer and disposal • Achieving recovery targets under producer responsibility obligations	Comply, and be able to demonstrate compliance to regulatory authority. Otherwise, risk prosecution and sanctions, and difficulty with other stakeholders.
Economic instruments	Provide economic incentive to encourage organisations to change behaviour or otherwise incur charges for using the environment. Alternatively, the loss of subsidy, tax break or market opportunity if investment in better practices is forgone when relevant schemes exist.	• Tax on waste going to landfill • Levy on energy use or use of virgin aggregates • Charges for providing parking spaces or for vehicle access into certain areas • Subsidy for uptake of certain technology • Tradeable permit market for greenhouse gas or acid species emissions	Balance the costs and benefits of action with flexibility to adopt options available – pay a tax or charge, or seek to reduce the charge paid by improving performance in the relevant area, eg minimise waste/energy use or find substitutes for virgin aggregates. Ability to sell or buy pollution permits.

Table 1.4.2
Policy approaches and their management implications

1.4.3 Tradeable permits

An example of an early tradeable permit scheme is that set up in the USA to deal with sulphur dioxide from large emitters such as power stations. They are also being used in the UK for dealing with greenhouse gas emissions from certain sectors. They are explicitly allowed under the Kyoto Protocol, a major international agreement seeking to reduce global greenhouse gas emissions. Effectively, these schemes are a hybrid between the strict regulatory approach and economic incentives.

Operators included in a tradeable permit scheme are allocated permits for a certain quota of emissions to be released. These permits are issued by a regulatory authority and set the quota for a designated period of time. Each quota is based on an overall emissions ceiling for the sector or region. A facility to trade permission is also set up which, subject to certain rules, allows:

- any excess permission from those operators who reduce emissions below the quota to be *sold* on the market
- any shortfall in permission for those operators who emit more than their quota to be *bought* on the market.

The basic concept is shown in Figure 1.4.3 – this is based on two businesses with the same emissions quota (the 'permitted level of emissions'). In reality there would be a number of operators with different permit levels and taking different actions to buy or sell permission.

Figure 1.4.3
The basic concept of tradeable emission permits

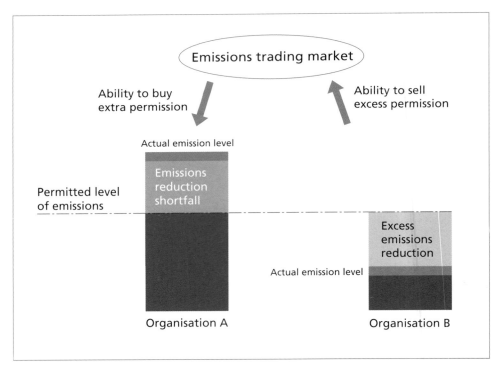

Tradeable permits allow operators to be flexible about how (and to what degree) they invest in emission reductions, and whether to aim to be a buyer or seller on the emission permit trading market.

Tradeable permit systems can, in principle, be developed for areas other than emission releases – for example, waste recovery and recycling quotas or effluent discharge volumes.

1.4.4 Environmental management schemes

Environmental management schemes also rely on market forces. Under such schemes, organisations can demonstrate to their stakeholders that they meet the requirements of an environmental management standard through certification by third parties who are accredited to carry out this role.

The two most significant schemes are:
- the ISO 14001 Environmental Management System standard, which sets out the specification for an environmental management system (EMS) – the key elements of ISO 14001 are described in detail in Chapter 3.1
- EMAS (EU Eco-Management and Audit Scheme), which sets out the requirements for an EMS equivalent to ISO 14001, but with the additional requirement of a public reporting statement on environmental performance.

These schemes require specific environmental issues – based on the organisation's obligations under applicable laws and an understanding of stakeholder concerns – to be identified and addressed as part of the ongoing environmental management process.

BS 8555

In the UK, the BS 8555 standard allows organisations to take a 'six steps' approach to a certificated EMS. It is particularly aimed at small to medium-sized enterprises (SMEs).

As an organisation introduces each step (or 'phase') in BS 8555, it can either assess itself through an internal audit, allow customers to assess it against selected criteria, or be assessed by a third party (such as a certification body). The standard allows an organisation to demonstrate progress to stakeholders, without necessarily having to undergo certification.

Each of the phases identified in Table 1.4.3 is supported by chapters and sections in this book.

Phase		Relevant chapters and sections in *Essentials* include...
1	Commitment and establishing the baseline	• 2.3 Environmental auditing and review • 3.2 Environmental policy
2	Identifying and ensuring compliance with legal and other requirements	• 2.2 Prioritisation – determining significance • 2.3 Environmental auditing and review • 4 Operational control
3	Developing objectives, targets and programmes	• 3.3 Environmental objectives and targets • 3.4 Environmental management programmes and procedures
4	Implementation and operation of the environmental management system	• 3.4 Environmental management programmes and procedures • 3.6 Allocating environmental responsibilities and providing training • 4 Operational control
5	Checking, audit and review	• 2.3 Environmental auditing and review
6	Environmental management system acknowledgment	• 3.1.5 Certification • 3.7 Communication on environmental issues

The sixth phase prepares an organisation either for certification to ISO 14001 or registration to the EU's Eco-Management and Audit Scheme (EMAS).

Details on implementing BS 8555 are available from the Institute of Environmental Management and Assessment (see Appendix 3).

2: Tools for environmental assessment and review

2.1 Identifying environmental aspects and impacts

The fundamental principle of environmental management is that those environmental interactions (either actual or potential) considered to be *significant* are the ones that are managed. As discussed in Chapter 1.1, these interactions are termed 'environmental aspects' and the changes that they cause are termed 'environmental impacts'.

Table 2.1.1 shows how ISO 14001 sets this out principle.

ISO 14001 requirement – environmental aspects
The organisation shall establish, implement and maintain a procedure(s) (a) to identify the environmental aspects of its activities, products and services within the defined scope of the environmental management system that it can control and those that it can influence, taking into account planned or new developments, or new or modified activities, products and services, and (b) to determine those aspects that have or can have significant impact(s) on the environment. The organisation shall document this information and keep it up to date. The organisation shall ensure that the significant environmental aspects are taken into account in establishing, implementing and maintaining its environmental management system.

Table 2.1.1 ISO 14001 requirement – environmental aspects

This chapter is concerned with the identification of aspects and impacts. Chapter 2.2 considers how to determine significance.

2.1.1 Distinction between aspects and impacts

When considering aspects and impacts it is useful to think in terms of 'cause' and 'effect' respectively (see Figure 2.1.1). Put simply, activities cause aspects (environmental interactions) which, in turn, cause environmental impacts (changes in the environment). The ISO definitions for environmental aspect and environmental impact are provided in Table 2.1.2.

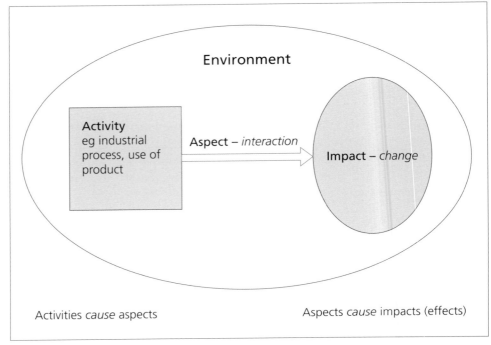

Figure 2.1.1 The activity–aspect–impact relationship

Environment

Activity
eg industrial
process, use of
product

Aspect – *interaction*

Impact – *change*

Activities *cause* aspects

Aspects *cause* impacts (effects)

Term	Definition
Environmental aspect	Element of an organisation's activities, products or services which can interact with the environment.
Environmental impact	Any change to the environment, whether adverse or beneficial, wholly or partially resulting from an organisation's environmental aspects.

The key words in these definitions are 'interact' for aspect and 'change' for impact. Examples are listed in Table 2.1.3.

Environmental aspect	Environmental impact
Chemical or oil spill	Water pollution or land contamination
Atmospheric emission, eg volatile organic compounds (VOCs)	Atmospheric pollution, eg tropospheric ozone creation
Noise	Noise nuisance

Assessing whether the interaction is 'significant' is covered in Chapter 2.2. However, at this stage it is important to note that whether an impact is considered to be adverse or beneficial, and to what extent, is largely dependent on the views of society (or parts of it). The existence of legal controls and other government policy measures, and the opinion of other stakeholders, are fundamental considerations when assessing significance (as discussed in Chapter 2.2).

When considering aspects and impacts it may be useful to refer to the list of environmental concerns and issues listed in Chapter 1.3.

2.1.2 Systematic approach

The identification and understanding of environmental aspects are essential for creating, developing and maintaining an effective environmental management process. Aspects that are determined to be significant should be the focal point for management and performance improvement – whether certification to a standard such as ISO 14001 is a goal or not. A systematic approach to identifying aspects and impacts is, therefore, a firm foundation for effective environmental management. The main steps in identifying aspects and impacts are summarised in Figure 2.1.2.

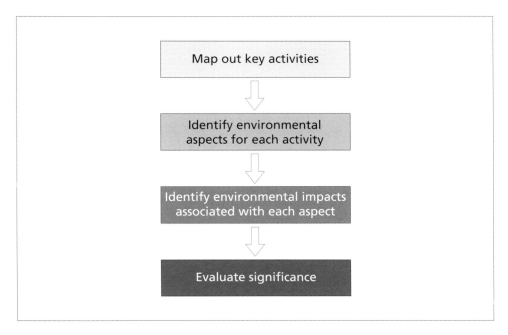

Figure 2.1.2
Principal steps in identifying aspects and impacts

Defining the scope of an environmental management system (EMS) is particularly important – this is returned to later in this chapter. Aspects related to the organisation's operations are normally given priority because they are directly associated with the core business and are under the company's control. However, environmental aspects associated with the use and disposal of a product, or provision of a service, should also be considered. For those organisations seeking certification to ISO 14001, this is an explicit requirement (see Table 2.1.1).

While emphasising that, in practice, it is important to consider products and services, for the sake of simplicity they are not covered further in this chapter.

2.1.3 Mapping out key activities

Activities can be analysed and aspects identified at a number of levels in an organisation. These can range from a general overview of the organisation's operations and business functions to a detailed breakdown of a specific process at a particular location. The aim is to obtain sufficient detail about what is happening, and to enable relevant actions to take place. Those with strategic responsibilities should therefore work on the overview, while those with operational responsibilities should adopt a more specific and detailed approach. For many organisations, the site level provides a convenient starting point, offering a range of readily identifiable activities associated with the site and its facilities. Table 2.1.4 provides examples of such site activities.

Table 2.1.4
Examples of site activities

Type of site	Typical activities might include:
Paper merchant warehouse	goods in; warehouse and site lighting; administration; packaging; despatch and delivery; storage of fuel (vehicle fleet); vehicle cleaning; catering.
Offshore oil exploration drilling rig	supply of fuel and materials; storage of fuel, chemicals and other materials; power generation; drilling operations; well testing; accommodation; administration; catering.
Consumer appliance manufacturer	goods in; storage of materials and components; production and assembly processes; packaging; administration; despatch and delivery; storage of fuel (vehicle fleet); vehicle cleaning; catering; (possibly) on-site power generation.
Park	horticultural practices, including planting, irrigation, soil conditioning, fertilising, mowing, pruning, pest control; storage of materials; visitor use, including events; building (eg pavilion, café, ranger's hut) services (lighting, heating and other services), landscaping.

2.1.4 Identifying aspects

Environmental aspects are the elements of activities that can interact with the environment. A particularly valid approach to identifying aspects is to establish the inputs and outputs from the activity in question (since inputs and outputs make up the environmental aspects of the activity). The importance of looking at aspects as *inputs* as well as outputs is that it allows attention to be paid to the use of materials, water, energy and land – not just to releases, or the risk of releases. This concept was briefly introduced in Chapter 1.1 and is expanded in Figure 2.1.3.

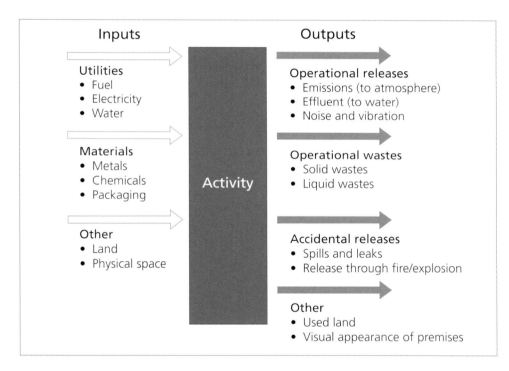

Figure 2.1.3
Typical interactions from any activity

A practical approach should be taken to identifying inputs and outputs since ultimately, the range of inputs and outputs can be large and unwieldy (especially when considered across several activities). Also, certain inputs and outputs may be more usefully considered at a site level, rather than an individual activity level, eg the total electricity or water consumption if no sub-metering exists, or the visual appearance of the site.

It is vital to think in terms of actual aspects (eg expected emission, effluent and waste streams for a given process) but also *potential* aspects (eg arising if something abnormal happens or something goes wrong such as a spill or leak, or waste is generated by equipment malfunction or other incident). ISO 14001's Annex A (which provides guidance on the standard) states that organisations should consider "normal operating conditions, shut-down and start-up conditions, as well as the realistic potential significant impacts associated with reasonably foreseeable or emergency situations" as part of the evaluation.

2.1.5 Identifying impacts

The next stage is to consider what impacts are associated with the identified aspects. Some practitioners choose to aggregate aspects from different activities before this stage. If this is done it is important that the link with key activities is not lost since the management of significant environmental aspects means examining how these *activities* are managed, and assessing what opportunities exist for improved performance.

In some cases, an aspect may have more than one impact – for example, emissions of nitrogen oxides can contribute to both tropospheric ozone creation and acid deposition (see Chapter 1.3). However, different aspects can also contribute to the *same* impact – for example, carbon dioxide and methane are both greenhouse gases implicated in global climate change (examples of global warming potentials of different emissions are provided in Table 2.4.2).

Importantly, the identification of impacts in environmental management normally requires detailed scientific evaluation only in a minority of cases and in specific situations. In the majority of general environmental management situations, it is sufficient to understand the overall issues and concerns associated with the organisation's aspects and be able to articulate this at a level comparable to that set out in Chapter 1.3. It is important to note that organisations can manage their environmental aspects and the activities leading to them – *in general*, they cannot directly control impacts.

The main environmental impacts are listed in Table 2.1.5. Note that this list explicitly includes *beneficial changes*, such as resource conservation, habitat creation or ecosystem conservation.

General impacts	Specific impacts
Atmospheric impacts	• Climate change • Stratospheric ozone depletion • Acid deposition • Tropospheric ozone creation • General air quality

Aquatic impacts	• Water pollution
	  ◦ Effects of toxic and hazardous substances
	  ◦ Eutrophication
	  ◦ Excess oxygen demand

Land impacts	• Land contamination involving effects of:
	  ◦ toxic substances
	  ◦ other hazardous substances

Community impacts	• Nuisance • Loss, or creation, of amenity
Specific ecosystem or species effects	• Loss, fragmentation or degradation of habitats • Conservation or habitat creation • Acute event, eg dead fish in a river, dead birds along a stretch of coast
Resource depletion/conservation	• Renewables • Non-renewables

Table 2.1.5
Key environmental impacts

2.1.6 Drawing up the list of activities, aspects and impacts

The analysis of activities, aspects and impacts is usefully presented as a matrix or table.

Developing the examples used earlier, the format could be as outlined in Table 2.1.6.

Table 2.1.6
Analysing
activities, aspects
and impacts

Type of site	Activity	Aspects	Impacts
Paper merchant warehouse	Warehouse lighting – electrical	Emissions of carbon dioxide (at power station) through use of grid electricity	Contribution to global climate change
		Use of electricity (fossil fuel generating plant)	Depletion of non-renewable resource
Offshore oil exploration drilling rig	Refuelling of rig – diesel transfer from supply vessel to rig storage tanks	Potential spill	Potential marine pollution event
	On-rig generation of electricity using diesel	Combustion emissions of carbon dioxide, nitrogen oxides, sulphur dioxide and particulates	Contribution to global climate change and other atmospheric pollution impacts
		Use of diesel (derived from fossil fuel)	Depletion of non-renewable resource
Consumer appliance manufacturer	Goods in – unloading materials	Noise	Nuisance
	Assembly – components	Waste generation (reject items)	Depletion of resources (unless recovered)
Park	Mowing	Generation of compost from green waste	Conservation of resources (through composting)
	Soil conditioning	Use of peat	Depletion of resources (sensitive/rare peat-forming habitats)

The table could be developed as the assessment of activities, aspects and impacts is carried forward. Additional columns could be added to identify significance, including relevant legislation, stakeholder concerns and magnitude of the aspect or impact (for instance, if parameters such as global warming potentials can be assigned – Chapter 2.4 provides examples).

Organisations may find it beneficial to aggregate information from different activities so that data on types of environmental aspect are grouped together, eg energy use, water use, solvents, different waste streams or types of emission. An alternative is to organise the information into environmental impact categories, eg global climate change, stratospheric ozone depletion, water pollution, resource use and nuisance.

Whichever format is chosen, it is important that the environmental aspects and the associated key activities are clearly identified and that the cause–effect relationships are not lost. Note that *activities cause aspects* and *aspects cause impacts* – environmental management action should normally focus on the key activities as the root cause of those aspects and impacts considered to be significant.

2.1.7 The scope of the assessment

Before beginning to identify environmental aspects and impacts an organisation should consider the scope of the environmental management being applied and therefore the scope of the assessment. Relevant questions to ask include:

• why is the organisation undertaking environmental management?
• how wide-reaching will the analysis of environmental interactions be?
• will it include products or just focus on site-based operations?
• where are the boundaries of the exercise?

As noted, for many organisations the initial emphasis tends to be on site-based activities directly under an organisation's control. Sites usually offer the advantage of a well-defined boundary – namely the perimeter fence. However, with time, the assessment of aspects and impacts should extend to areas beyond the site boundary – for example, to include transport issues, supplier activities and product-related aspects. This in itself can be part of the process of continual improvement.

Figure 2.1.4 summarises how the scope of environmental management, and therefore the analysis of environmental aspects and assessment of significance, can be broader than site-based activities.

Figure 2.1.4
The scope of the
aspect–impact
assessment

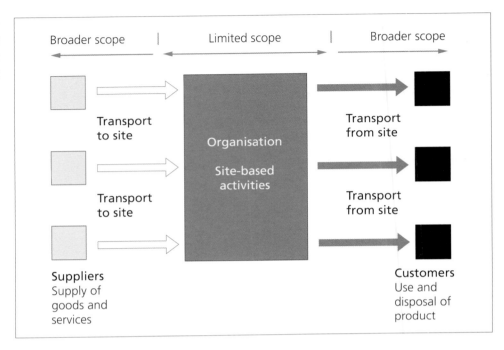

When considering the scope of the assessment it is useful to consider the distinction between direct and indirect aspects (see Table 2.1.7).

Table 2.1.7
The distinction
between direct
and indirect
aspects

Direct aspects	Indirect aspects
Are typically: • directly related to the organisation's operations • inputs and outputs of activities for which an organisation has responsibility and over which it has direct control. The majority are usually identified through a systematic examination of site-based activities and processes.	Are typically: • the result of the activities of others with which the organisation does business. • those over which the organisation should have a degree of influence, eg through product design, supplier selection, distribution options, employee commuting options. Their identification requires a broader view of activities, products and services beyond the site-based focus.

2.1.8 Screening aspects for management

The analysis of activities (and products or services) can potentially identify a large number of environmental interactions (environmental aspects) and associated impacts. The next, and again, fundamentally important, management step is to filter the aspects to identify the priorities for management action. In other words, an organisation needs to ask itself: 'which aspects are the most important?'. In terms of environmental management, it needs to assess which interactions with the environment are the most *significant*. This is the topic of Chapter 2.2.

2.2 Prioritisation – determining significance

Having identified the organisation's activities, aspects and impacts, the next step is to establish which are the most important issues to manage – in environmental management terms this means determining which environmental aspects are significant (see Table 2.2.1 for ISO definition).

Table 2.2.1
ISO 14001
definition –
significant
environmental
aspect

Term	Definition
Significant environmental aspect	A significant environmental aspect is an environmental aspect that has or can have a significant environmental impact.

2.2.1 Purpose of determining significance

Establishing significance is an early challenge for any organisation that is introducing or developing its EMS. Some organisations have made the process more difficult than necessary, but an organisation needs to decide on its criteria for significance, and to apply its criteria in a justifiable, consistent and transparent way. Experience has shown that several basic methods can be applied to help deliver these requirements.

The assessment of significance is a prioritisation process – its purpose is to determine which environmental aspects are most important to the organisation and therefore require management action. It enables organisations to understand their key environmental impacts and to concentrate resources and effort on the aspects (and activities, products or services) leading to them (see Figure 2.2.1).

Figure 2.2.1
The role of
evaluating
significant aspects
in the
management
process

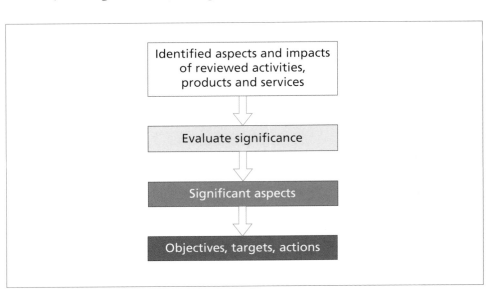

This is a key requirement of ISO 14001, as set out in Table 2.2.2.

ISO 14001 requirement – environmental aspects
The organisation shall establish, implement and maintain a procedure(s) (a) to identify the environmental aspects of its activities, products and services within the defined scope of the environmental management system that it can control and those that it can influence, taking into account planned or new developments, or new or modified activities, products and services, and (b) to determine those aspects that have or can have significant impact(s) on the environment. The organisation shall document this information and keep it up to date. The organisation shall ensure that the significant environmental aspects are taken into account in establishing, implementing and maintaining its environmental management system.

Table 2.2.2
ISO 14001
requirement –
environmental
aspects

2.2.2 Environmental significance in context

A key issue in an EMS is the extent to which the organisation's assessment reflects the actual environmental significance of the impact. The environmental aspects of the organisation will cause a change or set of changes in the environment (environmental impacts). While these impacts can readily be considered in general terms, establishing the significance of the organisation's actual contribution to these impacts can be difficult – particularly for smaller organisations. This is because of the complexity of the environment, other sources affecting the impact in question and incomplete (or even conflicting) scientific knowledge. However, some aspects will have a demonstrable impact (actual or potential) on the environment and therefore are more obviously significant – a spill of oil into a river which kills fish is one example.

A detailed assessment of the significance of impacts is sometimes required for specific major projects such as a new development (typically planned projects covered by Environmental Impact Assessment legislation such as roads, wind farms or oil production facilities) or specific industrial installations (eg those covered by Integrated Pollution Prevention and Control legislation). These situations sometimes call for advanced assessment techniques. Examples are predictive modelling of the impact of releases on ambient air quality, or evaluating disruption to protected habitats or species.

For most organisations developing an EMS, however, a more general approach is normally taken.

It is important to note that, ultimately, environmental concerns arise from society's view of what constitutes an adverse (or beneficial) situation or emerging problem. Also, what is considered to be a resource and what constitutes pollution ultimately depends on society's values.

Therefore, when assessing significance in an EMS, an approach that incorporates the concerns of key stakeholders is essential. This not only helps avoid the difficult task of defining significance in pure ecological or technical terms, but also helps ensure that those issues that are important for maintaining the organisation's 'operating space' (see Chapter 1.4) are addressed. In this way, environmental management is more likely to be properly integrated into the overall business process.

In determining significance, many environmental management practitioners have therefore found it useful to interpret 'significant' to mean 'important' when designing and conducting the evaluation of significant environmental aspects.

2.2.3 Factors in assessing significance

Taking the above into account, in general terms an environmental aspect should be considered to be 'significant' if it:

- is controlled by regulatory requirements
- is of concern to key stakeholders (or its associated impact is of concern)
- has the potential to cause a demonstrable impact on the environment
- has major financial implications – either positive (savings or market opportunities) or negative (costs).

An organisation may use additional criteria. It is for the organisation to design a method that works for its circumstances – there is no standard technique.

Key factors that could be used in assessing significance are set out in Figure 2.2.2. These can be developed into a recognised set of specific criteria (or filters) for an organisation, against which each aspect is evaluated.

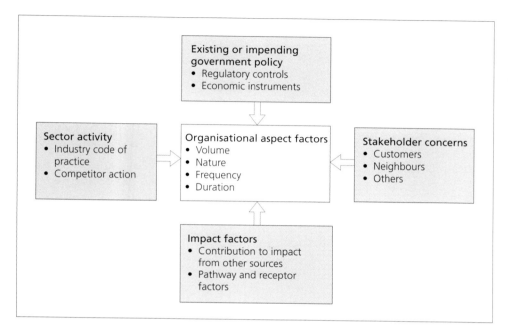

Figure 2.2.2
Factors in assessing significance

It is recommended that any aspect that is directly controlled by applicable legislation should be determined to be significant. Firstly, this reflects a situation where society has considered the aspect to be significant enough to require its control by passing legislation. Secondly, it is in the interest of the business that management controls are sufficient to ensure that the law is complied with. Indeed, for any organisation seeking certification to ISO 14001 this is a fundamental consideration, since commitment to regulatory compliance is one of the standard's main requirements.

Examples of aspects covered by legal controls include those listed in Table 2.2.3.

Environmental aspect	Regulatory control
Certain substances, eg hazardous chemicals or key ozone-depleting substances	Bans or restrictions on supply and/or use
Atmospheric emissions	Conditions in licences and permits, eg Air Pollution Control authorisation or Pollution Prevention and Control permit
Effluent discharges	Conditions in licences and permits, eg conditions in discharge consent (to controlled water or sewer)
Contained waste	Duty of care on handling, storage, treatment, transport and disposal of controlled waste
	Conditions in waste management licence/permit
Use of packaging	Recovery and recycling obligations
	Design and labelling of packaging

The assessment of significance, therefore, requires the organisation to have a thorough knowledge of the environmental legislation affecting its operations. It should also have a sufficient understanding of who the key stakeholders are and what environmental concerns they have.

2.2.4 Methods for assessing significance

There is no standard method for assessing significance and no guidance is given in ISO 14001. This provides organisations with flexibility with regard to how they conduct, and present, the assessment. It is, nevertheless, vital that the process is recorded. In particular, the reasons for the decisions reached should be consistent, clear and recorded so that:

- others in the organisation can understand why an aspect is considered to be significant when implementing environmental management
- the process can be reviewed to ensure its suitability and effectiveness in the context of internal performance and external developments
- accredited certifiers can understand the process (if certification of the EMS to ISO 14001 is an issue).

Techniques for assessing significance include decision diagrams, scoring systems and risk assessment. Environmental managers should develop an approach that is most appropriate to their organisation (for example, to fit with the decision-making processes and procedures of the business). In designing the assessment process, managers should build in the factors summarised above.

a. Simple 'pass/fail' filter method

One simple but often effective method is to develop a set of questions that is applied to each aspect. If the answer is 'yes' to any of the questions then the aspect is significant – so only one 'yes' response acts as the threshold of significance.

The flow chart in Figure 2.2.3 demonstrates the method. Other question boxes could be added – for example, concerning impending legislation, other stakeholders and demonstrable impacts – to make the process more comprehensive. Also, the questions as presented are relatively high level and could be more precisely defined. Additional (qualifying) boxes could be introduced to refine the process following any 'yes' response.

If kept simple (as represented in the flow chart), the method could also be applied in tabular form. Simple ticks could be inserted if the response is 'yes' to any of the questions posed.

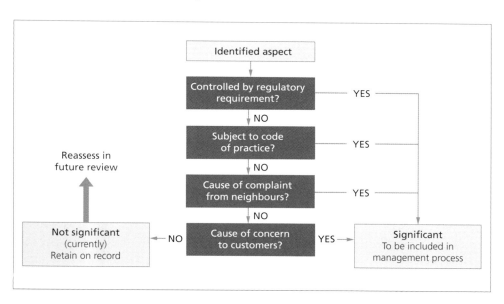

Figure 2.2.3
Simple 'pass/fail' decision flow chart

Whether the assessment is based on a flow chart or table, it is important to provide a brief account of why the answer is 'yes'. For example, summaries of which regulatory control applies, the extent to which complaints from neighbours make it significant, and details of the concerns being raised by customers. This will help ensure current and subsequent understanding.

b. Scoring matrix method

Another method is to allocate numerical 'scores' to each aspect. If the score exceeds a certain value then the aspect is considered to be significant; if it is below that threshold value it is not.

This represents a numerical approach imposed on what is essentially a subjective assessment. Consequently, it should be remembered that the score is only indicative. However, it enables different weighting factors to be introduced so that the organisation can assign levels of importance to different assessment criteria.

The scoring method involves comparing a given aspect against various criteria, with different scores allocated to the aspect, depending on the description which best matches it, eg 'none', 'high'. Weighting factors can then be applied to ensure that critical criteria attain a higher score than less critical ones. For example, a high weighting may be given for regulatory control issues and for neighbour concerns, but perhaps a lower weighting for general public stakeholder concern.

The matrix in Table 2.2.4 provides an example.

Table 2.2.4
An example
scoring matrix

Criteria	Score				Weighting factor	Total score per criterion
	0	1	2	3		
Regulatory control	none	possible	impending	existing	5	A
Stakeholder concern (neighbours)	negligible	some	moderate	major	4	B
Stakeholder concern (general public)	none	some	moderate	major	2	C
Magnitude of aspect	negligible	low	medium	high	3	D
Demonstrable impact	none	unlikely	possible	certain	4	E
					Total score	(A+B+C+D+E)
						(Then, compare to 'threshold' score)

The total possible score will depend on the number of criteria, the maximum scores available for the criteria (in the above example this is '3') and the weighting factors. The organisation would decide the 'threshold' score that indicates significance.

Other rows could be added to the matrix above, eg dealing with other specific stakeholders, reflecting the relevance of economic instruments, or major financial costs or opportunities. Further scores could be introduced beyond '0 to 3', or the scores could follow a scale different from '0-1-2-3' (eg '1-2-4-6'), although this can increase complexity.

Also, rather than using simple terms such as 'none' or 'major', further descriptions could be included in the matrix to make it more precise and transparent. Alternatively, this detail could be included in supporting guidance. For example, factors which could be considered when determining whether the magnitude of an aspect is 'low' or 'high' might include volume, duration, pollution potential of releases or the scope for recovery or recycling. Factors to be considered under demonstrable impact could include the magnitude of the aspect (actual or potential), pathways to sensitive receptors and the nature of the impact (actual or potential) on the sensitive receptor, as well as the state of knowledge about the impact.

Certainly, a brief account of why a score was arrived at should be recorded to help ensure understanding.

One issue with the matrix as presented is that an existing regulatory control might not automatically determine the aspect to be significant, even with high weighting against this criterion. This means the method may need to be adjusted so that, regardless of the total score, if a regulatory control applies then the aspect is treated as significant.

c. Risk assessment

Another approach, often considered by organisations attempting to align environmental management with health and safety, is to apply a risk assessment matrix, similar to that used in health and safety risk assessments. In environmental management terms, risk assessment involves determining the likelihood of occurrence of an aspect and assessing it against its consequence, as set out in the example risk assessment matrix in Figure 2.2.4.

In this example, those environmental aspects in the shaded areas would be significant, those outside not significant. The darker shaded areas determine higher priority – and even unacceptable aspects and associated impacts. Assignment to the relevant occurrence and consequence

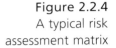

Figure 2.2.4
A typical risk
assessment matrix

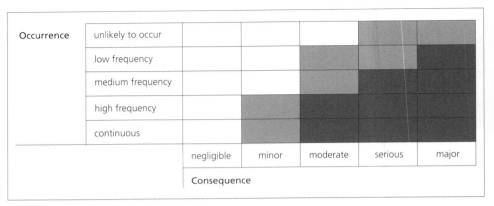

category can be carried out qualitatively or by using a numerical scoring system.

The above matrix uses simple terms such as 'continuous' and 'major'. Again, more detail could be included in the matrix for improved precision.

Alternatively, this might be included in a supporting guidance document. Once again, a brief account of why the occurrence and consequence category was assigned should be recorded to help ensure understanding.

Certain aspects can occur regularly or continuously, such as use of energy or process releases. Others, such as spills or leaks, should be infrequent. A method that requires the assessment of the precise ecological consequence of these outputs can be difficult, particularly if it requires detailed knowledge of the impact on environmental receptors. However, consequences can include numerous factors such as stakeholder concerns, financial impacts (eg when economic instruments apply), magnitude of the aspect (its nature and volume), the presence of sensitive receptors, and exposure to regulatory action.

It is important to note that risk assessments can include consideration of the presence (or absence of) appropriate controls. This approach determines so-called 'residual risk'. If controls are taken into account in the evaluation of significance, this must be made clear, and there must be a record of what the controls are. When assessing residual risk, it is very important to bear in mind that controls can fail.

This type of risk assessment methodology does not make it readily transparent that an aspect is covered by applicable legislation and therefore should be significant. However, such a risk assessment approach is particularly useful in determining whether the risk of incidents (eg spills, leaks) or local impacts (nuisance) is significant.

d. Hybrid methods
Organisations may decide to develop a hybrid of the above techniques. For example, it might be relevant to use:
• a simple pass/fail technique for regulatory controls (so that anything covered by such a control is automatically significant)
• a scoring system for aspects associated with normal operations
• a risk assessment approach for incidents and potential impact situations.

The approach may vary depending on whether the focus of the evaluation is strategic or operational.

However, it is important that the assessment is kept as simple and transparent as possible. Simplicity and transparency will improve the likelihood of subsequent action in the organisation to manage the significant aspects, and will help those who did not carry out the assessment to review its suitability.

2.2.5 Keeping the evaluation up to date
The identification of environmental aspects and impacts and the evaluation of significance should be reviewed on a regular basis, and normally at least once a year. This review will need to take into account:
• operational feedback, audit findings and internal performance to ensure it is a practical process that works
• new projects or substantial changes to existing activities, products or services
• external developments, including new regulatory controls, economic instruments, stakeholder opinions or emerging concerns.

2.3 Environmental auditing and review

2.3.1 Overview of auditing

'Environmental audit' is a term used for any systematic, objective and documented examination of environmental issues relevant to an organisation.

Even so, there are different types of environmental audit. Audits can be issue-specific (eg addressing waste, packaging or energy aspects) or more general, covering a range of environmental aspects and management practices. The term can also describe a study of external developments such as an 'audit' of new environmental legislation or best practice. Life cycle assessment (see Chapter 2.4) is also a type of audit. Examples of some specific types of audit are outlined in Table 2.3.9.

The focus of this chapter is on the two main types of general audit:
• the environmental review
• the environmental management (system) audit.

The role of management reviews, in which senior management considers the findings of internal audits and implications of external developments, will also be outlined (see section 2.3.6).

The different characteristics of these three key environmental management processes – environmental review, management audit and management review – are outlined in Table 2.3.1. Their role in a systematic approach to environmental management is illustrated in Figure 2.3.1.

Audit/review	Characteristics
Environmental review	This takes a 'snap shot' of the organisation (or part of the organisation). It collects and reports information in terms of the question 'where are we now?'. It is a planning tool. It is typically undertaken in preparation for implementing an environmental management system and the term 'initial review' or 'preparatory review' can be used in these circumstances. It identifies environmental aspects and applicable legislation and establishes what needs to be managed. It also identifies what system elements are in place, considers how previous incidents have been dealt with and where gaps exist.
Environmental management (or system) audit	This examines how the environmental management system (or parts of it) is performing. It collects information and reports in terms of 'how have we done?'. This audit is a checking tool. It is undertaken to establish how actual practices conform to the organisation's policy and procedures, including progress against set objectives and targets. Where mismatches exist, this should prompt changes to practices or system elements.
Management review	This examines the overall performance of the environmental management processes, the need for change and strategies for achieving change. The management review is a tool to ensure the ongoing suitability, adequacy and effectiveness of environmental management in the organisation. It receives and reviews conclusions and recommendations from internal audits and reviews. It also considers changing circumstances, including the implications of new projects and external developments. Inputs may therefore include surveys of stakeholder opinions and reviews of new and impending legislation. This information is reviewed in the context of the organisation's environmental policy, objectives and plans.

Table 2.3.1
Different types of
audit and review

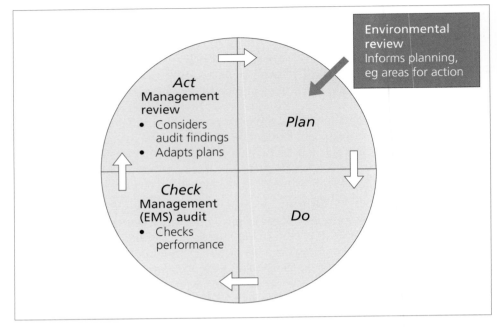

2.3.2 Audit characteristics

Environmental audits should be systematic, objective and documented (see Table 2.3.2). They can be conducted by internal or external environmental auditors.

Audit	
Systematic	This can be achieved through having a preset programme of functions, sites and activities to be audited. Checklists, protocols or questionnaires should be used to ensure all relevant issues are examined and nothing of importance is overlooked.
Objective	This requires that findings be based on factual information, which is obtained and reported without bias. For example, the outcome of interviews should be supported by documentary or observational evidence. For environmental management audits it is important that the auditors should be independent of the activities being audited. This is a requirement of ISO 14001.
Documented	This requires recording of the audit findings. In particular, the principal conclusions and recommendations should be clear and concise, and capable of being acted on.

Environmental management (system) audits should be scheduled so that the performance of the system is checked on an ongoing basis. The management audit process also requires prioritisation, to ensure that certain areas undergo more thorough auditing than others. This is returned to in section 2.3.5.

The International Organization for Standardization (ISO) has issued ISO 19011 as a standard on on quality and environmental management system auditing (see Appendix 2).

2.3.3 General audit process

Many of the elements of the audit process are relevant to all types of environmental audit or review. Common basic steps are set out in Figure 2.3.2.

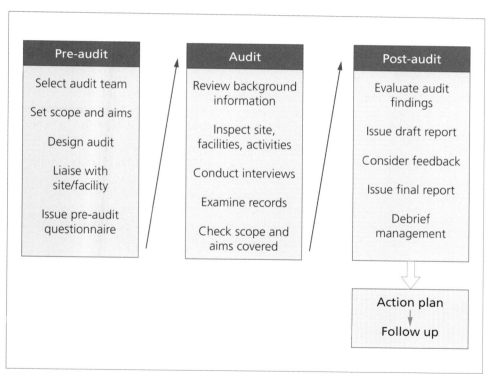

Figure 2.3.2
Basic steps in an environmental audit

a. Audit planning

Planning is vitally important if the audit is to be efficient and effective. Without planning, valuable on-site time is likely to be wasted and the findings may not be representative. Planning should include the actions listed in Table 2.3.3.

Table 2.3.3 The main components in planning an audit

Planning action	Elements
Assemble an audit team	This should include: • in-house personnel with a mix of skills and knowledge covering environmental issues, operational awareness, auditing techniques • external consultants to guide the internal team or fill any skills gap, if necessary.
Clarify the scope and aims of the audit	It is important to define what is wanted from the audit, including: • activities to be included (and excluded) • purpose and nature of the audit • priority issues to be investigated • manner of reporting findings/recommendations.
Design the format of the audit	Audit design will need to consider how to gather relevant information and include: • scheduling auditing activities, including meetings, site or facility inspections, reporting and feedback deadlines, data evaluation and report drafting time • auditor roles and responsibilities, eg certain auditors may be assigned specific activities or EMS elements • developing appropriate audit questionnaires, protocols and/or checklists • identifying interviewees and scheduling interviews.
Liaison with sites/facilities to be audited	Good relations with management and staff responsible for the areas to be audited are essential for a successful investigation. This can be assisted through: • timely liaison on meetings, interviews and information requirements • making sure personnel are aware of, and understand, the purpose and aims of the audit and how it helps their business • encouraging participation and feedback.
Issue pre-audit questionnaire	This should be returned before the visit. By obtaining background information in advance, it helps ensure that the time on site is used effectively so that effort is concentrated on the key areas of the investigation and that inspection is focused. It also helps direct questions to site personnel. Such a questionnaire can be particularly important when conducting an environmental review.

b. Conducting the audit

The on-site audit process can be broken down into two main parts: the opening meeting and the collection of information. In many situations, it is also sensible to have an orientation tour of the site, facility or activities being audited before starting the detailed investigation.

Activity	Elements
Conduct opening meeting	This should help promote the participation of those being audited. It can be used to: • introduce the audit team to the management and representatives of the area being audited • review the scope and aims; audit methodology; access requirements (facilities and personnel); and audit timetable • raise any issues at the outset, and agree a process for resolving any difficult issues • ensure the audit team is aware of site safety and emergency procedures.
Collect information	This will depend on audit aims but can include: • inspection of site, facilities, activities and surrounding area, as relevant • formal interviews and informal discussion with a cross-section of management and staff • examination of documents and records • observation of measurement processes and environmental controls • factual evidence to support interview information through observations, documents and records, additional discussions • ensuring all steps in checklists, protocols and questionnaires are completed.

Table 2.3.4
The main components in conducting an audit

c. Audit reporting

The nature of the report will depend on the type of audit, its objectives and its scope. Issues to address include those considered in Table 2.3.5.

Issue	Considerations
Opportunities for feedback	It is good practice to enable the site and functional management audited to provide feedback on the audit findings and draft report, for example, through: • a closing meeting to present findings and allow comment on their factual basis • the opportunity to review draft report and provide further comments.
Format of final report	This should include consideration of: • document structure, content and size • audience and distribution list • use of an executive summary • how to highlight key findings and recommendations for action • use of presentations to support the written report.

A mechanism also needs to be devised for addressing recommendations, dealing with problems identified and checking agreed actions have been implemented.

2.3.4 Environmental review

An environmental review is often the starting point for developing an EMS. Defining the scope of the review is particularly important because it will influence/establish the boundaries of the management system, ie the activities, products and services to be covered (see Chapter 2.2). The wider the scope, the more time and resources will be required.

An environmental review should cover four key areas (see Figure 2.3.3):
• legislative and regulatory requirements
• identification of significant environmental aspects
• examination of existing environmental practices and procedures
• evaluation of feedback from the investigation of previous incidents.

A comprehensive environmental review should enable an organisation to:
• establish an environmental policy or check the relevance of the existing policy
• assess the adequacy of current arrangements in dealing with significant aspects and identify where gaps exist
• draw up and implement an action plan to deal with the issues arising and establish an agenda for regulatory compliance and continual improvement.

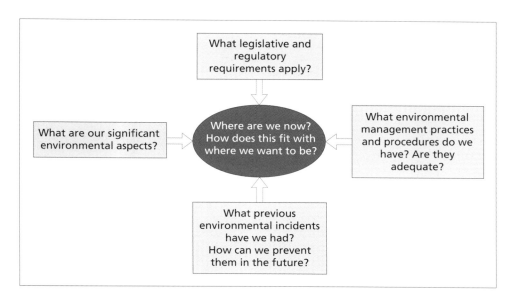

Figure 2.3.3
Key areas of an environmental review

The identification of aspects and impacts and the assessment of significance should follow the principles set out in Chapters 2.1 and 2.2. The review should seek to obtain as much quantitative information as possible – for example, annual data on the consumption of energy, water and materials, maximum storage volumes of oil and chemicals, amount of waste generated (including what happens to it), emission levels and the quantities of effluent discharges.

A useful starting point when conducting the review is to obtain a site plan and use it to highlight features with particular environmental relevance. Examples of such features are included in Table 2.3.6.

Table 2.3.6
Examples of
features that can
be identified
by/plotted on a
site plan

Type	Example features
Input points	• Mains water meter • Gas and electricity meters • Fuel delivery points • Material storage areas • Oil and chemical storage tanks
Key processes and activities	• Production, assembly and finishing facilities • On-site power generators • Refrigeration or air conditioning plant • Boilers and furnaces • Unloading, marshalling, materials transfer and loading areas • Packaging operations • Product storage • Laboratories • Administration offices • Car parking space • Site access
Output points	• Discharge points to sewer or directly to body of water • Stacks and chimneys • Skip yard, waste despatch points • On-site landfill
Environmental control facilities	• Effluent treatment plant • Oil–water separators • Emission abatement plant • Waste storage and segregation facilities • Waste treatment facilities • On-site waste incineration installations or reprocessing facilities • Site screening and landscaping features (dealing with noise/visual aspects)

A map of the local area will assist with the assessment of local impacts, notably by helping establish important environmental pathways and receptors. For example, it will be useful to know the proximity of the site and its access routes to:

- residential communities and sensitive neighbours, such as hospitals and schools
- local water courses, eg streams or rivers
- site exposure and orientation, eg relative to the prevailing wind – affecting airborne dispersion, and slope direction – affecting run-off
- local ecosystems such as woodland, lakes or ponds and especially nature reserves and special conservation sites
- local cultural heritage sites.

Ideally, the review should encourage the participation of site representatives, which will build (or reinforce) understanding of the key elements of environmental management at the operational level. It will also help direct the audit team to key areas for inspection and more detailed investigation.

During the review, information on the following should also be obtained:
- existing environmental policy, objectives and targets
- existing environmental responsibilities
- existing procedures and records relevant to environmental management (for example procurement, maintenance, stock control (including hazardous materials), energy management, waste management, monitoring and auditing)
- existing communication and training programmes
- historic use of site (to help determine whether contaminated land may be present)
- development plans (to understand what aspects may become significant in the foreseeable future)
- previous incidents such as spills, leaks, fires, regulatory non-compliance and complaints from neighbours or customers.

In-house documentary information sources for an environmental review might include those listed in Table 2.3.7.

Area	In-house documentation
Applicable legislation	• Process authorisation/installation permit • Discharge consent • Waste management permit • Register of relevant legislation/guides to legislation
General site	• Site plan • Map of surrounding area • Organisation chart • Process flow charts • Emergency response procedure • Previous audits or surveys, eg contaminated land
Material inputs	• Health, safety and environmental data sheets • Purchase records • Inventory records
Utilities	• Supplier invoices • Metering records • Fuel bills

Table 2.3.7
In-house documentary information sources for an environmental review

Table 2.3.7
In-house
documentary
information
sources for an
environmental
review
continued

Area	In-house documentation
Waste	• Duty of care transfer notes • Hazardous waste consignment notes • Waste management permit • Waste data (types and quantities) • Specifications of waste storage facilities/compactors
Effluent/emissions	• Authorisations/consents/permits • Monitoring records • Site drainage drawings and plans • Abatement plant and monitoring equipment specifications
Spills and leaks (actual/potential)	• Incident records (including identification of near misses) • Drawings of storage facilities, pipework systems • Maintenance records
Nuisance issues	• Complaints from neighbours • Correspondence with local authority • Local community opinion surveys
Products	• Product information sheets • Product studies
Existing practices and procedures	• Vision statement, written policy, objectives and targets • Organisational chart • Environmental action plans • Procedures for specific activities or aspects • Maintenance schedules • Auditing programme • Pollution control equipment specifications • Minutes of environmental committee meetings or equivalent • Training plans and records • Communication documentation
Previous incidents	• Incident and 'near hit/near miss' records • Follow-up reports on emergency response • Correspondence with regulators • Abatement notices
Contaminated land	• Archive records of operations or incidents on site • Historic site plans and maps • Contaminated land surveys

2.3.5 Environmental management audit

The purpose of the management (or system) audit is to ensure that the organisation's environmental management processes are properly implemented and working effectively. For those organisations aiming for, or seeking to maintain, certification to the ISO 14001 standard, the EMS audit is also used to ensure that the requirements of the standard are being met.

EMS audits should be scheduled to ensure that the performance of the system is checked on an ongoing basis. However, this does not mean that the whole system needs to be audited at once, or even within an annual cycle. ISO 14001 requires that the audit programme is based on the environmental importance of the operations and the results of previous audits. This clearly acknowledges that auditing should address priorities, and that different parts of the organisation can be audited with different frequency and detail. This can also allow auditing personnel to be used more efficiently.

Figure 2.3.4 provides a framework that might be used to help identify priority areas. This involves a matrix that covers both significance (low, medium or high) and recent (or anticipated) performance (good, fair or poor). Since environmental management should be addressing all the aspects determined to be significant (Chapter 2.2), it follows that all the activities, products and services and relevant management arrangements contributing to these significant aspects should be audited at some stage. However, some will be more significant than others, and could be allocated to low, medium or high categories. Previous audits or other monitoring mechanisms (eg performance indicators, regulator correspondence or customer feedback) should be used to identify whether performance is poor, fair or good. Top and high priority areas should be given a more detailed and frequent audit (at least annually, and more frequently if necessary).

Facilities and areas which require more frequent and detailed auditing might therefore include:
- activities which can lead to high environmental impact (in normal or abnormal situations)
- operations with high incident rates, eg spills, leaks or breach of emission limits
- areas with previous high levels of environmental management non-conformance
- aspects which have missed (or are likely to miss) important improvement targets.

Other factors might include:
- activities subject to high or new levels of regulatory scrutiny
- areas where particularly challenging targets have been set
- areas to which the scope of environmental management has recently been extended and performance is still uncertain, eg new operations, critical suppliers.

It can also be useful to show key stakeholders – including regulators, certifiers and key customers – how auditing is being prioritised, as this can help build confidence in the organisation's approach to environmental management.

Figure 2.3.4
Prioritising areas for environmental management audits

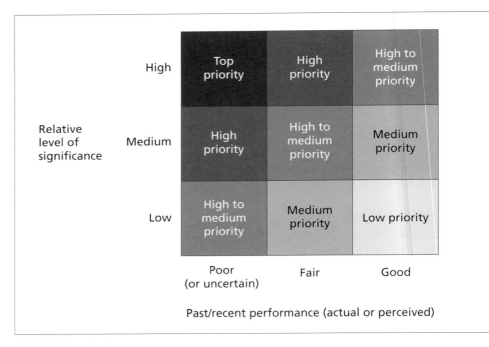

An audit programme should be drawn up, taking into account priorities, the need to inform the management review (section 2.3.6) and the availability of competent personnel. Inevitably, these factors will differ between organisations. The programme should allocate audit team members to areas of the organisation to be audited at scheduled dates. Environmental management audits tend to be much more valid and useful if those who are auditing are independent of the area being audited. This is also a requirement of ISO 14001. It means, for example, that the person responsible for auditing a particular facility should not be the person who operates it or is directly responsible for it.

Term	Description
Audit cycle	The period over which all parts of the organisation are audited. Normally this should be at least annually for high priority areas.
Audit programme	The timetable of individual audits projected over the audit cycle. This should also assign responsibility for the audits.
Audit plan	The details for an individual audit. This should include the: • scope and aims • schedule for the audit, including the opening and closing meetings • personnel to be involved • audit methodologies and procedures • method of reporting • audit report distribution.

Table 2.3.8
Management
audit terms

A key outcome of the audit is the identification of non-conformance to the management system in place. Non-conformance typically relates to:
• failure to meet targets
• failure to implement an action plan
• inadequate document control
• lack of staff awareness of what to do
• inappropriate procedures or other system elements.

Non-conformances should be recorded and reported. This should include agreement with the person responsible for that area to take:
• corrective action – so that the existing problem is rectified within an agreed timescale
• preventive action – so that it does not happen again.

A follow-up mechanism should be established to confirm that the corrective and preventive actions have been implemented – or to explain why not. A single form can often achieve all the requirements (ie non-conformance reporting, corrective and preventive action statements and confirmation of action).

Another output of the audit should be an overview of how the system is performing and what improvements could be made. This, together with an overview of number and types of non-conformance, should be fed into the management review.

The main elements of an environmental management audit are shown in Figure 2.3.5.

Figure 2.3.5
Environmental
management
audit

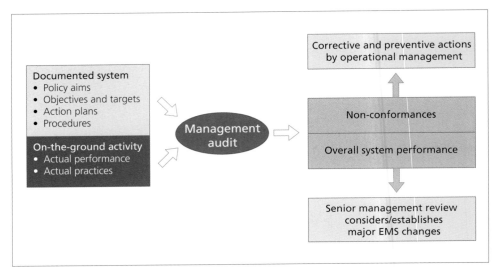

Auditing has a vital role in ensuring the effectiveness of an EMS. To underline this, bodies that certify organisations to ISO 14001 invariably focus on the robustness of the internal auditing regime in the early stages of the certification assessment. This includes an evaluation of the audit programme, audit plans, protocols and methodologies, auditor competence records, audit reports and corrective action follow-up as part of their overall assessment.

2.3.6 Management review

A senior management review should be undertaken at regular intervals. Normally, this means at least annually, but the frequency may vary depending on the organisation's existing governance, or the issues being managed. The review should ensure that the organisation's environmental management processes are still relevant. It should also ensure that any major problems or missed opportunities as a result of under-performance of existing system elements and practices are addressed. It should aim to be largely proactive, considering external developments and internal plans, and the change mechanisms needed to address them. This is summarised in Figure 2.3.6.

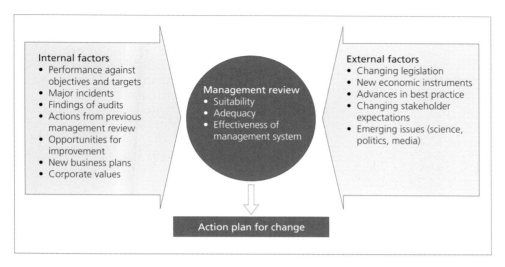

Figure 2.3.6
Management
review

The management review is a senior management activity, although co-ordinated reviews at site and functional level are also good practice.

Given the range of internal and external factors that the review may need to consider, it needs a well-structured agenda, concise and clear papers supported by 'sharp' presentations, and clear recommendations and/or requests for decisions. The management review is not a forum for simply circulating the full environmental management audit report.

Pertinent information from internal audits should be reviewed, but other input may need to be considered. For example, this might include:
• a survey of stakeholder views and expectations
• a review of new, impending and proposed regulatory controls and economic instruments
• an audit of good or best practice – perhaps through a benchmarking study with comparable (peer) organisations.

The management review should be documented, noting clearly the decisions reached and the action points determined. A documented management review is a requirement of ISO 14001. The action points should drive the next round of improvements in the organisation's EMS. As will be seen in Chapter 5.2, an effective management review process is particularly important in helping an organisation to address sustainability issues.

2.3.7 Examples of specific types of audit

As mentioned in section 5.2.1, environmental auditing can include various types of audit. Some examples are outlined in Table 2.3.9. These can help supplement a general audit, eg by providing more detail on specific aspects such as greenhouse gas emissions or on legal compliance.

Type	Approach	Example coverage
Management activity audits/ reviews	An audit of a specific management activity. The audit aims to identify the extent to which the activity implements good practice, and to highlight any inadequacies.	• Emergency response • Employee competence on environmental matters • Maintenance regimes • Target setting and performance reporting • Supplier assessment
Aspect and impact audits/ reviews	A detailed audit of a specific release or other aspect and the issues across the organisation (or a specific area) that affect it. The audit may include quantifying the 'footprint' of an aspect, eg all greenhouse gas emissions as units of carbon dioxide equivalent.	• Energy • Greenhouse gases • Waste • Packaging materials • Timber • Water • Hazardous substances
Code audits	The extent to which an organisation is meeting a code of practice it has signed up to. The audit would consider each commitment or criterion in the code and assess whether it is being met or exceeded.	• Government code of practice • Industry sector code • Independent code • Corporate code across a group or multinational operations
Permit 'licence' audits	The extent to which an organisation is meeting the specific requirements set out in environmental permits, or licences or other authorisations, eg in terms of release limits and reporting requirements.	• Conditions in permits, licences and authorisations
Compliance audits	As for permit audit, but with wider scope: auditing the extent to which the organisation can meet forthcoming legal requirements or is meeting existing regulatory requirements.	• Producer responsibility obligations • Carbon reduction commitments • Waste duty of care requirements • Green claims
Environmental policy statement audit/review	A specific examination of the organisation's environmental policy statement. The audit aims to ensure the policy stays aligned to its activities, products and services, and to its environmental management processes.	• Scope • Commitments • Review processes • Link to objectives, targets and other management arrangements • Best practice, including ISO 14001 or BS 8555 requirements

Table 2.3.9
Examples of specific environmental audits

Importantly, the key findings of these audits should also be considered by the management review process (section 2.3.6). A review or audit of greenhouse gas emissions is particularly important for organisations seeking to measure and report their 'carbon footprint' (Chapter 5.1) and establish a greenhouse gas (or carbon) management strategy (Chapter 5.2).

2.4 Life cycle assessment

Life cycle assessment (LCA) is used to help design products and services so that they have improved environmental performance across their entire life cycle, ie 'from cradle to grave'.

This chapter provides a brief introduction to LCA and, importantly, introduces the general concept of 'life cycle thinking' that helps organisations understand environmental issues beyond their immediate operations. LCA enables organisations to identify their significant *indirect* environmental aspects, and provides a holistic approach to environmental assessment.

Those organisations wishing to obtain detailed guidance on formal LCA should consult the set of ISO standards dealing with LCA (see Appendix 2). Specialist technical help should also be considered if undertaking detailed LCA studies.

2.4.1 Overview of LCA

Life cycle assessment can be extremely useful but it can also be complex and difficult to interpret. It attempts to identify and, where possible, aggregate the various material, energy and waste flows to evaluate the environmental impacts associated with the provision of a product or service throughout its entire life cycle. For a product, the full life cycle spans the extraction of raw material (often referred to as the 'cradle') through various stages to the end-of-life of the product, when it is discarded (the 'grave'), although increasingly sustainability suggests that it should be 'cradle' to 'cradle' (with products or parts reused or materials recovered). The life cycle concept is illustrated in Figure 2.4.1.

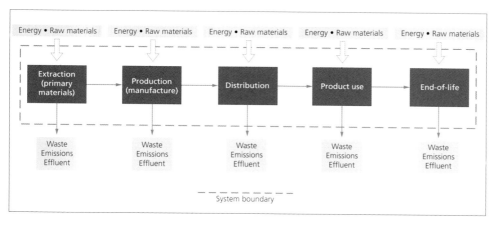

Figure 2.4.1
Main life cycle system stages for a product

It differs from many other forms of environmental assessment, such as environmental reviews, since these tend to consider a particular site, facility or stage of the life cycle (eg manufacturing, storage or transport operations) rather than the wider picture.

2.4.2 Application of LCA

LCA seeks to quantify significant aspects and impacts over the whole life cycle. These impacts are sometimes referred to as the 'environmental footprint' of a product or service. It can be used to ensure that improved environmental performance at one stage is not achieved at the expense of significantly worse performance elsewhere.

It also helps with environmental comparisons between different product or service systems. Therefore, a useful application of LCA might be to determine the environmental footprints of different packaging systems using different materials – for example, to compare the footprints of different packaging options that provide a quantity of liquid product (eg a litre of milk) in a glass bottle, plastic bottle or cardboard carton.

In summary, the key uses of LCA in business include:
- identification of where the most significant environmental aspects of providing a product or service exist in the life cycle. This will direct action (eg design, redesign, procurement decisions, supply chain initiatives) to improve performance in the stage (or stages) most relevant. It helps with prioritisation. For example, for the product represented in Figure 2.4.2, the impact is highest in the 'use' stage. This suggests that action on this stage should be the priority, rather than putting most effort into reducing impacts during manufacturing
- comparison of the relative environmental performances of alternative product or service systems which provide the same function, to help make informed decisions as to which is the best practicable environmental option.

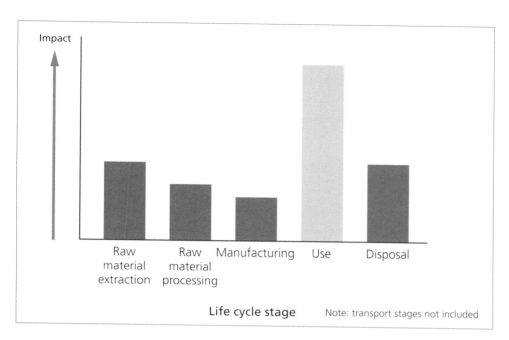

Figure 2.4.2
Product LCA and
prioritisation for
action

LCAs can be conducted over part of the life cycle. For example, an assessment may be carried out for the 'upstream' stages (before manufacture) to look at resource issues such as selecting different timber materials or energy supplies. Alternatively, it might focus on the detail nearer the end-of-life stage, to identify different impacts between reuse, recycling or disposal options (including transport, reprocessing and treatment). How LCA is used depends on:

- the problem in question
- the resources available
- the time available for reaching a decision.

2.4.3 Phases in conducting an LCA

There are four phases to conducting a formal LCA. These are:

- goal and scope definition
- life cycle inventory (LCI) analysis
- life cycle impact assessment
- interpretation.

Their relationship is shown in Figure 2.4.3.

Figure 2.4.3
Life cycle
assessment:
factors and phases

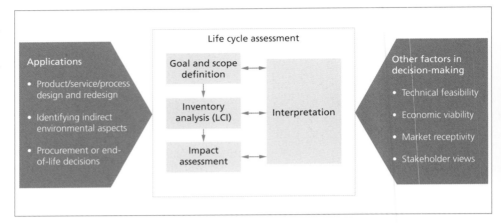

2.4.4 Goal and scope definition

The complexity of LCAs depends mainly on the reason for undertaking the assessment and what the organisation wants from the exercise. An LCA can be general (eg considering key inputs and outputs across the main stages), or can focus on one key issue (eg the global warming potential or carbon footprint of the system), or be detailed and comprehensive (detailing inputs and outputs through a thorough breakdown and analysis of each stage).

Conducting an LCA can be a vast exercise – taken to its logical (but impractical) conclusion it would be never-ending. It is therefore vital to have a clear definition of the goal and scope of the assessment. This helps to ensure that the information collected for the LCA remains relevant.

The definition of the *goal* depends on the following factors:
- the intended application of the LCA, eg whether it is to develop an improved product or service or to compare different products or services
- the reason for conducting it and the intended audience, eg whether it is to be used for internal purposes or used for discussion with external stakeholders
- what specific decisions the LCA will be used to help with.

The *scope* must be linked to the goal. The scope should define the breadth (ie the stages covered) and depth (ie the detail of each stage and the inputs and outputs to be included) of the assessment needed to address the goal. The key is to make the LCA detailed enough to be meaningful but not so detailed that the task becomes too large and complex to be conducted, or for its findings to be of use.

The scope should include:
- definition of the function of the system being investigated (ie the function of the product or service), including the 'functional unit' (see Table 2.4.1)
- definition of the system boundaries, eg which stages, inputs and outputs are to be included or excluded
- methods for gathering the data, eg direct measurement or estimates, specific or generic data
- key assumptions and limitations – this is essential to allow transparency of the exercise.

Functional unit
The functional unit is the measure of performance of the main functional output of the system being investigated. It enables comparisons to be made since it forms the unit of comparison for two or more product or service systems fulfilling the same function. For example: • packaging used to deliver a quantity of liquid product, such as a litre of milk   • unit area of wall surface covered by paint or wallpaper.

Table 2.4.1
Definition of functional unit

Consideration of the functional unit is vital when defining the goal and scope of the LCA.

A simple linear sequence of stages from extraction through manufacturing, distribution, use and end-of-life of a product (see Figure 2.4.1) is a useful concept for life cycle thinking, but is an oversimplification when considering most formal LCAs. In reality, LCAs often deal with complex life cycle webs. This is another reason for striking a balance at the planning phase between simplicity and complexity.

Figure 2.4.4 illustrates the main stages of a system in which a glass bottle with a metal cap delivers a quantity of liquid product. The diagram is simplified – for example, it omits the various transport stages (such as the metal ore to the smelter, and the metal to the bottling plant). However, it identifies the main material streams contained in the glass bottle and metal cap. If the purpose of the LCA is concerned only with the packaging, then the liquid product stages could be excluded from the assessment since they have no relevance. For the glass bottle, there may be different end-of-life options that warrant more detailed assessment – or they may, of course, form the main focus of the assessment.

This system might be compared with alternative packaging systems such as cardboard cartons and plastic containers. All these packaging systems will have different impact profiles along their life cycles associated with different materials, processing and end-of-life options.

Figure 2.4.4
Simplified life cycle
stages of a glass
bottle (with a
metal cap)
containing a liquid
product

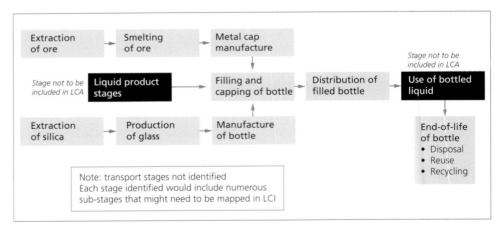

2.4.5 Inventory analysis

Inventory analysis involves the compilation and quantification of the material, energy and waste flows (environmental aspects). It maps the system stages and the inputs and outputs in accordance with the goal and scope. Often, as the exercise proceeds, the mapping itself reveals insights which may mean that the scope of the exercise needs to be updated – for example, new aspects may be discovered or data difficulties encountered.

The data on materials, energy and wastes (including emissions and effluent) can be either 'situation-specific' or generic. Situation-specific data can be from on-site collection, measurement or estimation. Data may be directly obtained from suppliers – as measurements or estimates. Databases are also being developed to provide generic data on the inputs and outputs across life cycle stages of key materials and products, in recognition of the potentially huge task that LCI analysis can entail.

Once obtained, the data need to be expressed in terms of the unit flow of product through each stage of the system and, ultimately, to the functional unit. Allocation of data may be necessary where operations are shared with other products which are not part of the LCA. This increases the complexity of the study.

LCI analysis may be undertaken without the impact assessment phase being conducted.

2.4.6 Impact assessment

This phase aims to evaluate the significance of environmental impacts using the results of the LCI analysis. The level of detail, choice of impacts evaluated and the methods used depend on the goal and scope of the investigation.

Impact categories (classification)

A key step in impact assessment is the selection of impact categories. These might include global climate change, acidification, air quality (eg ground-level ozone), stratospheric ozone depletion, biological oxygen demand (BOD), eutrophication, toxicity of substances and resource depletion.

Data on the inputs and outputs (aspects) are assigned to one or more of these categories. For example, CFCs are both ozone-depleting substances and greenhouse gases, so release figures for these substances may be assigned to both categories.

Some LCAs go no further than this step.

Characterisation
This step applies numeric 'indicators' related to the impact category. For example, they exist as ozone depletion potentials, photochemical ozone creation potentials and global warming potentials.

Combining the contribution from each aspect that is associated with the same environmental impact category helps to quantify the overall impact of the system with respect to the impact in question. For example, to assess global warming impact the emissions of different greenhouse gases over different parts of the life cycle would each be aggregated and converted by their global warming potentials and typically reported as CO_2 equivalent.

Examples of global warming potentials (GWPs) are provided in Table 2.4.2, noting that CO_2 has a GWP of 1.

Table 2.4.2 Global warming potentials (GWPs)

Emission	Global warming potential
Carbon dioxide	1
Methane	21
Nitrous oxide	310
HFC-125 (pentafluoroethane)	2800
Perfluorobutane	7000
Sulphur hexafluoride	23900

Valuation
This step is highly subjective. It attempts to give 'value' to the data so that different (often markedly different) impacts can be compared, eg climate change compared to eutrophication. This might be, for example, through ranking or weighting.

This stage requires clear explanation of how the ranking or weighting scores (or other values) are arrived at, so that the process is transparent.

2.4.7 Interpretation
This phase involves the review of the findings of the LCA, checking that they are consistent and that the assumptions are sound. Again, transparency is key to this phase.

Interpretation must be linked to the goal and scope of the LCA. It will typically seek to identify priorities for improvement and the feasibility of options for improvement. LCA is a decision-making aid that considers environmental parameters. Therefore, other factors will need to be considered, including stakeholder views, technical and economic feasibility of options for improvement, and market conditions.

2.4.8 Life cycle thinking

While a formal LCA is a potentially powerful tool for examining environmental aspects and impacts and for identifying areas for improvement, it has important limitations. These include:
- accuracy of the findings can be limited by accessibility to appropriate data or by data quality
- LCAs cannot prove conclusively that one product or service system is better than another; they can only provide an indication based on the scope of system assessed
- detailed and comprehensive LCAs can require significant resources and expertise.

However, the life cycle approach helps identify environmental issues beyond the stage where the organisation is operating. Even 'rough and ready' assessments can help with strategic thinking through an improved understanding of direct and indirect aspects and impacts.

Life cycle thinking can help drive an organisation to 'think outside the box'. It assists in:
- breaking down the product or service system to identify key environmental issues, priorities and areas providing opportunities for improvement
- understanding the broad, general trade-offs between the life cycle stages or between key environmental aspects and impacts
- ensuring important issues are identified upstream and downstream of the organisation's activities
- identifying areas for supplier or customer initiatives (see Chapter 5.1).

A useful element of environmental management is to identify possible issues associated with key life cycles relevant to the organisation (such as for existing or planned products and services or facilities). For example, putting key issues into a table (one similar to Table 2.4.3) can indicate whether more detailed action (including further research) is necessary.

Table 2.4.3
Quick map of key life cycle issues – upstream and downstream of an organisation's activities

Product system	Stage					
OR...	Raw material extraction	Production/ manufacture	Product distribution	Product use	Disposal/ recovery	Transport between stages
Facility system	**Stage**					
	Raw material extraction	Manufacture of plant/ construction materials	Construction of facility	Operation of facility	Decomm-issioning	Transport between stages
Key inputs • Materials • Energy • Land						
Key outputs • Waste • Effluent • Emissions • Other, eg visual, noise						
Key impacts/ issues/ concerns associated with inputs and outputs						

This can be a useful 'ready-reckoner' for identifying opportunities for continual improvement in environmental management.

2.4.9 Embodied carbon

An area where the life cycle approach that is being increasingly used is the assessment of 'embodied carbon' or 'embodied energy'. This has become of particular interest in relation to climate change.

It describes the amount of carbon emissions generated or energy required for a product (or a service or installation) during specific parts of its life cycle, typically other than those emissions generated or energy required during use (or service provision). Importantly, it does not describe whether a product has any carbon or carbon compounds in it. Embodied carbon can also be a part of developing the 'carbon footprint' of a product or service (see Chapter 5.1).

It is, for example, becoming a key parameter for assessing the impact of products such as electrical and electronic equipment. Here the focus might have previously have been on the carbon dioxide (CO_2) emitted or energy required during use. However, embodied carbon/energy helps to address other important stages (including production or 'end-of-life') and can support a move to products and services with inherently less embodied carbon or energy.

An associated concept is that of carbon or energy payback. This, for instance, can be expected to be important for renewable energy systems, eg photovoltaics or wind turbines. Carbon or energy payback provides data on how long it takes the generation of the renewable energy or carbon saved to fully payback the energy used or CO_2 (equivalent) released to produce, install, maintain or decommission such plant. In the future, this might have more widespread application and could become an important metric in developing products and services that are more sustainable.

3: Environmental management system processes

3.1 Overview of environmental management systems

An environmental management system (EMS) is a set of logical processes to help an organisation manage its environmental issues effectively. Important models include ISO 14001, the international EMS standard, and the European Union Eco-Management and Audit Scheme (EMAS). EMAS sets out a standardised approach to environmental management, including an EMS equivalent to ISO 14001. There are other national EMS schemes, but ISO 14001 is predominant, and internationally recognised.

Environmental management system
The part of the overall management system that includes organisational structure, planning activities, responsibilities, practices, procedures, processes and resources for developing, implementing, reviewing and maintaining the environmental policy; and managing environmental aspects.

Table 3.1.1
Definition of an environmental management system

3.1.1 The 'plan, do, check and act' cycle

A systematic approach to environmental management should be based on the 'plan, do, check and act' (or Deming) cycle. This cycle is the basis of ISO 14001 and other management models seeking continual improvement.

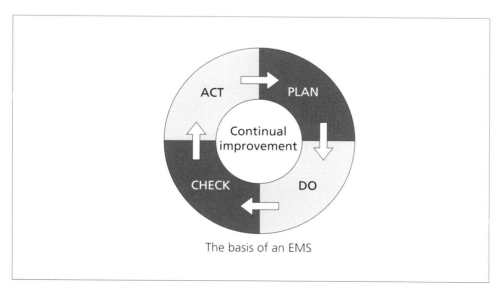

The basis of an EMS

Figure 3.1.1
The 'plan, do, check and act' cycle

The four stages can be broken down further, as outlined in Table 3.1.2.

Table 3.1.2
The four stages of
the continual
improvement cycle

Cycle stage	Management activities/steps	Relevant environmental management tool
Plan	• Identify priority issues (significant aspects) • Establish (or modify) policy to address issues • Identify performance standards/improvement opportunities (legal requirements, best practice solutions) • Agree key performance indicators • Set objectives and targets to meet desired performance levels • Prepare action plans, programmes and procedures for achieving performance/ meeting objectives and targets	Environmental review (initial or subsequent
Do	• Implement actions	
Check	• Monitor results • Evaluate performance against policy aims, objectives, targets, plans, programmes and procedures • Determine reasons for deviations, eg non-conformances	Environmental management audit
Act	• Take corrective action for non-conformances • Reflect on performance and adequacy of system elements in delivering desired levels of performance • Ensure changing circumstances are identified • Modify system elements: policy, objectives and targets, plans, programmes and procedures, as necessary	Management review

3.1.2 Environmental management systems in outline

The principal elements of an EMS are outlined in Figure 3.1.2. Although this diagram is different from that conventionally used to describe ISO 14001 (see Figure 3.1.4), it shows the main elements. ISO 14001 also provides extra detail – for example, in terms of responsibilities, training, communication and documentation.

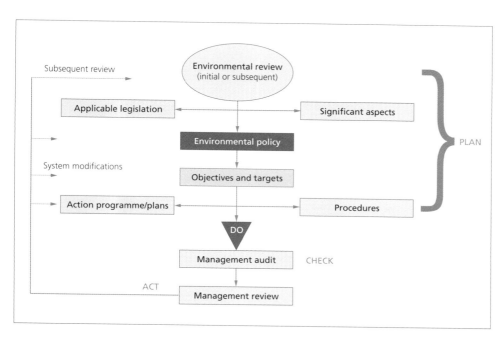

Figure 3.1.2
The main
elements of an
EMS

Important features of an EMS are:
- the environmental policy statement is fundamental to the system – it sets the framework for environmental management
- the environmental policy should address significant environmental aspects and requirements of applicable environmental legislation (note: legislation should in any case be used as part of the assessment of significance – see Chapter 2.2)
- the policy is given purpose through appropriate objectives, targets, action plans, programmes and procedures
- performance is checked through auditing, and rectified where non-conformances are identified
- there are feedback mechanisms through the management review. This ensures that the system is kept relevant and fit-for-purpose, and can deliver continual improvement
- the environmental review is an important first stage for those organisations without a formal EMS. Subsequent environmental reviews may be sensible if circumstances significantly change, eg new activities, products or services, or external developments.

3.1.3 Purpose of environmental management systems
One of the main drivers to develop and maintain an EMS is to minimise the organisation's business risks associated with environmental issues through the systematic management of its significant environmental interactions (aspects).

Figure 3.1.3
Business risks
associated with a
lack of effective
environmental
management

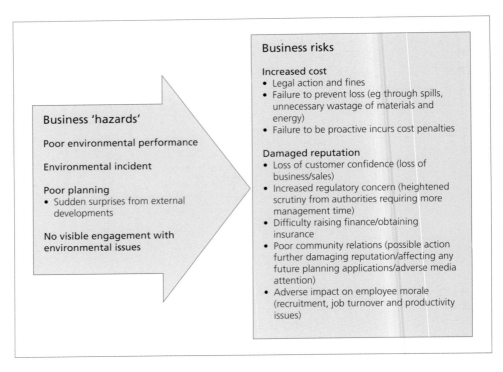

Business 'hazards'

Poor environmental performance

Environmental incident

Poor planning
• Sudden surprises from external
  developments

No visible engagement with
environmental issues

Business risks

Increased cost
• Legal action and fines
• Failure to prevent loss (eg through spills,
  unnecessary wastage of materials and
  energy)
• Failure to be proactive incurs cost penalties

Damaged reputation
• Loss of customer confidence (loss of
  business/sales)
• Increased regulatory concern (heightened
  scrutiny from authorities requiring more
  management time)
• Difficulty raising finance/obtaining
  insurance
• Poor community relations (possible action
  further damaging reputation/affecting any
  future planning applications/adverse media
  attention)
• Adverse impact on employee morale
  (recruitment, job turnover and productivity
  issues)

It is entirely possible to operate an EMS without certification to a management standard such as ISO 14001. However, certification to such a standard has a number of benefits:
• it provides independent recognition that the organisation is managing its environmental issues in accordance with a recognised standard
• it provides an internal discipline for the organisation – the business understands that its system is being audited not only through the internal management audit, but also through accredited external verifiers.

Environmental reports (particularly those verified by a third party) may also be important in helping demonstrate an organisation's engagement and performance with environmental matters. These reports (covered in more detail in Chapter 3.7) will be more robust where they draw on information from a comprehensive and systematic approach to managing environmental issues, ie an EMS.

The flip side to business risk is business benefit. The potential business benefits of establishing and maintaining an effective EMS are shown in Table 3.1.3.

Benefit area	Specific benefits can include:
'Licence to operate'	• makes it easier to obtain regulatory permits, licences, consents, authorisations (including planning consents and operational licences) • maintains and enhances community relations • improves relations with regulator • avoids enforcement or civil actions
Cost control	• avoids fines and damages awarded from legal action through criminal or civil courts • avoids hidden costs of legal action, including substantial draw on management time • improves operational and process efficiency • provides ongoing annual savings in materials, water, energy and waste costs where minimisation programmes are functioning • has a direct contribution to the bottom line
Access to product markets	• assures customers of commitment to responsible environmental practices • helps understand (and meet or exceed) customer's requirements • creates improved or new products and services with market opportunities
Access to labour markets	• improves morale and productivity • attracts prospective employees to the organisation
Access to capital markets	• satisfies investor criteria • allows insurance to be obtained at relatively reasonable cost
General public	• helps build a positive reputation/enhanced image

Table 3.1.3
Potential business benefits of an effective EMS

These business benefits relate to the concept of operating space discussed in Chapter 1.4.

3.1.4 ISO 14001

This standard was first issued by ISO in 1996 and a revised version was published in 2004. ISO 14001 is part of a comprehensive suite of environmental management standards that provide guidance on various topics, including environmental performance indicators, life cycle assessment and environmental communications.

ISO 14001 is a "specification with guidance for environmental management systems". It is a standard specification of the requirements for an EMS which need to be in place and functioning in order to obtain official certification – it is not therefore a non-certifiable guideline. However, organisations that design their EMS to conform to the standard are not obliged to obtain certification.

Figure 3.1.4
The ISO 14001
approach

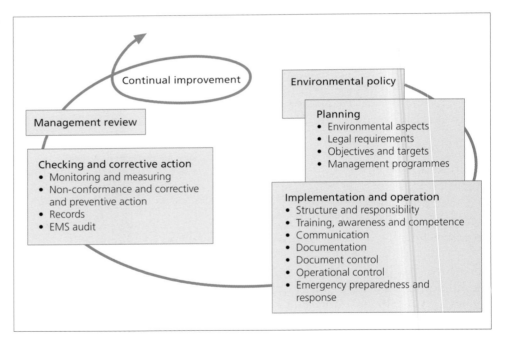

Importantly, ISO 14001 does not establish absolute requirements for environmental performance. It does, however, require the organisation to make explicit commitments in its policy statement to:
- comply with applicable legislation
- strive for continual improvement
- prevent pollution.

The prevention of pollution requirement does not attempt to define pollution levels. Prevention of pollution can include source reduction or elimination, process, product or service changes, efficient use of resources, material and energy substitution, reuse, recovery, recycling, reclamation and treatment (see Table 3.1.4).

Commitment	Definition
Continual improvement	Recurring process of enhancing the environmental management system in order to achieve improvements in overall environmental performance consistent with the organisation's environmental policy.
Prevention of pollution	Use of processes, practices, techniques, materials, products, services or energy to avoid, reduce or control (separately or in combination) the creation, emission or discharge of any type of pollutant or waste, in order to reduce adverse environmental impacts.

Table 3.1.4
ISO 14001 key commitments and definitions

Defining scope
ISO 14001 requires that an organisation defines the scope of its EMS and that it ensures that its environmental policy matches that scope. Among other things, this aims to give stakeholders (who should be able to access the policy) a clearer picture of what the EMS covers (and what it does not cover).

3.1.5 Certification
Certification is the process by which an independent third party organisation (certification body or certifier) checks that an organisation's EMS conforms to a standard such as ISO 14001, and certifies that this is the case (see Figure 3.1.5). For the EU EMAS, the terminology is slightly different – the process is referred to as verification and those conducting it as verifiers.

To ensure credibility, organisations seeking certification to ISO 14001 should commission certification bodies that are accredited by government agencies to be able to undertake certification work. In the UK, this is the UK Accreditation Service (UKAS).

Certifiers usually undertake at least an initial assessment of the system followed by the main assessment before awarding a certificate. The process includes examination of documentation, interviews and site visits. If non-conformances with ISO 14001 are found, the organisation will be advised which changes are necessary and these areas will be checked again before the certificate is awarded. Should non-conformances be discovered during a subsequent certification surveillance audit, then typically the organisation is given a timescale to take corrective action. If action is not taken or if the non-conformance is substantial, then the organisation may lose certification status.

Figure 3.1.5
Overview of the
certification
process

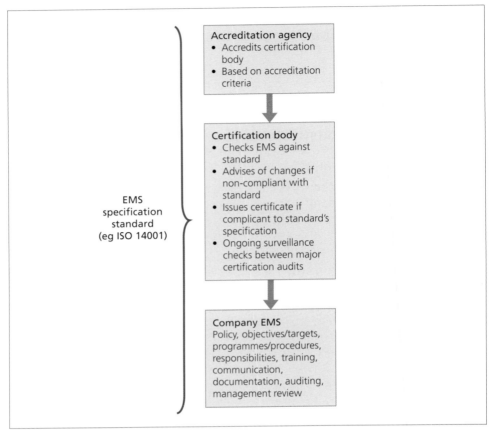

3.1.6 Management manual

For those organisations aiming for certification to ISO 14001, it is vital to provide a summary of how the EMS works. This is also good practice for those not seeking certification since it provides a central point of reference. It can be achieved by producing a management manual which is either paper-based or in electronic format. Its contents should include:

- the organisation's environmental policy statement
- an organisational chart mapping out responsibilities for environmental issues and relevant committee structures for decision-making, performance monitoring and review
- an overview of environmental objectives and targets, and of any key performance indicators
- an overview of the system elements, including assessment of significance of environmental aspects, list of applicable legislation, auditing and review mechanisms
- copies of programmes and procedures to manage significant environmental aspects, communicate progress and train employees on environmental matters.

Where detail would make the manual too cumbersome, the manual should summarise the core elements and signpost where detailed documentation can be found.

3.1.7 External reporting

External reporting of environmental performance is becoming increasingly important. A public statement (independently verified) is an important requirement of the EU Eco-Management and Audit Scheme (section 1.4.4).

There is also particular pressure for organisations to report their green house gas emissions, ie their carbon footprint. For example the UK government has issued detailed measurement and reporting guidelines, including the importance of defining the scope of activities as part of this activity. This is returned to in Chapter 5.1.

External reporting is also further considered in Chapter 3.7. An important factor is for such reporting to provide meaningful performance data highlighting key facts, trends and the extent to which targets have been achieved.

3.2 Environmental policy

The environmental policy is the foundation of environmental management, whether certification to an EMS standard is the goal or not. It outlines the organisation's aims and commitments and sets the framework for more detailed objectives and targets to be developed. It also demonstrates the level of commitment to environmental management to the workforce and, since it should be publicly available, to external stakeholders.

Table 3.2.1 shows the ISO 14001 definition of an environmental policy. It is important to design the policy with care – it should not commit the organisation to anything it does not expect to deliver in the foreseeable future. Also, if certification to ISO 14001 is a goal, then the accredited certifiers will be using the policy statement as the basis of their assessment of conformance with other elements of the management system.

Table 3.2.1
ISO 14001
definition –
environmental
policy

Term	Definition
Environmental policy	Overall intentions and direction of an organisation related to its environmental performance as formally expressed by top management. *Note: The environmental policy provides a framework for action and for the setting of environmental objectives and environmental targets.*

3.2.1 Developing an environmental policy statement

ISO 14001 provides a good model for developing a policy statement. The standard requires that it:

- is defined by top management, within a defined scope
- is appropriate to the nature, scale and environmental impacts of the organisation's activities, products and services
- includes a commitment to compliance with applicable legal requirements and with other requirements to which the organisation subscribes which relate to its environmental aspects
- includes commitments to continual improvement and to prevention of pollution (see Table 3.2.2)
- provides the framework for setting and reviewing environmental objectives and targets
- is documented, implemented and maintained, and communicated to all employees and others working on behalf of the organisation
- is available to the public.

The policy should also address, at a high level, the significant environmental aspects of the organisation.

Term	Definition
Continual improvement	Recurring process of enhancing the environmental management system in order to achieve improvements in overall environmental performance consistent with the organisation's environmental policy. *Note: the process need not take place in all areas of activity simultaneously.*
Prevention of pollution	Use of processes, practices, techniques, materials, products, services or energy to avoid, reduce or control (separately or in combination) the creation, emission or discharge of any type of pollutant or waste, in order to reduce adverse environmental impacts.

Table 3.2.2
ISO 14001 definitions related to environmental policy

Other requirements to which an organisation might subscribe include codes of practice (eg established for the trade or sector) and official voluntary resource efficiency schemes.

When developing the policy statement, the organisation should consider its vision, stakeholder expectations and its capability to deliver the commitments made (see Figure 3.2.1).

Figure 3.2.1
Factors in drafting an environmental policy

The policy should provide strategic direction – it should ensure that the organisation actively addresses environmental issues rather than just reacts to them.

The statement should also be kept short – anything more than one side of A4 may well be too long. It should be clear, so that those reading it can understand it and identify its commitments. The document should be endorsed by the managing director or above, and dated.

Policies may need to be changed. To allow this, the policy should be regularly reviewed through the management review process (see Chapter 2.3) to check that it remains suitable, adequate and effective.

3.2.2 Examples of policy commitments

While the issues addressed in the policy statement will depend on the nature of the organisation, policy commitments might, for example, be developed from the following:

- comply with or exceed applicable environmental laws
- strive for continual improvement in environmental performance through setting objectives and targets and developing key performance indicators
- prevent pollution, reduce waste and minimise the consumption of resources (materials, fuel and energy)
- commit to the reuse and recovery of waste, as opposed to disposal, where feasible
- take into account the environmental impacts of raw material sourcing on habitats, species diversity and natural beauty
- identify and manage key risks and have arrangements in place to respond to all foreseeable emergencies
- ensure environmental factors are included in all key business decision processes, specifically, for example, the design of new products and services, the planning and commissioning of new sites and installations, the acquisition of new businesses or the investment of reserves
- embody life cycle thinking in key business processes
- ensure staff and contractors are aware of environmental performance requirements and are trained and competent in environmental matters
- influence suppliers, contractors and other business partners to adopt environmental best practices/subscribe to equivalent environmental standards
- communicate/engage in dialogue with interested parties
- produce an annual environmental report to set out progress to employees and stakeholders.

These commitments would need to be suitably modified to match corporate vision, external expectations and internal capabilities.

Organisations may also consider including a commitment to sustainable development. If such a commitment is included, then the organisation should have carefully evaluated the implications of the commitment and considered the required actions in both the short and longer term. Commitments made without substance can be counter-productive and may be referred to by some stakeholders as 'greenwash'.

In addition, the precise wording provides a sense of the degree of commitment or engagement.

3.2.3 Environmental policy statement
As already discussed, an environmental policy statement should normally be short, simple and to the point.

It should contain the elements listed in Table 3.2.3.

Statement element	Description
Clear heading	This should clearly identify that this is the environmental policy statement of the organisation.
Scope of the policy	This should clearly indicate the areas or operations covered by the policy – for example, it covers worldwide or UK operations, or a particular site or business unit.
Concise statement of principle	This should provide recognition that the organisation's activities, products and services impact on the environment, or that environmental protection is relevant to the organisation. It should provide a sense of the importance of environmental issues to the business, and linkage to the corporate vision.
Policy commitments	These should set out the broad environmental management aims of the organisation.
Declaration of who the policy is addressed to	Depending on organisation culture, this might be used to reinforce the message that the policy is for all staff and that managers have responsibility to implement the policy. It might also be used to state that the policy is publicly available.
Endorsement and date	The statement should be signed by the managing director or equivalent, and dated.

Table 3.2.3
Key structural elements of an environmental policy statement

A straightforward example of a policy statement is shown opposite. This illustrates how an effective statement can be presented and it refers to a fictitious small, one-site manufacturing company.

The statement should give a sense of the organisation's values and culture. For example, it wants environmental management to be about business success. Also, it suggests that the organisation is reasonably well engaged with stakeholders – although, except in the case of suppliers and distributors, there is no *explicit* commitment to have dialogue with other stakeholders. Such dialogue is implied in that the environment report will go to regulators, customers, suppliers and neighbours, but unless this invites feedback, it is a limited communication exercise. Certainly, the local community is considered to be important (bullet point two). Also, the role of employees is clearly significant – bullet point six explicitly commits to *involving* them, not just training them or making them aware, and the declaration towards the end of the statement emphasises the importance of teamwork and open communication.

This policy statement represents one example of many possible statements. Each organisation should tailor its statement to reflect its own culture and performance objectives.

HEMINGFORD TOOLING LTD

ENVIRONMENTAL POLICY

This policy applies to all operations at our North Road site in Bristol, UK.

Hemingford Tooling manufactures machine tools for the engineering industry, with principal markets in the UK, Germany and USA. We recognise that all our activities interact with the environment and are committed to minimising adverse impacts and improving process efficiency. In particular, this will be achieved through our commitment to:

- comply with all applicable environmental legal requirements, and other relevant requirements to which we subscribe
- review regularly the actual and potential environmental aspects and impacts of all our activities, including those affecting our local community
- strive for continual improvement in environmental performance through setting objectives and targets and developing key performance indicators
- employ best practice to prevent pollution, minimise waste and maximise the efficient use of resources (materials, fuel and energy)
- identify and manage key risks and have arrangements in place to respond to all foreseeable incidents and emergencies
- involve employees and contractors in our environmental programmes and provide training to enable them to discharge their responsibilities
- engage in dialogue with suppliers and distributors to encourage their participation in environmental best practice
- produce an annual environmental report to set out progress to employees, regulators, customers, suppliers, neighbours and other interested parties.

Every employee has an individual responsibility to help meet the requirements of this policy. All are invited to contribute ideas for better practices, for example, through their quality team meetings, HSEQ co-ordinator, line manager or directly to myself.

Simon White – Managing Director
December 2010

This policy is publicly available, on request

3.3 Environmental objectives and targets

Objectives and targets are the springboard for action to improve environmental performance (see Figure 3.3.1). Environmental management is, essentially, the management of an organisation's significant environmental aspects, and this means that objectives and targets should provide a clear and demonstrable link to the significant aspects. They should also reflect the environmental policy since this sets the general aims and direction for environmental management. Objectives and targets are defined in Table 3.3.1

Figure 3.3.1
Role of objectives
and targets

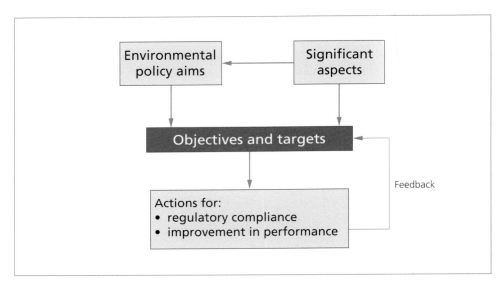

Table 3.3.1
ISO 14001
definitions –
objectives and
targets

Term	Definition
Environmental objective	Overall environmental goal, consistent with the environmental policy that an organisation sets itself to achieve.
Environmental target	Detailed performance requirement, applicable to the organisation or parts thereof, that arises from the environmental objectives and that needs to be set and met in order to achieve those objectives.

3.3.1 Relationship between policy, objectives and targets

Objectives and targets set specific goals for action. They also provide standards against which the degree of success can be measured or progress monitored.

There is a 'hierarchical' relationship between policy aims, objectives and targets, although the distinction between objectives and targets is not always 'hard and fast'. Policy aims set the overall corporate context and objectives flow from them. It is useful to think of targets as the means by which overall objectives will be attained and against which operational actions will be assessed. Objectives tend to be longer term, corporate and relatively broad. Targets should be short term (typically annual), operational and specific. Targets should be an integral part of action plans and programmes at the level of the business unit. This is considered in Chapter 3.4.

The relationship between the three types of goal is illustrated in Figure 3.3.2, with an example provided in Table 3.3.2.

Policy commitment	Objective	Targets (for 2011)
To minimise the consumption of resources (materials, fuel and energy)	To reduce energy consumption by 10 per cent on 2010 levels by 31/12/2015	• To reduce electricity consumption in office A by 10 per cent in 2011 compared to 2010 • To reduce gas consumption in production unit X by five per cent in 2011 compared to 2010 • To reduce oil consumption in warehouse Y by seven per cent in 2011 compared to 2010 • To send all (100 per cent) operational supervisors (grade E and above) in business units P, Q and R on an energy efficiency awareness course by the end of 2011 • To conduct a detailed energy audit of business unit Z. Report required for July 2011 to assist with improvement target-setting cycle for 2012

Table 3.3.2 Example of the link between a policy commitment, objective and targets

In the above example, the 2011 targets, and actual performance in relation to these targets, contribute to the overall five-year objective. The targets set in 2012 and subsequent years, and satisfactory performance against these targets, would also contribute to achieving the objective by December 2015.

Figure 3.3.2
Relationship between policy, objectives and targets

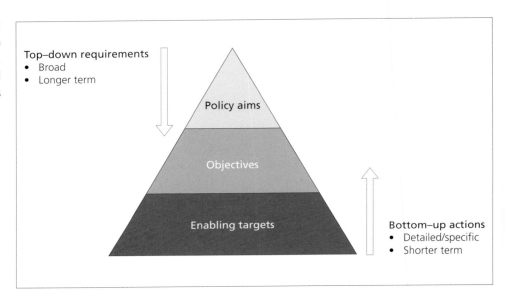

3.3.2 SMART by nature

An essential management principle is that objectives, and especially targets, should aim to be 'SMART' (see Table 3.3.3).

Specific	They should be clear and unambiguous. They should be expressed in terms of specific results required. Responsibility should be assigned for their achievement.
Measurable	They should be quantifiable so that the degree of progress can be readily gauged and achievement or failure quickly identified. Where possible, they should be linked to performance indicators.
Agreed	Individuals and/or teams responsible for achieving the goal should have the opportunity to comment on it and to understand and accept its value. This is particularly important for targets.
Realistic	They should be challenging but achievable. While objectives and targets should not be too easily achieved (as this will fail to motivate performance), they should not be too difficult. If they are too difficult, individuals and teams responsible for achieving them will become demoralised. They may give up hope or divert too much attention to achieving the goal at the expense of other business goals. Objectives and targets must be realistic in terms of resources available and the demands of other business priorities.
Time-bound	They should have a date by which the goal should be achieved. This helps ensure action takes place in that timeframe. Where the timescale for achieving an objective is long, it may be advisable to set interim milestones to monitor and assess progress.

Table 3.3.3
Definition of
SMART

3.3.3 Continual improvement

Objectives and targets specify continual improvement goals. However, simultaneous continual improvement is rarely practical across an organisation's entire range of significant aspects. This is reflected in the definition of continual improvement in ISO 14001 (see Table 3.3.4).

Term	Definition
Continual improvement	Recurring process of enhancing the environmental management system in order to achieve improvements in overall environmental performance consistent with the organisation's environmental policy. *Note: the process of continual improvement need not take place in all areas of activity simultaneously.*

Table 3.3.4
ISO 14001
definition –
continual
improvement

Objectives and targets should help drive continual, year-on-year improvement in overall environmental performance. However, not all of them need to define specific environmental improvement goals. For example, if an aspect is being effectively managed, an improvement goal may not be required but rather an objective or target should be applied to ensure that current controls continue to work well. Furthermore, the organisation might not be in a position to implement improvement actions because it first needs to understand the nature of an aspect and to identify and evaluate options for improving performance in that area.

It can be useful to think of three types of objective/target (see Table 3.3.5).

Table 3.3.5
Different types of objective (target)

Type of objective/target	Description	Example
Improvement	These explicitly aim to deliver improvement in the management of one or more of the significant environmental aspects and to demonstrate improved performance.	To reduce waste going to landfill by 10 per cent over 2011 compared to 2010 levels.
Management	These aim to ensure that controls relating to an aspect or set of aspects are systematically applied on an ongoing basis. They do not explicitly aim for improved environmental performance but stipulate an ongoing required standard of performance to be achieved.	To ensure that controlled waste is handled in accordance with the duty of care code of practice.
Investigation	These aim to investigate, research or monitor a situation before appropriate action is taken. They recognise that for certain aspects it may be inadvisable for actions to be taken without understanding the nature of the aspect and/or the options for its management in greater detail. In other words, there is a need to research the situation, to investigate what is going on and to identify practical and economic solutions.

This type of objective/target could also include the requirement to undertake technical research and development projects or demonstration pilots. Certain techniques or technologies may be in the development stage and therefore a suitable objective may be to monitor progress. | To undertake waste minimisation audit by July 2011 to identify cost-effective on-site and off-site waste reduction, reuse and recovery opportunities. |

Figure 3.3.3 sets out a simple method for establishing which type of objective or target is most relevant for a significant environmental aspect.

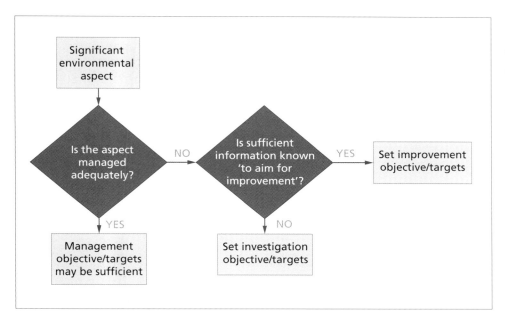

Figure 3.3.3
Deciding on the types of objective/target

In practice, an aspect may be assigned a combination of target types. For example, at the operational level it would be necessary to manage waste in line with the duty of care as a minimum standard (eg as required by law in the UK), so that this would be a management target. However, an investigation target might also be set to determine what types of waste are generated and in what quantities, and to identify what opportunities exist for process efficiency. This would be as a precursor for setting appropriate waste minimisation (ie improvement) targets in subsequent years.

3.3.4 Setting objectives and targets
Deciding whether a significant aspect is sufficiently managed, or the degree of improvement and the timescale over which this should happen, will depend on a number of factors. Typically:
• risk of breaching legal requirements through current operating practices
• planning to meet or exceed impending (or anticipated) regulatory standards
• degree of concern of stakeholders in the aspect
• degree of risk of an incident leading to a breach in the law, civil claim, demonstrable environmental impact
• implications of economic instruments affecting the aspect

- opportunities for improvement – particularly low cost/rapid payback/easily implemented changes, or capital projects leading to high returns
- technological options and developments in best practice for controlling the aspect
- financial and other resources of the business
- other business priorities
- degree to which the organisation wishes to be seen to be a leading edge or responsible operator regarding the aspect in question.

Ultimately, the setting of objectives and targets is about balancing the costs and benefits of action or inaction.

Priority grids can be used to assist the target-setting process. Two simple techniques are outlined below.

a. Urgency/importance matrix (Figure 3.3.4)

Significant aspects (or action areas) are allocated 'cells' according to the agreed level of importance and urgency. Reasons should be given (and recorded) as to why something is allocated to a particular cell in terms of both its importance and urgency.

Figure 3.3.4
The urgency/
importance matrix

	not urgent	moderately urgent	urgent
very important	priority level 4	priority level 2	priority level 1
important	priority level 5	priority level 3	priority level 2

It should be noted that there are no 'not important' cells in the matrix. This is because the assessment of significance has already screened out what is currently not considered to be important, ie what is 'significant' is 'important'.

b. Benefit/ease of action grid (Figure 3.3.5)

Significant aspects (or action areas) are allocated points on the grid according to the agreed position on each axis depending on ease (or difficulty) of action and the degree of benefit. Reasons should be given (and recorded) as to why something is allocated its position on the grid.

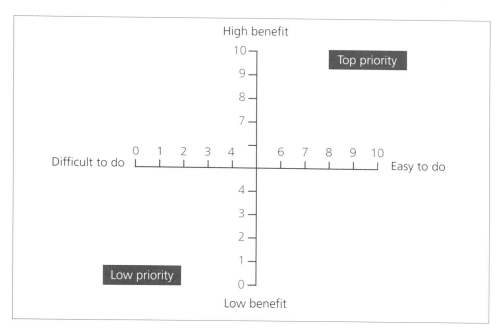

Figure 3.3.5
The benefit/ease of action grid

Benefits can include environmental, financial (eg rapid payback) or reputational factors.

Priority grids can assist with the ranking of areas for action. This can be particularly relevant where a range of improvement areas may be available but there are limited resources. Alternatively, it can assist in identifying priorities for future budgeting. They could help set timescales – for example, anything allocated a high priority ranking would require immediate action.

3.3.5 Environmental performance indicators

Environmental objectives and targets should ideally be linked with performance indicators. This also has the advantage of helping ensure that the objectives and targets are SMART.

Environmental performance indicators (EPIs) are specific parameters which provide information about an organisation's environmental performance. Two classes of EPI are outlined in Table 3.3.6.

	Aspect (or operational) performance indicators	Management performance indicators
Table 3.3.6 Examples of performance indicators	These provide information about the performance of the organisation's activities, products and services in terms of environmental aspects. Examples include: • quantity of energy used per year • quantity of energy used per unit of production or office area • quantity of water used • quantity of recycled materials used (as opposed to virgin materials) or reused components • quantity of waste produced per year • quantity of specific substances released (effluent or emissions) • quantity of greenhouse gas emissions per year (as carbon dioxide equivalent) • quantity of carbon dioxide equivalent releases per unit of production or office area • percentage of waste sent for disposal, reuse and/or recovery • number and volume of spills • area of land used for different purposes • area set aside as nature reserve.	These provide information about management efforts to influence an organisation's environmental performance. Examples include: • number of achieved objectives and targets • number of audits conducted • number of products with environmental labels • number of suppliers audited • number of contractors inducted • number of employees trained • number of non-compliances with regulatory requirements • number of unresolved corrective actions • number of emergency drills • number of complaints • rating score from community surveys.

When considering EPIs, and when setting improvement objectives and targets, it is important to consider the distinction between absolute performance and *relative* performance.

Absolute performance indicators relate to the actual quantity, number or volume of the parameter in question – for example, tonnes of carbon dioxide (CO_2) emitted in a year, kWh of energy used per year or total hours of training provided in a given period of time. Absolute indicators provide information on the actual size of an interaction, initiative or achievement.

Relative performance indicators compare the data in relation to another parameter – for example, tonnes of CO_2 emitted per unit of production, kWh of energy used per m^2 office space, total hours of environmental training per total hours training or total people trained out of those needing training. Relative (or ratio) indicators provide information on the efficiency of an activity, or the quality of an initiative or achievement.

Relative indicators allow different scales of operation to be compared. They can be particularly useful for businesses that are changing the size of their operations and which are planning to set meaningful longer-term objectives.

3.4 Environmental management programmes and procedures

Environmental management programmes are action plans that enable an organisation, or part of it, to work towards achieving its environmental objectives and targets. They are supported by procedures and relevant documentation.

3.4.1 Management programme

A programme should be inextricably linked with the setting of targets (see Figure 3.4.1). The management programme should set out:

- the context for action, eg corporate objective, significance of aspect, priority issues
- the activities that will be necessary to achieve each target
- how these will be resourced in terms of people and money
- timescales for each action to be completed or milestone reached.

Figure 3.4.1
Actions necessary to achieve targets and objectives

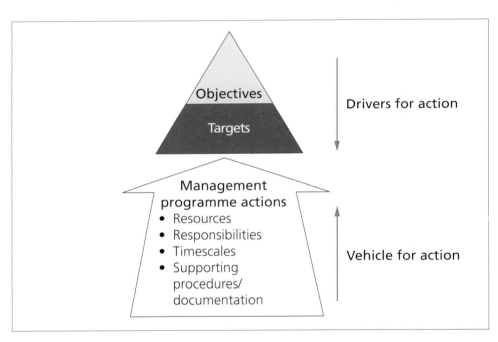

Consultation on the programme is essential so that those who are responsible for its implementation can contribute to its formulation and support the allocated actions.

Table 3.4.1 contains an extract from a 2010 management programme.

Significant aspect	Controlled waste		
Context	Subject to regulatory control under the Environmental Protection Act 1990 Part II and needs to be managed in line with the regulatory duty of care. Audit findings have identified areas of non-conformance and other inadequacies. Waste sent to landfill incurs landfill tax – measures to reduce this form of waste disposal will reduce the cost of disposal. General waste minimisation should result in other cost-saving opportunities for the organisation and contribute to resource conservation at the societal level. The corporate policy aim is to reduce waste and commit to recovery and recycling, as opposed to disposal, where feasible.		
Target	Actions to achieve	Responsi-bility	Completion date
To ensure that controlled waste is always handled in accordance with the duty of care code of practice	• Obtain code of practice • Review waste segregation, storage and transfer procedures • Review audit records to detail recent waste non-conformances • Review transfer documentation • Identify waste carriers and obtain copies of licences • Discuss amendments to procedures with operatives • Produce specifications for new storage facilities • Develop 'toolbox talks' on waste handling and transfer • Order new storage facilities • Give 'toolbox talks'	JW JW/DM JW/DM JW/DM JW/PH DM JW/PH JW/DM PH DM	30/1 30/3 30/3 30/3 30/3 15/4 30/4 30/4 10/5 30/5
To undertake waste minimisation audit by October 2010 to identify on-site and off-site waste reduction, reuse and recovery opportunities	• Identify potential consultants to undertake audit • Invite consultants to tender for work • Select consultants (experience, availability, price) • Issue contract • Conduct waste minimisation audit • Draft report issued • Final report and presentation • Review opportunities	JW JW/PH JW/PH PH Consultants Consultants Consultants PR/JW/DM	30/1 15/2 30/3 10/4 30/6 30/7 30/8 30/9

Table 3.4.1 An example extract from a management programme

Additional sections or columns could be added, for example, regarding budget.

Progress against the management programme should be monitored regularly.

3.4.2 Environmental procedures

An environmental procedure is a documented explanation of how to undertake an activity with respect to environmental management. For those organisations integrating environmental matters into business processes, this will not necessarily mean stand-alone or exclusive environmental procedures but rather the incorporation of environmental matters into all procedures, as required. Where environmental procedures *are* stand-alone, it is important that they complement those in other areas of management.

Environmental procedures typically fall into the categories listed in Table 3.4.2.

Procedure	Examples
Operational	• Waste management • Process control • Use of abatement plant • Start-up and shut-down operations • Materials handling and storage • Night-time operations
Decision-making	• Assessment of significance • Product design • New facility planning • Investment appraisal • Supplier and contractor appraisal • Research and development project evaluation
Monitoring and auditing	• Collecting and reporting data on environmental aspects, eg releases (emissions and effluent), contained waste (solid and liquid), energy and material use, greenhouse gas emissions/carbon footprint • Planning, conducting and reporting audits
Emergency response	• Preparedness and response to spills, fires and accidental releases
Personnel	• Induction • Training • Appraisal • Communication • Employee suggestions
External communication	• Dealing with complaints and concerns of stakeholders • External reporting on environmental management
System maintenance	• Document control • Corrective action • Management review

Table 3.4.2
Types of environmental procedure

The main purpose of procedures is to set out standard ways of doing things. People can then refer to these for instruction or guidance. They help ensure that what needs to be done is done. They inform employees or contractors and other relevant people what is expected of them. Procedures can contain standard forms and explain how these should be completed.

To help ensure that they are followed, the number of procedures should be kept to a minimum. Each procedure should also be as short as possible and written in simple language.

There is a balance to be struck between providing enough detail to ensure work is done correctly and the risk of the procedure being too cumbersome for effective use. The use of flow charts, diagrams, tables, photographs and bullet point actions can improve comprehension.

Procedures should be drafted, tested and reviewed with those who are responsible for implementing them, to help build understanding, support and ownership.

A written procedure typically contains the following elements:
- procedure name and reference
- purpose – what the procedure intends to achieve
- scope – what activities or areas are covered by the procedure
- description of the procedure
- allocation of responsibilities
- definitions of any specific or unusual terms used
- process for modifying the procedure
- interface with related procedures
- date issued and version number
- authorisation.

Procedures are key features of an EMS and they are examined in environmental management audits (see Chapter 2.3). It is important that procedures are readily available and kept up to date, and that obsolete versions are removed or easily identified as such.

3.4.3 Environmental record-keeping

Proper consideration should be given to the purpose of any records being kept, particularly with a view to keeping the number of EMS records under control. However, key actions and decisions should be recorded.

Records can:
- provide information to help set future targets
- enable monitoring of progress against a target or standard
- assist with the auditing of procedures by helping verify their implementation
- demonstrate compliance with a legal requirement
- confirm that agreed actions have been undertaken
- provide a reference point for important information, such as legal requirements or audit findings.

Records can be kept in either paper or electronic format, but they must be readily accessible to relevant individuals. Records can take many forms – for example, charts and graphs, forms, tables, registers, log books, reports and minutes.

Environmental records might include:
- a list of applicable legislative and regulatory requirements
- a list of environmental aspects and identification of significance
- organisation charts setting out responsibilities
- agreed objectives and targets
- monitoring information – emissions, discharges, waste, energy, water, materials, greenhouse gas emissions
- inspection, maintenance and calibration records
- process and product information
- supplier and contractor information
- training records
- permits, licences, consents and authorisations
- copies of official forms submitted to regulators
- correspondence with regulators or other stakeholders
- incident reports
- complaints from neighbours, customers or other stakeholders, and follow-up actions
- audit reports, non-conformance reports and corrective actions
- minutes of environmental committee meetings/outcome of management review
- photographs to show the situation 'before and after' action, or to show good or poor practice
- external reporting.

Again, a balance needs to be struck between providing sufficient detail, the effort required to maintain the records, and the complexity of the records. Records need to be a useful resource and not a paper-generating exercise.

Furthermore, the importance of people actually doing things needs to be borne in mind during the development of programmes and procedures, and the keeping and use of records. Ultimately it is people that ensure environmental actions are undertaken and that any management system is successfully designed and implemented. This is returned to in Chapter 3.6.

3.5 Environmental emergency preparedness and response

An emergency incident can lead to an immediate environmental impact, or an increased risk of an impact. Depending on the type of incident, the severity of the impact can vary enormously. This chapter will look at emergency incidents with the potential to escalate into a serious impact. When an emergency incident occurs, rapid and correct decisions have to be made to minimise the impact. It is therefore important that environmental management processes consider what incidents could happen and what contingency measures should be in place if incidents occur, to help ensure that serious impacts are either avoided or minimised. The main stages in developing a contingency plan are illustrated in Figure 3.5.1.

ISO 14001 requires an organisation to establish and maintain procedures to identify the potential for, and to respond to, accidents and emergency situations, and to prevent and minimise the environmental impacts that may be associated with them.

3.5.1 Identify potential incidents
Typical incidents that could cause an emergency are spills, leaks, accidental releases, fire or explosion.

Figure 3.5.1
The main stages in developing effective contingency plans

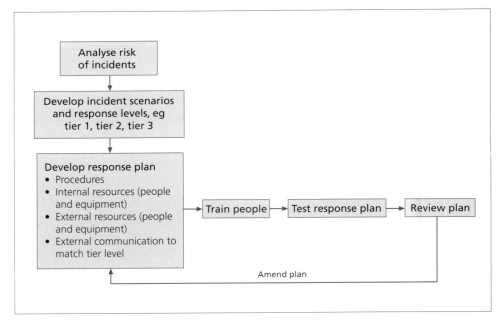

The identification of potential incidents is usually determined by applying the types of risk assessment used for health and safety hazards. This involves systematically assessing what could go wrong (related to the hazard) and determining the likelihood of the event and its consequence (the risk).

To establish what could go wrong it is important to identify both the intrinsic hazards of substances, and hazardous situations. Particular emphasis should be given to the storage, handling, processing or treatment of hazardous substances – for example, toxic and flammable substances. It should be remembered that, in terms of environmental management, hazardous substances can be both inputs (materials and fuel) and outputs (wastes and pollutants). Consideration of the possible causes of incidents is integral to the assessment of hazardous situations. Typical causes include:

- corroded pipework and storage facilities
- rupture of pipework or storage facility, eg through collision with a vehicle or puncture by a sharp object
- faulty couplings when transferring chemicals or fuel
- process upset
- equipment failure, including failure of emission or effluent abatement plant
- operator error or misuse
- vandalism.

An analysis of previous incident statistics, including near hits/misses, can help with this process. Note that the causes above are often derived from other, 'root' causes, such as lack of training or communication, or resources.

Once a list of potential events is established, the events should be classified according to the likelihood of occurrence, and the consequences should they actually occur. The risk assessment matrix in Figure 3.5.2 provides an example.

Likelihood					
	unlikely to occur	negligible risk			
	low likelihood	low risk			
	medium likelihood		less serious risk		
	high likelihood			serious risk	critical risk
		minor	moderate	serious	major
	Consequence				

Figure 3.5.2
An example of a risk assessment matrix

The consequences could be established in terms of environmental impact, cost of rectification, legal actions, damage to reputation and so on. Other consequences could include damage to plant and equipment, loss of production, and health and safety impacts. Consequence factors are important when developing worst case scenarios (see section 3.5.2).

It may be useful to conduct two parallel risk assessments, particularly when preparing for emergency response planning. The first assessment can identify risks without any controls in place, and the second can cover risks with existing controls in place, to indicate the 'residual risk'.

Before building this assessment into the contingency planning process, its role in (and the need for) risk management should be considered. A competent, systematic and comprehensive risk assessment should be used to support risk management – the management of the significant (or unacceptable) risks so that the residual risk of an incident is as low as reasonably practicable. All significant risks should be managed by either management or improvement targets (see Chapter 3.3) aimed at preventing the incident from happening. Risk management is closely related to the processes of evaluating significant aspects and setting objectives and targets.

The risk assessment process will help to evaluate the risk of incidents and should ensure control mechanisms are in place to prevent occurrence. It provides a firm foundation for establishing emergency response procedures since it should ensure that any hazards are well understood and types of potential incident are documented. However, even if the likely occurrence of an incident is low, there still remains the possibility that it could happen – and it may have a high impact. Emergency preparedness (also known as contingency planning) considers what would need to be in place if a significant incident actually occurred, despite risk management measures being in place.

3.5.2 Develop incident scenarios

Using the risk assessment as a foundation, scenarios should be developed based on the following questions:

- what are the worst things that could happen?
- following an incident, what are the potential pathways to critical receptors?
- how could an incident escalate into a crisis event?
- at what stage would external assistance be vital?

For example, for a diesel spill from a refuelling operation, factors to consider would include:

- the total volume being transferred and transfer rate
- the existence of pathways to the environment, such as drains, slope of ground, permeability of ground surface, surface and subsurface hydrology, evaporation rates at different times of the year
- the existence of receptors such as coastlines, rivers or other watercourses, aquifers, downstream nature reserves, water extraction points, fisheries or watersports facilities
- what would happen if the oil reached these receptors, and any particularly sensitive times, eg fish breeding season, period of maximum water extraction or particular leisure or other use
- ignition hazards to turn the spill into a fire or explosion
- health and safety risks associated with the incident.

Risk management might include:	*Emergency response* might include:
• self-sealing couplings in case disconnection occurs • inspection of hose and connections before refuelling to ensure no wear or tear that could facilitate rupture or disconnection • alarm on storage tank to prevent overfill and overflow • transfers undertaken in kerbed area to contain any minor spills • installation of oil–water interceptors (separators) to prevent any spill contaminating the surface water drainage system.	• drain protectors to be placed on drains to prevent fuel entering drains, eg if secondary containment is breached • access to emergency services to intercept drains if spill is progressing towards river, eg if any interceptor is overwhelmed • if spill reaches river, access to emergency services to deploy booms and pump out oil • if river wildlife is at risk, access to agencies to rescue wildlife such as birds and fish • oil waste and debris storage and disposal facilities.

Table 3.5.1 Distinction between risk management and emergency response (example: refuelling oil spill)

3.5.3 The tiered response concept

It is useful to develop contingency plans based on a 'tiered response'. This recognises that incidents can have various consequences and therefore different response requirements. It also recognises that incidents can escalate to emergency status.

For some organisations, a certain type of tiered response may be required by legislation. Otherwise, organisations can tailor these tier levels to fit their circumstances. Three tiers are often effective, as illustrated in Table 3.5.2.

Tier level	Description	Typical consequence category	Possible example
1	The incident can be managed by staff in the immediate operating area using available resources. There is no immediate threat to the environment as the incident is relatively easily contained. An incident report is raised for internal monitoring purposes.	Minor	Small oil spill that does not reach drains and can be cleaned up by oil spill kit in operating area.
2	The incident requires support from a response team and resources from across the site. Emergency services may be alerted and the environmental regulators notified as there is a risk of an environment impact and possible regulatory non-compliance if the incident escalates. Public relations measures may be necessary. Detailed internal post-incident investigation and report will be necessary and possibly a report submitted to regulator.	Moderate/risk of approaching serious	Ongoing leak of oil threatening to breach secondary containment and overwhelm localised drain protection.
3	The incident requires external support from the emergency services and/or technical specialists. The environmental regulators must be notified since the law has been breached and/or there may be threat of secondary impacts. Under tier 3, public safety may also be at risk and public relations measures are a necessary part of the response. Detailed internal post-incident investigation will be necessary and possible regulatory investigation depending on severity.	Serious or major	Large oil spill reaches river and is carried downstream, putting amenity, ecological resources and livelihoods at risk.

3.5.4 Develop an emergency response plan

The organisation should produce a plan so that it is prepared to handle foreseeable emergency situations. The aim should be to minimise the impact of incidents and reduce the risk of their escalation through rapid and effective response mechanisms.

The contingency plan should:
- outline the steps to be taken in the event of key incidents based on the tiered response, including personal protection for those involved in the response. Checklists can be particularly useful
- allocate roles and responsibilities, including the set-up of on-site rapid response teams and emergency response centre, as appropriate
- ensure that response can occur at any time so that there is out-of-hours capability and coverage for key personnel during holiday periods
- identify where equipment and materials to deal with the incident are located or can be readily obtained, together with additional personal protective equipment for those dealing with the situation
- contain up-to-date contact details (including hotlines) for key members of staff and external organisations, including the emergency services, technical specialists, regulatory authorities, community groups and media
- include emergency call-out procedures
- contain copies of forms for notifying relevant authorities of the incident and the actions being undertaken
- include stand-down and restart procedures or checklists.

Organisations should consider setting up an emergency response centre (ERC) for serious or potentially serious incidents. Using the example tiered approach, this would be initiated for any incident approaching tier 2 or above. A staged approach could be used with core centre members called in for a tier 2 incident (or tier 1 where there is a risk of escalation) and other personnel put on alert in case the incident should move towards tier 3 status. The full team would be mobilised in the event of a tier 3 incident. It is important that back-up members are assigned, for example to provide rest for primary team members.

The ERC is a focal point for information on the incident and for decisions and communication concerning the response. It also ensures that managers and key staff are released from other activities so they are able to focus on the emergency.

Key contact points for an ERC dealing with a serious environmental incident are identified in Figure 3.5.3. Individual team members should be allocated specific co-ordination and communication roles under the co-ordination and direction of an emergency manager. Some organisations (eg in the offshore oil industry) might choose to have a dedicated room permanently set up for ERC purposes. Alternatively, it may be feasible to convert an existing (nominated) office into the ERC. Hardware for the ERC might typically include dedicated communication equipment and lines, boards to chart information and contact details, emergency response manuals and checklists for individual members of the team, and desk positions for emergency services or regulatory authorities (in the case of a major incident).

Figure 3.5.3
The role of an emergency response centre

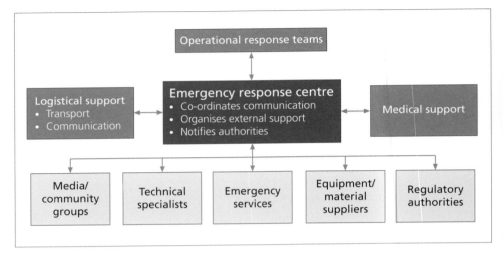

Dedicated contact with technical specialists and suppliers of critical equipment and essential materials may be necessary depending on the nature of the incident.

Additional contacts are likely to include:
- relatives who may be concerned for the safety and wellbeing of family members. This will be especially necessary where there have been any casualties
- normal suppliers and contractors, eg to avoid unnecessary deliveries to the site during the incident or the presence of unnecessary personnel This will be particularly important in a major environmental emergency
- customers, especially if loss of production has occurred or there is concern that it has been, or may be, disrupted.

3.5.5 Training, testing and review
It is vital that all employees who may be involved in the response to an environmental emergency – either operationally or as members of the ERC – fully understand what steps to take, where equipment is located, and who to contact. Training is therefore essential.

Regular practice drills should be conducted to consolidate training and to test the effectiveness of the response plan. Drills should simulate a serious incident and involve key external organisations such as the emergency services and regulatory authorities.

The contingency plan should be reviewed in light of experience with practice drills, and amended as necessary. The plan should also be reviewed following any actual emergency as part of the investigation of why the incident happened, how it was dealt with and whether the response could have been better. The plan should also be revised regularly to take account of any changes to on-site activities, facilities and personnel, and changes related to external bodies such as enforcers or emergency services. It is particularly important that contact details of essential individuals and organisations are always up-to-date.

3.6 Allocating environmental responsibilities and providing training

Groups of people make environmental management practices and processes work. However, individuals need the skills and knowledge to undertake their various responsibilities.

Environmental management therefore needs to be supported by:
- appropriate organisational structures
- processes to identify and deliver relevant training
- effective internal communication (see Chapter 3.7).

3.6.1 Defining environmental roles and responsibilities

Environmental roles and responsibilities depend on a number of factors, including the:
- existing structures and reporting chains or networks
- size of the organisation
- organisational culture
- intended degree of integration of environmental management into line management and business functions
- existing level of environmental management expertise
- existence of individuals who are aware of and motivated by environmental issues and can act as champions to take the environmental management process forward.

It is vital that the overall structure for environmental roles and responsibilities is documented (including organisational charts) and communicated. It is useful to consider the main activities in the 'plan, do, check and act' management cycle (see Chapter 3.1) when mapping this out (and ensuring any gaps are filled).

At the operational level, roles and responsibilities should be clearly defined in action plans, programmes and procedures to ensure that action actually takes place.

There are two main categories of responsibility – general and specific (see Table 3.6.1).

Type	Description
General responsibilities	Overall responsibility of all personnel to understand their general role, accountability and involvement in contributing to meeting the aims of the organisation's environmental policy.
Specific responsibilities	Specific, clearly defined roles, responsibilities and accountabilities to implement the environmental policy, check on progress, rectify any problem areas, identify improvement opportunities, or review the suitability, adequacy and effectiveness of the policy.

Table 3.6.1
The main types of
responsibility

When establishing or reviewing responsibilities, it is good practice that they should be:
- developed and agreed with those allocated or to be assigned to the role
- incorporated into job descriptions and individual performance and appraisal mechanisms
- clear and able to identify interfaces with other parties, both internally and externally.

Table 3.6.2 indicates the individuals or groups that might have environmental responsibilities in an organisation.

Table 3.6.2
Examples of
environmental
responsibilities

Area of environmental responsibility	Typical individuals/functions or groups
Overall vision and direction on environmental issues	Chief executive officer/managing director/board/senior management committee
Agree and endorse policy and corporate objectives	Chief executive officer/managing director/board
Develop and recommend policy commitments and corporate objectives Review action plans and targets	Environmental steering group, task force or committee
Provide professional support on environmental issues (including significant aspects and legislative requirements) and co-ordinate and facilitate environmental programmes and initiatives	Environmental manager/environmental team/health, safety, environmental and quality (HSEQ) manager/HSEQ team
Develop environmental targets and action plans for operational activities	Operational managers and supervisors
Develop environmental targets for products or services	Design and marketing teams
Research new processes and products with reduced environmental impacts	Research and development function
Develop environmental targets for procurement and requirements of contractors and suppliers	Procurement and purchasing team in liaison with operations personnel
Identify, evaluate and recommend ideas for improvement programmes and targets	Improvement teams (interdisciplinary and interdepartmental), including employee representatives and environmental champions/members of the environmental team
Identify training needs and maintain environmental skills base	Human resources function in liaison with the environmental manager/ environmental team
Comply with legal requirements	Operational managers and supervisors
Comply with policy and procedures	All managers and supervisors
Identify customer expectations	Sales and marketing teams

Area of environmental responsibility	Typical individuals/functions or groups
Monitor government policy, new laws and economic instruments	Environmental manager/environmental team/corporate or regulatory affairs departments
Identify external stakeholders and their environmental expectations	Corporate affairs function/environmental manager/environmental team
Develop and maintain investment appraisal procedures to cover environmental costs and benefits	Finance manager
Monitor environmental performance and management system delivery	Environmental manager/environmental team/health, safety, environmental and quality (HSEQ) manager/HSEQ team
Review overall environmental performance Identify strengths, weaknesses, opportunities and threats and recommend changes	Environmental steering group/task force or committee, supported by environmental manager/environmental team
Review overall environmental performance Agree on changes required and direct action	Chief executive officer/managing director/board/senior management committee
Produce external communication tools	Corporate affairs function with environmental manager/environmental team
Produce internal communication tools	Corporate affairs function/human resources function with environmental manager/environmental team
Comply with environmental procedures	All personnel
Work to achieve regulatory compliance and continual improvement	All personnel

Table 3.6.2
Examples of environmental responsibilities
continued

Effective environmental management is truly interdisciplinary. It requires an interdepartmental team approach and input and feedback from all levels of the organisation. Effective communication is vital to its success.

3.6.2 Environmental training

Those with environmental responsibilities must have sufficient training and resources to undertake them effectively.

ISO 14001 requires that organisations identify training needs and that all personnel whose work may create a significant impact on the environment should have appropriate training.

It is useful to follow a training cycle – the key elements of which are set out in Figure 3.6.1.

Figure 3.6.1
The training cycle

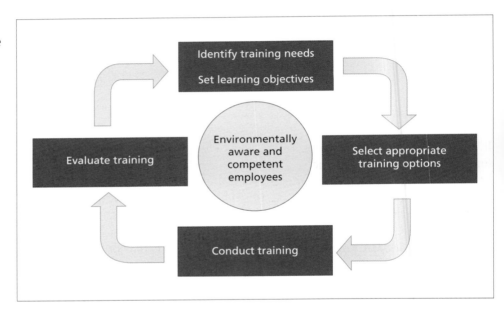

Training needs can range from general awareness to specific knowledge and skills (see Table 3.6.3).

General awareness requirements	Specific needs
To provide or enhance the general context for environmental management	To provide or enhance knowledge and skills to conduct specific tasks
Typical areas might be: • environmental issues and their implications for the organisation • overview of stakeholder pressures, government policy and legislation • explanation of environmental policy aims and corporate objectives • awareness of system elements to deliver policy.	Examples include: • techniques for identifying significant aspects or for undertaking environmental audits • controls for specific aspects such as emissions, effluent and waste • detailed understanding of regulatory requirements • procedures for responding to incidents • techniques for improved process design, waste minimisation, energy efficiency • environmental communication tools.

Table 3.6.3
Examples of environmental training needs

It is good practice for learning objectives to be agreed with the person undergoing training. This helps provide a clear understanding of what will be required from that person during and after the training. The attainment of learning objectives can be assessed after training and any additional training requirements can then be identified.

The options for training include those contained in Table 3.6.4.

Table 3.6.4
Typical options for
delivering
environmental
training

Option	Example	Advantages	Possible issues
'Tailor-made' internal course	Half-day course on waste minimisation	• Tailor-made to organisation/function • Opportunity to share ideas with colleagues • Tends to be cost-effective	• May fail to expose ideas from outsiders (especially if internal trainer used)
Short external course	Five-day course on environmental auditing	• Mixing with those from other organisations can stimulate new ways of thinking • Can be reasonably cost-effective	• Areas of the course may not be immediately relevant • Delegates may have to 'sell' new ideas on return to work
Training at the workplace	Supervisor instructing new operatives on waste segregation procedures	• Practical and relevant to operational requirements • Provides highly targeted training	• Best practice opportunities may be missed • Those providing instruction may need 'train the trainer' course
Academic courses	Certificate or diploma in environmental management	• Formal recognition of competence • Provides detailed knowledge • Helps build capacity	• Areas of the course may not be immediately practical or relevant • Relatively high cost
Open-learning materials	Distance learning on environmental management topic or full course	• Allows delegates a flexible form of study • Tends to be cost-effective	• Areas of course may not be immediately practical or relevant • Dialogue with others could be limited • Requires a high degree of motivation for individual being trained

For environmental managers developing their own training courses (or assessing course suitability), it should be recognised that there are different training methods. Typically, in any course it is useful to have a variety of such methods. The methods are listed in Table 3.6.5.

Method	Description	Advantages	Possible issues
Presentation	• Trainer presents information supported, for example, by overheads and flip chart	• Consistent information provided • Time management relatively easy	• Lack of active participation means that the attention span of learners is limited
Case study	• Information about a realistic situation is provided, typically to small groups • Learners present feedback on findings and conclusions	• Active involvement for learners • Can stimulate participation and creativity • Learning by doing	• Takes time for learners to analyse problem and present feedback
Group discussion	• Learners discuss subject and may present conclusions	• Can stimulate participation and creativity • Ability to collect range of ideas and share experience	• Time management and good facilitation are required
Demonstration	• Learners are shown a piece of equipment or visit a site and are instructed on the relevant issues or controls	• Provides observation of practical situations and applications • Provides 'real world' experience	• Group size should be restricted
Practical application exercise	• Learners undertake a practical exercise, eg actual or simulated operation of equipment, or application of a technique, eg auditing, cause–effect analysis, risk assessment	• Active participation for learners • Learning outcome can be tested easily	• Takes time for learners to analyse problem and complete exercise
Reading	• Information provided in written or graphic format	• Useful as reference material and to reinforce other training methods • Can provide additional or background details	• Limits interaction with others and takes time

Table 3.6.5
Examples of environmental training methods

It is important to evaluate the effectiveness of training. At the organisation level, this helps with the development of future training programmes so that successful approaches can be built on and ineffective methods avoided.

Various techniques exist for evaluating training, including course assessment sheets, tests and examinations, post-training appraisal interviews and observation of improved behaviours or performance.

Typical areas for evaluation include:
- were the training needs and objectives met?
- did the learner find the training useful?
- was the training relevant to the learner's current (or future) work?
- did the learner put the training into practice as part of their day-to-day work?
- how has the training contributed to regulatory compliance, improved environmental performance of significant aspects, or improved practices and procedures?

Records should be kept of training – this is essential for those organisations aiming for certification to ISO 14001. Training records should include details covering the:
- topic
- content
- purpose
- individuals trained (learners)
- dates
- costs
- names and organisations of the trainers (and whether internal or external)
- evaluation of effectiveness
- recommendations for future training.

3.7 Communication on environmental issues

Communication is key to the effective functioning of any organisation, on any issue. Furthermore, environmental management is of potential interest to a range of stakeholders. As such, effective communication is a crucial element in the environmental management process.

Communication allows the organisation and individuals within it to understand what needs to be done, decide how to do it, and to monitor and review progress. In other words, it is the vehicle for progressing the 'plan, do, check and act' cycle.

A key function is to understand what external stakeholders expect of the organisation and also what the organisation expects from, and can deliver to, external parties. It is the means by which others are informed of organisation values, policies, practices and performance.

Effective communication is essential to:
• initiate and sustain action
• build awareness and stimulate motivation
• demonstrate intention and performance
• form opinions and establish reputation.

3.7.1 The communication process

The basic elements of the communication process are set out in Figure 3.7.1. It is very important to recognise that various barriers exist between the source of a message and its recipient. How the recipient perceives the message will affect that recipient's behaviour and this may not reflect what the source intended, as a result of these barriers. A one-way message can be regarded as information. Communication is, at the very least, a two-way process.

Figure 3.7.1
Outline of the
communication
process

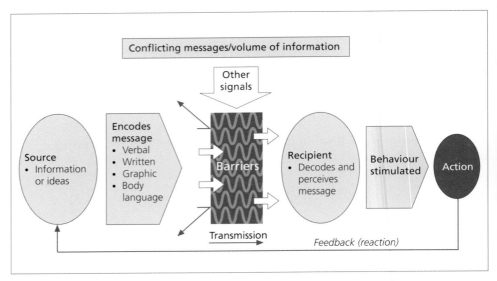

Barriers can include the amount of knowledge, or the attitudes and values of the recipient (or audience). These barriers can lead to rejection or distortion by the recipient, and therefore misperception and misunderstanding of the message. Cynicism can be a common attitude that acts as a barrier to environmental initiatives. Other resistance can be caused by beliefs related to environmental issues – for example, that environmental improvement measures are for other sectors to carry out or that such measures only have costs, not benefits.

The message may be wrongly encoded, such as that contained in a detailed memo or email, when a concise and convincing face-to-face verbal explanation would be more effective. For those giving verbal presentations, inappropriate body language can act as a barrier. Additionally, other signals can interrupt the message being transmitted. Messages may conflict and therefore cause confusion, or the sheer volume of messages may mean that key points are lost or acquire low priority.

A key principle in any communication, including environmental, is that the message should be encoded and transmitted in ways that seek to avoid barriers. The message and its medium should match the recipient or audience.

Noting that communication should be two-way, feedback is very important but it can also be subject to barriers. At one level, feedback can help the source of the information or idea to determine if the recipient understood the message as intended. At another level, it allows the recipient to contribute to the development of the information and ideas, and thereby gain ownership and enhance motivation.

3.7.2 Internal communication

Effective internal communication is required to:

- promote awareness of all relevant developments
- encourage staff involvement and participation in environmental matters
- monitor progress through reporting and feedback.

Table 3.7.1 provides examples of important areas for internal communication on environmental matters and the different internal audiences.

Internal environmental information and ideas communicated might include:	Categories of internal audiences might include:
<ul><li>general awareness</li><li>specific information</li><li>environmental policy aims and what they mean in practical terms</li><li>environmental objectives and targets</li><li>promotion of initiatives, schemes, projects or programmes</li><li>specific procedures or work instructions</li><li>performance indicators and information requirements</li><li>progress reports on performance</li><li>feedback on feasibility, eg objectives, targets, initiatives, programmes</li><li>submission of performance data</li><li>regulatory requirements</li><li>business and operational implications of government policy and policy measures</li><li>information on best practice</li><li>ideas for better practices and improved performance</li><li>environmental audit programmes</li><li>updates on stakeholder concerns.</li></ul>	<ul><li>executive/senior managers</li><li>middle managers</li><li>supervisors</li><li>operatives</li><li>professional and technical staff</li><li>employees in different functions, eg<ul><li>production</li><li>warehousing and distribution</li><li>procurement and purchasing</li><li>marketing and sales</li><li>facilities management</li><li>research and development</li><li>corporate communications</li><li>other corporate functions</li></ul></li><li>employees in different sites</li><li>employees in different countries</li><li>on-site contractors</li><li>part-time staff.</li></ul>

Table 3.7.1 Internal environmental messages and audiences

Each category of internal audience can be expected to have different cultures, attitudes, knowledge bases and competences, and therefore different communication needs.

3.7.3 External communication

Effective external communication should seek to:

- understand expectations and capabilities on a mutual basis
- keep abreast of relevant developments
- build good relations with key stakeholders
- demonstrate vision, plans and progress on environmental issues.

Different stakeholders tend to have different environmental interests in the organisation. Some examples are given in Table 3.7.2.

Stakeholder	Typical areas of environmental interest
Business customer	• General policy, practices and performance • Compliance with specific customer requirements or concerns • Information on environmental credentials of products and services
Consumers	• General policy, practices and performance • Information on environmental credentials of relevant products and services
Suppliers	• General policy aims, objectives and targets • Specific targets or requirements affecting suppliers • Supply chain initiatives
Investors	• General policy, practices and performance • Information on how environmental-related threats or opportunities to financial return are being managed • Corporate governance arrangements on environmental matters and potential business risks • How specific concerns are being addressed
Government	• General policy, practices and performance • Information on how organisation is addressing national environmental policy objectives and complying with environmental laws • Feedback on feasibility of government policy measures and best practice
Regulators	• General policy, specific practices and performance • Information on how organisation is complying with environmental laws and regulatory requirements • Feedback on feasibility of regulatory requirements and best practice
Neighbours	• General policy, specific practices and performance • How the organisation deals with community concerns/complaints, including contact methods • Level of corporate engagement with local community
Media	• Good news and bad news stories, image (also not just 'one off' stories but ongoing coverage and public relations input)
Pressure groups	• General policy, practices and performance • Views on, and management of, specific issues and concerns • Ability to engage with difficult issues

Table 3.7.2
External stakeholders and their typical areas of interest

When communicating, it should be remembered that external stakeholders may not have a comprehensive understanding of the organisation or sector, and there will be different levels of awareness of environmental issues. What may be obvious to those initiating communication (eg the nature of operations, sector jargon or acronyms, organisation achievements, business constraints and environmental trade-offs) may not be obvious or even known to external stakeholders.

3.7.4 Generic considerations when communicating

Factors to consider when choosing the appropriate medium for, and format and frequency of, communication include the:

- aim and purpose
- size, nature and needs of the target audience
- corporate image and design rules
- formality (or informality) and tone, eg aligned with organisation and stakeholder cultures
- cost and budget available
- timescale available (and its relationship to the different lead times of communication media and tools)
- timing with other initiatives (they may complement or conflict)
- internal resources/media available, eg competent people, reprographic facilities, audio-visual facilities, web design/IT capability
- need for external resources, eg to design and print publications, to produce video, to design and update websites
- language (eg technical/non-technical), including the need for different language versions where stakeholders (internal and external) are international or from minority groups
- environmental aspects and impacts of different communication tools, eg use of paper, type of paper, printing or production aspects, energy use in bringing communicators together
- effectiveness of the methods (written, diagrammatic, photographic, electronic, paper-based, verbal, face-to-face, audio-visual, teleconferencing, group sessions, one-to-one sessions, lectures, workshops).

3.7.5 Communication tools

Table 3.7.3 contains an indicative list of communication tools.

Internal	External
• Presentations or lectures (in-house and visiting speakers) • Workshops and seminars • Employee focus groups • Memos/emails • Posters • Videos/CD-ROMs/DVDs • Intranet • Paper or electronic reports • Brochures and leaflets • Documented programmes and procedures • Helpline (to professional function) • In-house magazines or newsletters • 'Toolbox' talks/team briefs • Pay slip 'mail shots' • Surveys and questionnaires • Staff suggestion schemes • Environmental competitions (based on business-relevant issues) • In-house exhibitions • Display panels	• Stakeholder dialogue workshops • Conferences (attending, presenting at or hosting) • Exhibitions (attending, presenting at or hosting) • Extranet (which allows controlled access), eg to primary stakeholders such as key customers and/or suppliers • Paper or electronic reports • Internet (general public), possibly including social network links and podcasts • Contracts with suppliers • Environmental interface documents with contractors • Brochures and leaflets, eg product information • Surveys and questionnaires • Stakeholder hotline • Press releases • Media articles (TV/radio/press) • Advertisements (TV/radio/press/poster/mail shot/web-based) • Videos/CD-ROMs/DVDs • Newsletters (eg for neighbours/suppliers/customers) as printed copies and/or web based • Open days supported by displays, leaflets, guided tours or other forms of communication or 'interpretation' (see Appendix 1)

Table 3.7.3 Examples of communication tools

A mixture of communication tools can reinforce a message – for example, posting overheads and feedback points on the intranet following a series of internal environmental workshops, or producing a leaflet for distribution to neighbours following a meeting with local residents. When making environmental claims (for example, in advertising material), care should be taken that these are clear, can be validated and follow any relevant code of practice on 'green' claims.

3.7.6 Corporate environmental reports

Governments, environmental groups and other stakeholders prompt organisations to report publicly on how they are managing their environmental issues. For those organisations aiming for EMAS, the provision of a statement on environmental performance is the main additional requirement beyond ISO 14001. EMAS sets out specific requirements for producing the statement.

The corporate environmental report (CER) can be an important communications tool. It is essential that any organisation intending to produce an environmental report must have a clear understanding of which stakeholders are (or may be) interested in the organisation's policy, practices and performance. The content, format and design of the report should be based on the interests, attitudes and knowledge base of the key stakeholder groups.

While corporate environmental reports can be a useful external communications tool, the internal audience is also important. The CER can be a helpful reference document for employees and assist with greater understanding of environmental issues, organisation policy, aims and objectives. Familiarity with the CER can help motivate continual improvement in performance.

One difficulty in producing a CER can be how to address the diversity of stakeholder groups. In such circumstances it will be necessary to prioritise stakeholders. Figure 3.7.2 provides an example method.

Figure 3.7.2
Considering the target audience for the CER

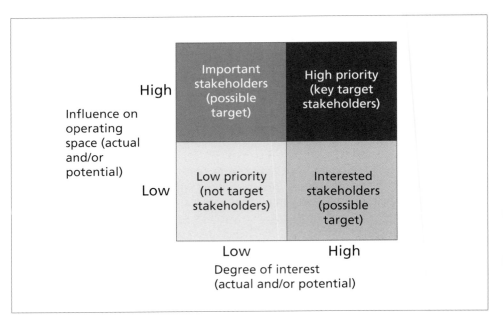

Communications objectives will depend on the target audience for the report. However, a good practice report would normally be expected to contain the sections listed in Table 3.7.4.

CER section	Features
Organisation profile	This helps the reader put the organisation and the rest of the report in context by providing an overview of the organisation, its activities and nature of its business. It should clearly indicate the scope of the report, eg businesses and operations covered, countries where operations are located. It should provide a summary of principal products and services, and the nature and geographic extent of the main markets served. It should also contain headline financial data (eg turnover and profit), number of employees, production volume or other means of indicating the level of activity. A clear statement of the reporting period is also required. Maps and diagrams can be useful.
Contents list	This enables the reader to navigate the report easily.
Executive summary	This provides the user with a balanced overview of the report, the organisation's environmental issues and its performance in key areas.
Statement from the managing director or other senior organisation representative	This helps demonstrate commitment from the top to both external and internal audiences. Also, this is the section that should present the organisation's vision and strategy for addressing environmental issues and, wherever possible, how environmental management is adding value to the business. This could also be the section that highlights the organisation's views on environmental issues to contribute to public debate. The statement should address key achievements but also any significant failures or stakeholder concerns with performance.
Environmental management	The report should set out how environmental management is undertaken in the organisation. This should outline the corporate governance structure (eg committees, steering groups, interface with the board) for environmental management. The policy may be included here or, so it can be easily referred to, as a separate section, eg towards the end or front of the report. The environmental management system elements should be outlined, together with a statement as to whether it is certified or modelled on any EMS standard, eg ISO 14001. Employee training and stakeholder communication elements should also be referred to. The use of diagrams can help with the understanding of this section. Photographs of the management team might be appropriate here.

Table 3.7.4

Typical sections in a CER

Table 3.7.4
Typical sections in
a CER
continued

CER section	Features
Significant issues	This section should outline the organisation's key environmental aspects and their associated impacts. It should also provide an explanation of the main activities that contribute to these aspects. This should also mention any significant issues along the supply chain, including relevant suppliers, distributors, products and services. A brief explanation of why these issues are considered important should be given.
Objectives and targets	The report should set out corporate-level objectives and targets for the coming reporting period. Importantly, performance against those set for the previous reporting period should also be detailed. Where an objective or target has not been met this should be acknowledged, giving reasons why (if possible) and, importantly, addressing how the situation may be resolved in the future.
Performance	For each significant issue identified, there should be a section that addresses performance and plans for that issue. This should include reference to relevant performance indicators (see Chapter 3.3) over at least the previous reporting period and, if possible, over previous years (eg up to five years' historic data) to help demonstrate trends. Useful formats for these data are graphs and charts or simple tables. Sections might be organised by environmental impact categories, eg climate change, water pollution, contaminated land, resource depletion, biodiversity, nuisance. Alternatively, sections could be arranged by environmental aspect categories such as energy use, material use, water use, emissions, effluent, waste, noise, light and incidents. There should be a section (or reference in each section) on compliance with relevant environmental legislation.
Data	While the performance section should include an analysis of the data and present key facts and trends, detailed data are usually best represented in a separate section towards the end of the report (or in a separate report). This should typically be in tabular format and include data for previous years. Readers then have an opportunity to review the data, which might otherwise introduce unnecessary detail and loss of clarity to the performance section of the main report. If the report covers a range of operating sites or countries, it might be useful to produce separate, detailed data sheets for individual sites or countries. These could then be provided to stakeholders, as relevant.
Environmental policy statement	This is essential since it sets out the organisation's aims and commitments. Claims made elsewhere in the report should be related to the policy aims.

CER section	Features
Glossary	This can be useful to explain technical (industry and environmental) terms to non-technical readers. This is essential if acronyms are used in the report.
Case studies	These could include major achievements, the progress of initiatives and programmes, or an account of an incident and how action was taken to minimise its impact and prevent recurrence. Case studies might include: initiatives with suppliers, contractors or employee involvement; product design projects or stewardship measures; research, development or demonstration projects; community or nature conservation schemes; stakeholder dialogue programmes; pollution prevention or waste minimisation projects; award schemes or events; description of an improved decision-making technique; or an emergency response structure. Plans for responding to new legislation or an impending economic instrument can also be included. Typically, case studies should be spread throughout the report and provide opportunities to include representative photographs.
Verification statement	The credibility of the organisation's CER can be improved by independent verification of the reliability of claims, completeness of data and the robustness of information collection systems. The verifier's opinions are set out in a signed and dated verification statement. Verification statements are an obligatory requirement for public reporting under EMAS.
Feedback mechanism	Communication is a two-way process and the objective of the report is to help engage with stakeholders, so a feedback mechanism should be included. This could involve provision of a contact address (postal or email) to which to submit comments or, more specifically, inclusion of a feedback questionnaire that can be returned in paper form or electronically. The questionnaire could invite open questions or ask for scores against the main elements of the report, eg clarity of text, clarity of data, whether it covers important issues, usefulness of verification statement. It would be sensible to ask for comments on how the report might be improved in the future.

Table 3.7.4
Typical sections in a CER
continued

Environmental reports can be in printed or electronic format – either on a DVD or available through the organisation's website – or all of these, to cover individual stakeholder preferences. Web-based versions offer greater flexibility, for example, by presenting details about individual sites and countries. If a printed version is produced, consideration should be given to the environmental suitability of the use of paper and the printing process being used.

The reporting period of a CER is usually annual, and it is sensible to match the organisation's financial reporting cycle. Web-based reports provide the opportunity for intermediate updates, to reflect corporate communication culture and objectives.

Guidance on environmental communications – both internal and external to organisations – has now been set out in ISO 14063:2006 (see Appendix 2). This guidance standard is recommended reading not only for those working towards ISO 14001 certification or recertification, but also for any organisation that wants to communicate effectively on environmental matters.

Increasingly, organisations are being encouraged to measure and report their greenhouse gas emissions and this should take account of technical guidance together with the communication considerations set out in this chapter. The measurement and reporting greenhouse gas emissions is also considered further in Chapter 5.1.

4: Operational control

4.1 Principles of pollution prevention and control

The term 'pollution' was introduced in Chapter 1.3. It is the general term for a range of adverse environmental impacts arising from outputs from processes and other activities (environmental 'aspects'). Pollution results from the introduction of a substance or energy into the environment that will be detrimental to human health and comfort, harm valuable species and ecosystems, interfere with the food chain, damage property, impair amenity or otherwise interfere with legitimate uses of the environment. This chapter discusses the principles supporting the management of pollutants as outputs from business activities.

ISO 14001 requires that organisations make a commitment to the prevention of pollution. The standard defines prevention of pollution as the "... use of processes, practices, materials or products that avoid, reduce or control pollution, which may include recycling, treatment, process changes, control mechanisms, efficient use of resources and material substitution".

4.1.1 The fate of waste outputs
Activities can give rise to gaseous, liquid and solid wastes as a result of normal operations. There are three broad strategies immediately available for dealing with these outputs – release, treat or contain. These are summarised in Figure 4.1.1.

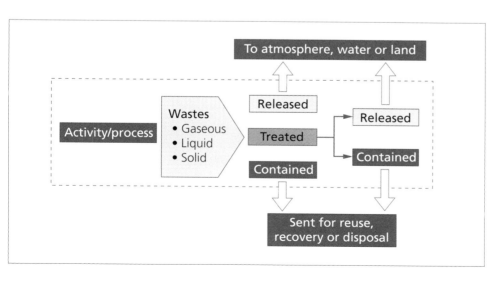

Figure 4.1.1
The fate of planned wastes

In principle, a waste output can be released directly into the environment (emitted into the atmosphere, discharged directly into a body of water or indirectly via a public sewer, or deposited on or into land). This was typically the route taken for waste outputs during the Industrial Revolution. The historic practice of dumping waste has left parts of countries such as the UK with a substantial legacy of contaminated land.

Alternatively, the waste (typically liquid and solid) can be contained (eg in drums, tanks or skips) so that it is not released into the environment but sent for reuse, recovery (eg recycling) or controlled disposal (eg landfill or incineration). An interim option is to treat the waste output so that it is transformed into a less problematic form. The outputs from the treatment process may be partly released and partly contained, depending on their nature.

Which options are acceptable for the waste output in question will depend on the significance of the waste output, particularly as framed by:
• its associated impacts in different environmental media
• applicable legal controls and specific regulatory requirements
• concerns of key stakeholders
• technical and economic considerations
• developments in best practice
• values and policy aims of the organisation.

4.1.2 Legal controls and policy measures
Legal controls have become increasingly prescriptive about which wastes can and cannot be released into the environment and, if they can, under what conditions. Legal controls are not the same in all countries, though there is increasing harmonisation between many countries. Overall, the amount of control has increased substantially, or is in the process of increasing.

Legal controls and policy measures may:
• ban the uncontrolled dumping or tipping of solid or liquid wastes on or into land
• ban the discharge of certain substances into specified bodies of water, eg public sewers, rivers, lakes, sea and/or ground water
• place severe restrictions on effluent discharges from industrial and commercial premises into specified bodies of water
• place restrictions on the quantity or concentration of substances that can be discharged into specified bodies of water
• place restrictions on the quantity or concentration of substances that can be emitted into the atmosphere

- set out a code of practice/duty of care to ensure that wastes that cannot be released are handled in a responsible manner, that they remain securely contained, and that they are only sent to disposal facilities that are licensed to take the waste in question
- classify certain wastes as hazardous so that strict controls apply to their containment, handling, transfer and disposal.

Such controls can be prescribed in specific laws or stipulated in regulatory permits for a particular activity, process, facility or installation.

Also, as mentioned in Chapter 1.4, governments are increasingly using policy measures other than legal controls, such as economic instruments to influence business behaviour. One example is a 'landfill tax' that seeks to encourage waste management options such as waste minimisation and recycling, so that the amount of waste sent to landfill is greatly reduced.

4.1.3 Managing operational waste streams

Figure 4.1.2 provides a useful hierarchy for managing operational waste streams; it is explained in greater detail in Table 4.1.1.

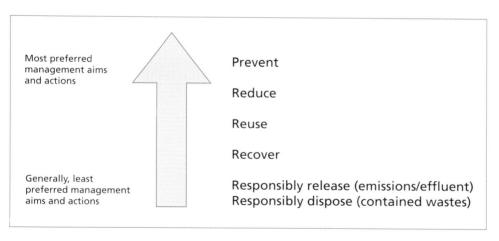

Most preferred management aims and actions

Prevent

Reduce

Reuse

Recover

Generally, least preferred management aims and actions

Responsibly release (emissions/effluent)
Responsibly dispose (contained wastes)

Figure 4.1.2 Management hierarchy for waste outputs

The hierarchy should be used as a broad indication of environmentally preferable solutions, and not as a 'hard and fast' set of rules. For example, certain hazardous wastes are best dealt with by responsible disposal options such as specialised landfill or incineration.

Nevertheless, the overall priority is to reduce the amount of waste produced. A priority could be the elimination (or a reduction in quantity) of problematic waste streams such as those that contain hazardous substances, are subject to stringent regulatory controls or incur high discharge/disposal costs. Chapter 4.4, which considers process efficiency, is relevant to this approach.

Reuse and recovery seek to obtain value from waste outputs that would otherwise be released or disposed of. This can be through the use of these materials either on or off site.

Table 4.1.1
Methods of
implementing the
waste
management
hierarchy

Method	Approach
Prevention	Change in process design, operation or substance/material/fuel use so that certain waste outputs are eliminated.
Reduction	Streamlined processes, improved maintenance, improved efficiency of operation so that the amount of waste output is reduced.
Reuse	Waste outputs are put back to use instead of being released or sent for disposal – for example, the reuse of cooling water instead of using it once and then discharging it as effluent, or reuse of pallets instead of sending them to landfill.
Recovery	• Reprocessing of waste outputs so that use can be made of them/value obtained from them • Recycling waste materials so they become usable input materials, eg resmelting of metal, repulping of paper • Composting organic waste to create compost for soil improvement applications • Using combustible waste materials as fuel or processing organic waste into a fuel (energy recovery)
Responsible release or disposal	Ensure releases or disposal meet required standards. Treatment may be required to render the release harmless, typically defined by conformance to relevant standards (set in accordance with regulatory requirements, stakeholder views and best practice).

Before they can be responsibly released into the environment, certain waste streams (eg emissions, effluent) need to be treated to render them harmless. This is often referred to as 'end-of-pipe' abatement or treatment. A major problem with end-of-pipe abatement is that while it may reduce the impact of the release to one medium, it typically leads to the creation of other waste outputs, either to the same medium or others. End-of-pipe abatement does not help to reduce inputs to the process (it often requires extra resource inputs, particularly energy). This re-emphasises the need to prevent and reduce waste at source through cleaner technology or process efficiency measures which design out the generation of waste.

An essential principle of environmental management is to ensure that responsible release or disposal routes are selected for planned waste streams.

If a responsible release or disposal route is not taken, then the output could lead to a demonstrable environmental impact, breach of legislation, nuisance impact and/or loss of trust with key stakeholders. It may require remediation measures to lessen or rectify the impact. For example, if organic liquid waste is discharged without treatment into a small lake it could result in high biological oxygen demand (BOD), leading to the death of fish and other organisms. There will be a need for remediation, in this case aeration of the lake and restocking with fish once oxygen levels recover. Remediation tends to be difficult and costly. It offers no opportunities for cost savings, unlike investment in process efficiency improvements or cleaner technology, which often yields ongoing financial returns.

4.1.4 Pollutant releases from unplanned events

The management of potentially problematic releases associated with unplanned events (incidents) should be based on risk management and contingency planning (see Chapter 3.5). This approach needs to consider the risk of the unplanned event occurring and there may be a strong link to safety management. However, an environmental management approach should also consider those pathways and receptors which may increase the risk of significant, and possibly longer-term, environmental consequences. This can include adverse effects on human livelihoods as well as ecological damage.

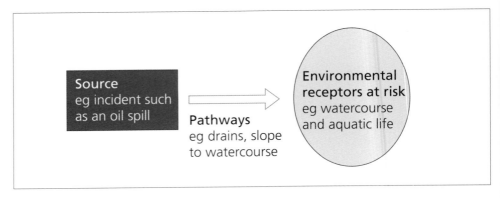

The overall aim should be to prevent incidents that could lead to serious consequences. The management hierarchy for such events (summarised in Figure 4.1.4) is to reduce the risk of occurrence, be capable of effective response so that the incident does not escalate and its consequence is minimised and, if there is a significant impact, take effective measures to rectify the damage.

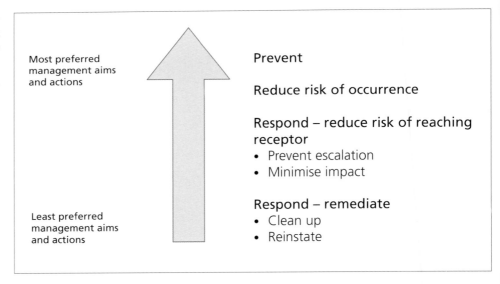

Table 4.1.2 outlines what might be included in the example of an oil spill.

Management approach	Specific actions
Measures to minimise risk of the spill occurring	• Proper handling procedures • Operator training on proper handling • Maintenance to ensure the integrity of the oil storage and transfer system
Response measures to prevent spill reaching receptor	• Secondary containment, eg kerbed areas or bunding • Spill response kits to contain and recover the spilled material, drain protectors to prevent the spill entering the drains • Deployment of booms across watercourse to contain the spill with recovery through adsorption systems or skimmers
Response measures to remediate any damage	• Clean-up or removal of contaminated sediments, damaged aquatic vegetation and injured or dead wildlife • Restocking with fish and other wildlife

Table 4.1.2 Management approaches to dealing with an oil spill

Note that the process of responding usually generates other waste streams that require responsible disposal.

4.1.5 Pollution control concepts

Government policy incorporates two important approaches to pollution prevention and control:
• the 'source-oriented' approach, through setting release (emission and discharge) standards, restrictions on what can be released, or the prescription of disposal routes
• the 'effects-oriented' approach, through the setting of environmental quality or impact standards.

The source-oriented approach is of direct relevance to those organisational activities and processes for which the standards are set. However, the effects-oriented approach can also be relevant. For certain (typically larger) installations and processes there may be a regulatory requirement to ensure that releases do not lead to local air quality or water quality standards being breached. Determining this will typically require detailed modelling work to establish ambient conditions and dispersion mechanisms, the contribution from the installation or process in question, and the effect of releases from other sources. The effects-oriented approach also highlights the pollutants that are considered to be priority concerns by government and by society at large.

Both the source- and effects-based approaches are used in the EU Directive on Integrated Pollution Prevention and Control (IPPC), first adopted in 1996 and updated in 2008. The Directive applies to prescribed industrial and other activities. However, its general provisions can provide a useful benchmark for those activities not covered by the Directive. The pollutants covered in the Directive are listed in Chapter 4.2.

Two central principles apply to pollution prevention and control: 'best available techniques' (BAT) and 'best practicable environmental option' (BPEO). These principles are incorporated into the policy and regulatory framework in the UK. While in law they apply only to certain activities or situations, the principles are generally used by environmental managers as they provide useful reference points for the wider environmental management agenda. Another relevant principle is 'as low as reasonably practicable' (ALARP). These terms are explained in more detail in Table 4.1.3.

Principle	Definition	Context and application
Best available techniques (BAT)	As defined in EU IPPC Directive (2008): "... the most effective and advanced stage in the development of activities and their methods of operation which indicate the practical suitability of particular techniques for providing in principle the basis for emission [release] limit values designed to prevent and, where that is not practicable, generally to reduce emissions [releases] and the impact on the environment as a whole: • techniques... include both the technology used and the way in which the installation is designed, built, maintained, operated and decommissioned • available techniques... mean those developed on a scale which allows implementation in the relevant industrial sector, under economically and technically viable conditions, taking into consideration the costs and advantages, whether or not the techniques are used or produced inside the Member State in question, as long as they are reasonably accessible to the operator • best... means the most effective in achieving a high general level of protection of the environment as a whole."	This is a core principle of the IPPC Directive. It is used to establish emission limits and controls on releases (this includes substances, thermal emissions and noise). Significantly, it refers to techniques and so is not restricted to technology, though often important (eg it might include the use of less hazardous substances, use of raw materials, accident prevention, maintenance and training). It also recognises the need for technical and economic feasibility.

Table 4.1.3
Pollution control principles and their application

Table 4.1.3
Pollution control
principles and
their application
continued

Principle	Definition	Context and application
Best practicable environmental option (BPEO)	As defined by the UK Royal Commission on Environmental Pollution in 1988 (12th Report): "A BPEO is the outcome of a systematic consultative and decision-making procedure which emphasises the protection and conservation of the environment across land, air and water. The BPEO procedure establishes, for a given set of objectives, the option that provides the most benefits or least damage to the environment as a whole, at acceptable costs, in the long term as well as the short term."	This principle takes into account both the environmental and economic costs and benefits of different options. It recognises that finding the solution to one environmental problem may lead to the creation of others – pollution may be transferred from one medium to another. This is relevant to the control of releases or the management of waste, eg abatement of atmospheric emissions will create liquid and solid wastes and require extra energy inputs, while moving from landfill to incineration may increase atmospheric pollution. BPEO considerations were originally a specific regulatory requirement for Part A processes prescribed under the UK's Environmental Protection Act 1990. This has subsequently been superseded by the requirements of the EU's IPPC Directive. BPEO is still an important consideration in government policy development and should be a guiding principle in environmental management generally, including waste management (see section 4.3.2).
As low as reasonably practicable (ALARP)	ALARP is a fundamental regulatory requirement in the UK where legal case law and policy measures exist defining ALARP for managing health and safety risks. ALARP compares the cost of harm that may result from the risk with the cost of trying to reduce the risk. It aims to reduce unacceptable risks to as low as reasonably practicable.	In environmental management, this principle is particularly useful as the basis of managing the risk of unplanned events/ incidents. Related terms are as low as reasonably achievable (ALARA) and as low as technically achievable (ALATA).

4.1.6 Technical and economic feasibility

BAT, BPEO and ALARP incorporate the need for pollution control options to be both technically viable and economically feasible. Indeed, EMAS states that it aims to reduce environmental impacts through the economically viable application of best available technology (EVABAT). Reference to 'technology' in EVABAT is not restricted to equipment. It also includes the broader concept of techniques, eg housekeeping, training.

Pollution prevention and control techniques can be categorised as minimal cost, low cost and capital cost measures, as indicated in Table 4.1.4.

Type of measure	Examples	Emphasis
Minimal cost	These include 'good housekeeping' measures, simple changes to working practices and procedures or adjustment to existing equipment – for example, effective implementation of planned maintenance programmes, 'toolbox' talks on a problem area, resetting controls, ensuring effective procedures are followed.	Based on the behaviour of people using existing equipment.
Low cost	These involve improvements to existing systems – for example, installing new monitoring equipment or simple control technology, designing and implementing a detailed training programme, obtaining new waste containers, undertaking a comprehensive overhaul of outdated or ineffective procedures, simple material input modifications.	This requires a combination of investment in low cost measures (which may include technological improvements) and involvement of people.
Capital cost	These involve investment in new, efficient and intrinsically cleaner technology, abatement or treatment plant. Examples include on-site combined heat and power.	The emphasis is on a high level of investment in technology, though the people element (eg training to operate new plant) should not be overlooked.

Table 4.1.4
Categories of pollution control by cost

Projects that involve capital expenditure or a significant change in existing practices should be subject to rigorous technical and economic appraisal. This may require input from external consultants. Payback calculations (cost of project divided by annual savings) can provide a simple evaluation of options being considered and can be interpreted to give tangible financial information, ie years in which project costs are recovered:

$$\text{cost/annual savings} = \text{payback}$$
$$\text{eg } £20,000/£10,000 = \text{two years}$$

However, this simple calculation takes no account of savings after the payback period, or the effects of inflation over time. Payback calculations can be useful, however, for helping to prioritise simple projects or for initial screening of more major projects (see benefit/ease of action grid in Chapter 3.3).

For major projects, the financial aspect of the appraisal should consider using 'return on capital' analyses over the project's lifetime, including discounting to take account of inflation. Even so, it is vitally important that the overall appraisal acknowledges that many of the benefits of environmental investment may be real but financially intangible – for example, improved compliance with legislation, enhanced environmental performance and improved stakeholder relations. These intangibles can be more difficult to communicate to top management than financial information.

When action is agreed, pollution prevention and control initiatives should be incorporated into the setting of improvement targets (see Chapter 3.3) and environmental management programmes (see Chapter 3.4). Furthermore, as will be seen in Chapter 5.2, innovation is an important factor in preventing and controlling pollution as part of the wider sustainability agenda. Innovation is important in not only significantly reducing impacts but also retaining an organisation's competitive edge.

4.2 Control of releases

This chapter provides an introduction to the operational control of releases into the environment, including the management of atmospheric emissions and effluent discharges. While Chapter 4.1 covers the general management principles of pollution prevention and control (including releases), this chapter gives further detail as to the type, source and control of key operational releases.

4.2.1 Categories of release

Releases into the environment can result in a range of environmental impacts, principally those summarised in Chapter 1.3. There are various ways of categorising releases. Table 4.2.1 provides one approach, which can be particularly useful when considering an industrial process or commercial site.

Category	Description
Normal releases	These arise from processes and activities under normal operating conditions. They are planned and designed to occur. Typically, the release is from a point source, eg emissions from an exhaust stack or chimney, or effluent from a pipe.
Abnormal releases	These are other releases that may occur for a short time during the operation of a process for specific non-routine reasons. Nevertheless, these releases are part of the overall operation of the process. As they may involve high release rates it is important that they are considered. Typical examples are releases from safety control devices such as pressure release valves. This category may also include releases associated with infrequent start-up and shut-down operations, and non-routine maintenance. As with normal operations, these releases are often from a point source such as a stack or pipe.
Fugitive releases	These are the many and varied ad hoc releases that can occur in a process or around a site. Key examples include losses from pipe joints and glands, and evaporative losses from storage tanks. Such releases are particularly relevant for volatile substances, eg light fuel oil and solvents. While each point source may amount to only a small release, there may be numerous sources which add up to a significant release overall.
Accidental releases	These result from incidents that can lead to the uncontrolled escape of pollutants into the environment. Common causes are equipment failure or operator error. Typical examples are spills, leaks and the releases associated with fire or explosion. These releases are unplanned and may be difficult to control. Risk management is required to reduce the risk of such incidents occurring and response plans should be in place to deal with any accidental releases.

Table 4.2.1 Categorising releases according to operational parameters

Releases can also be classified according to impact category (see Table 4.2.2), which can be useful as part of identifying and aggregating aspects and impacts.

Table 4.2.2
Categorising
releases according
to environmental
impact

Impact	Principal pollutants (actual or potential releases)
Global climate change	Emissions of: carbon dioxide (CO_2), methane (CH_4), nitrous oxide (N_2O), hydrofluorocarbons (HFCs), perfluorocarbons (PFCs), sulphur hexafluoride (SF_6)
Stratospheric ozone depletion	Emissions of: chlorofluorocarbons (CFCs), HFCs, hydrobromofluorocarbons (HBFCs), halon, carbon tetrachloride (CCl_4) 1,1,1-trichloroethane, methyl bromide (CH_3Br). Note that key ozone-depleting substances are now banned
Acid deposition	Emissions of: sulphur dioxide (SO_2), nitrogen oxide (NO), nitrogen dioxide (NO_2)
Tropospheric (ground-level) ozone creation	Emissions of: nitrogen oxides (NO_x), volatile organic compounds (VOCs) and unburnt hydrocarbons, including alkanes and alkenes
General air quality	Emissions of: particulates (smoke and dusts), carbon monoxide (CO), nitrogen oxides (NO_x), SO_2, VOCs, benzene, 1,3-butadiene, lead
Water pollution – eutrophication	Discharge, spill, leak or migration of nutrients such as nitrates and phosphates, eg as fertiliser, fertiliser run-off, or in sewage
Water pollution – dissolved oxygen depletion	Discharge, spill, leak or migration of substances which exert a high oxygen demand, in particular organic matter such as sewage, spilt milk and other readily biodegradable materials, which lead to enhanced microbial activity in the body of water, thus reducing dissolved oxygen levels. Also, oil and detergents forming surface film on the water, which then hinders oxygen transfer from the atmosphere. Heated discharges can also reduce oxygen levels
Land contamination	Deposit, spill or leak of a range of hazardous substances, including heavy metals, asbestos, combustible and explosive substances, toxic chemicals. Note that if mobilised, these can migrate to cause water pollution
Nuisance	Release of: noise, vibration, light, smoke, dusts, fumes, litter, odour

4.2.2 Priorities for management
The identification and prioritisation of releases for subsequent management action should be an integral part of the identification of environmental aspects and impacts (see Chapter 2.1) and the evaluation of

significance (see Chapter 2.2). It should also be linked to the objective-
and target-setting process (see Chapter 3.3).

Key factors related to prioritisation are shown in Table 4.2.3.

Factor	Example
Whether the release is controlled by regulatory requirement	• Subject to release limits or other conditions in a licence, permit or consent • Ban on the substance being released – to air, directly to water and/or via public sewers • Abatement notice on an activity causing nuisance
The degree to which the release is subject to stakeholder concern	• Complaints from neighbours concerning smoke, dust, fumes, noise, vibration, litter • Pressure group representations or media attention over problematic releases
Whether the release is subject to sector voluntary agreement or code of practice	• Sector agreement to reduce emissions by a given level or percentage • Sector code on best practice to control a particular release or address a specific impact
The implications of economic instruments intended to encourage behaviour to reduce releases	• Direct tax, levy or charge on volume of substance being emitted • Tax, levy or charge on inputs that are associated with particular releases, eg energy tax to encourage more efficient use of fossil fuel-based energy or fuel switching to low carbon sources with consequent reduction in carbon dioxide emissions; or road charging to discourage use of road vehicles with consequent emission benefits.
The risk of an unplanned event leading to an unacceptable consequence, eg demonstrable environmental impact, clean-up costs, legal action, public protests	• Risk of spills, leaks and windblown material associated with materials or waste handling, a process upset or plant or equipment failure (including failure of pollution abatement technology) • Risk of mobilisation and migration of contaminants from a parcel of contaminated land threatening a receptor, including ground water, surface water or user of the land
Cost-effective opportunities for improving process efficiency	• Opportunities for preventing or reducing the emission or discharge, or for transforming it into a useful by-product (see Chapter 4.4) as part of a process of continual improvement. This may include a reduction in fugitive releases

Table 4.2.3
Factors to consider
when prioritising
releases

For certain processes or installations (ie those considered by society to have the highest potential to pollute), detailed environmental impact assessments (EIAs) may be required by law. This could include modelling of dispersion and dilution of emissions and discharges in the air or water flow. It may also include modelling to determine the impact on ambient concentrations of pollutants and whether any environmental quality standards could be threatened by the additional releases. The impact assessment would determine priorities for action.

For any organisation reviewing its environmental aspects, the indicative list of pollutants set out in annex III of the IPPC Directive (2008) is a useful checklist of potential priority releases to air and water, even for organisations not covered by the Directive (see Table 4.2.4). This list helps identify those releases considered important across the EU member states. It could be used by most organisations for initial screening purposes when reviewing releases from their activities. A notable exception from the list is the greenhouse gas CO_2.

Table 4.2.4 Indicative list of main polluting substances in the Integrated Pollution Prevention and Control Directive (2008)

Air	Water
1 Sulphur dioxide and other sulphur compounds	1 Organohalogen compounds and substances which may form such compounds in the aquatic environment
2 Oxides of nitrogen and other nitrogen compounds	2 Organophosphorus compounds
3 Carbon monoxide	3 Organotin compounds
4 Volatile organic compounds (VOCs)	4 Substances and preparations which have been proved to possess carcinogenic or mutagenic properties or properties which may affect reproduction in or via the aquatic environment
5 Metals and their compounds	
6 Dust	
7 Asbestos (suspended particulates, fibres)	5 Persistent hydrocarbons and persistent and bioaccumulable organic toxic substances
8 Chlorine and its compounds	
9 Fluorine and its compounds	6 Cyanides
10 Arsenic and its compounds	7 Metals and their compounds
11 Cyanides	8 Arsenic and its compounds
12 Substances and preparations which have been proved to possess carcinogenic or mutagenic properties or properties which may affect reproduction via the air	9 Biocides and plant health products
	10 Materials in suspension
	11 Substances which contribute to eutrophication (in particular, nitrates and phosphates)
13 Polychlorinated dibenzodioxins and polychlorinated dibenzofurans	12 Substances which have an unfavourable influence on the oxygen balance (and can be measured using parameters such as BOD, COD and so on)

4.2.3 Managing releases

Releases should be managed in accordance with the general principles set out in Chapter 4.1. The guiding principle should be to prevent significant releases (actual or potential), or where this is not practicable, to reduce them.

Figure 4.2.1 identifies the main factors that determine the impact of a release. For certain processes (typically larger processes), a detailed analysis as well as modelling may be necessary. This analysis would be expected to incorporate such factors when considering control options. However, consideration of these factors is useful for any operation, as is the need to recognise that end-of-pipe abatement solutions can lead to the transfer of impacts.

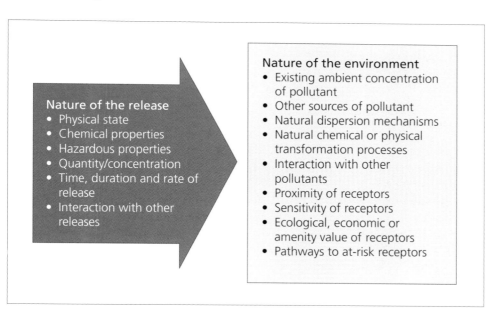

Nature of the release
- Physical state
- Chemical properties
- Hazardous properties
- Quantity/concentration
- Time, duration and rate of release
- Interaction with other releases

Nature of the environment
- Existing ambient concentration of pollutant
- Other sources of pollutant
- Natural dispersion mechanisms
- Natural chemical or physical transformation processes
- Interaction with other pollutants
- Proximity of receptors
- Sensitivity of receptors
- Ecological, economic or amenity value of receptors
- Pathways to at-risk receptors

Figure 4.2.1
Key factors affecting the impact of releases

Useful guiding principles are 'best available techniques', 'best practicable environmental option' and, in some situations, 'as low as reasonably practicable' (as discussed in Chapter 4.1). It should also be remembered that all these concepts incorporate technical viability and economic feasibility.

4.2.4 Controlling releases

The following considers methods used for controlling a range of releases.

a. End-of-pipe abatement

This section provides a very general overview of some of the main end-of-pipe technologies for emissions and effluent. It is vitally important that the output of these treatment processes is monitored (whether by sampling or continuous measurement techniques, as appropriate) to ensure standards are being met, and in particular to demonstrate compliance with emission limit or effluent discharge parameters set by regulators. It is also important to remember that abatement equipment – and associated monitoring – can fail. Regular inspection, maintenance and recalibration may be required, and this must be incorporated into management procedures.

Table 4.2.5
Example of abatement technology – waste gas streams

Technology	Pollutants abated	Brief description
Activated carbon	Solvents/VOCs (including odorous substances)	Waste stream passes through large surface area of activated carbon material, which may be in the form of pellets or applied to the surface of a filter. The organic compounds are adsorbed onto the surface of the carbon. Various methods are available to desorb the organic material so that it may then be recycled (eg solvent), if appropriate.
After burner	Incomplete combustion products, eg carbon monoxide (CO), unburnt hydrocarbons	The waste stream from the main combustion process is passed through this device. It typically introduces gas fuel and may increase oxygen levels as it aims to obtain virtually complete combustion. The result is that the CO and unburnt hydrocarbon are transformed to CO_2 and water vapour.
Bag filter	Particulates, eg dust and fume	Waste gas stream passes through filter system (eg suspended felted textiles) which intercepts particulates and builds up layers of dust. At intervals this is dislodged and collected as solid waste.
Bio-filters	Organic gases giving rise to odour	Waste gas stream passes through a substrate containing microbes such as bacteria and fungi. These break down the organic matter and in doing so reduce/remove the odour.

Technology	Pollutants abated	Brief description
Catalytic reactor (or converter)	Gaseous pollutants: VOCs, CO and NO_x	Waste gas stream is passed over a catalyst (eg platinum, palladium or rhodium) in the form of pellets, honeycomb structures or mesh (to provide large surface area). This then permits an increased rate of complete combustion at lower temperatures so that CO and VOCs are converted to CO_2 and water vapour, with reduced NO_x levels.
Condenser	Solvents (VOCs) in high concentration	Waste gas stream is cooled by cooling fluid or through device that encourages heat loss. This allows the solvent to be recovered and, if not contaminated with impurities, be available for reuse.
Cyclone	Particulates, eg grit and coarse dust	Waste gas stream enters funnel-shaped device tangentially. The spiral path of the stream in the device causes particulate matter to hit the walls and fall out of the stream. It is collected as solid waste.
Electrostatic precipitator	Particulates, eg smoke and fume	Particulates in waste gas stream become charged and are attracted to oppositely charged plates. These are then removed by vibration or spray to become solid waste or sludge.
Scrubber	Various depending on type, including noxious gases, particulates, mists	Waste gas stream passes through a system of sprays, across a wet surface (comprising a large surface area, eg by using spheres, rings or perforated plates) or into a wet rotor or mop. These devices remove the pollutant as effluent or sludge.
Thermal oxidiser	Combustible pollutants, eg VOCs, including odorous compounds	Waste gas stream is mixed with air or oxygen, and perhaps fuel gas. The pollutants are incinerated at high temperatures in a furnace and are transformed into simple combustion products (eg CO_2 and water vapour), which can then be released to the atmosphere.

Table 4.2.5
Example of abatement technology – waste gas streams *continued*

Table 4.2.6
Example of
abatement
technology –
effluent treatment

Technology	Pollutants abated/purpose	Brief description
Activated sludge	Organic effluent with high BOD	The effluent passes into tanks aerated by agitators that maximise the dissolved oxygen content to encourage microbial growth, which consumes the organic matter. The microbes are introduced in the form of activated sludge, which is recycled from earlier treatment and contains high levels of bacteria and protozoa.
Bio-oxidation	Organic effluent with high BOD	Effluent is passed through a structure (eg bio-tower or filter beds) containing large surface area, which encourages a microbial film to develop. This consumes and breaks down the organic matter in the effluent as it percolates down.
Cyclones	Sand, silt and suspended solids	Effluent enters a funnel-shaped device tangentially. The spiral path of the stream in the device causes particulate matter to hit the walls and fall out of the stream. It is collected as sludge or solid waste.
Electrochemical equipment	Metal salts	Effluent is passed into vats containing electrodes. The metals are removed by being deposited on the cathode from which they can be reclaimed and recycled.
Filter press	Removal of water from sludge	Device compresses sludge between filter plates to produce filter cake, which is collected as solid waste.
Micro/ultra-filtration	Small particles and micro-organisms	Effluent is passed into extremely fine filter units operating under high (micro-filtration) to very high (ultra-filtration) pressures. This removes the fine material, which is collected as sludge.
Oil–water separator	Removal of oil from waste water	Effluent enters tank and is held for sufficient period to allow the oil to form a separate layer on the surface of the water. This can be removed intermittently by pumping, to become waste oil. This may be sent for recovery. Separator technology should be located so that ad hoc oil releases (eg from factory yards, car parks and maintenance areas) are intercepted and not discharged into the drainage system.
Settlement tank	Removal of solids – organic and inorganic	Effluent enters tank and is held for sufficiently long period to allow the solid material to fall out under gravity. This may be assisted by coagulants and flocculants, eg to precipitate out dissolved materials). The material is then removed as sludge.

b. Fugitive releases

Fugitive releases are *ad hoc* releases, such as leaks and evaporation. To establish control it is important to understand the extent of the problem, ie to confirm how much is being lost and from where. One useful technique is to conduct a mass balance. Figure 4.2.2 shows how a mass balance technique can be used for solvents.

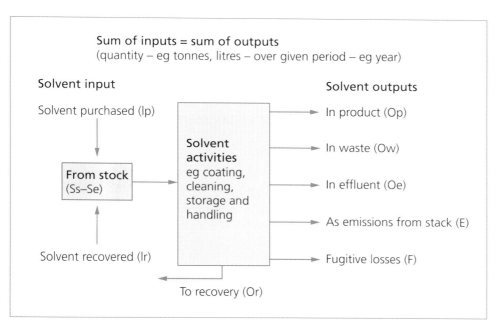

Figure 4.2.2
Use of mass balance to establish fugitive releases

Fugitive releases can be calculated for a given period by establishing the 'unaccounted for' figure, using the basic formula:

$$F = I - (Ss - Se) - O - E$$

where
F = the fugitive releases (unaccounted for)
I = the solvent purchased over the period
Ss = the stock held at start of period
Se = the stock held at end of period
O = the outputs other than stack emissions
E = the emissions via stack

Some of the output (O) figures may have to be estimated. This component includes solvent in contained wastes, solvent in effluent, solvent in product and solvent sent for recovery. It may be useful to identify these in the calculation (eg Ow, Oe, Op, Or) separately, together with separate figures for solvent purchased (Ip) and recovered (Ir) as inputs. Also, the destruction of solvent in any abatement (Oa) plant, before emission release, might require separate identification. The calculation then becomes more detailed:

$$F = (Ip + Ir) - (Ss - Se) - (Ow + Oe + Op + Or) - (E + Oa)$$

It can be useful to represent the quantities on a Sankey diagram (see Chapter 4.4). The size of fugitive emissions (unaccounted for figure) could be surprisingly large. This may warrant further investigation to establish the main sources of fugitive release and help prioritise action.

Common sources of fugitive releases are losses from valves, seals, joints, open filling nozzles and pressure relief systems. Causes range from wear, corrosion, incorrect specification or installation, to incorrect or poor working practices.

Typical controls, therefore, include improved inspection and maintenance, replacement of inappropriate seals, modification of seal and valve arrangements, revised working procedures and operator training. This approach is consistent with process efficiency techniques outlined in Chapter 4.4.

c. Emissions from fossil fuel combustion

The combustion of fossil fuel (coal, oil and gas) results in a range of atmospheric emissions depending on the fuel used, the combustion process and the efficiency of the application using the energy.

Common emissions are sulphur dioxide (resulting from sulphur in the fuel), nitrogen oxides (from nitrogen in the fuel or from reactions with atmospheric nitrogen in high temperature flames), unburnt hydrocarbons and, importantly, CO_2.

Emissions of SO_2 can be controlled through the selection of low sulphur content fuels. The level of unburnt hydrocarbons and NO_x can be dealt with through modifying combustion conditions or applying catalysts to clean the exhaust gases. However, CO_2 and water vapour are the natural end products of fossil fuel combustion:

hydrocarbon + oxygen = carbon dioxide + water

and there is no practical end-of-pipe solution for abating CO_2 emissions.

The combustion of fossil fuels is the main source of man-made emissions of CO_2. Energy use is an area relevant to all organisations since energy is fundamental to the operation of all activities, including transportation. Even though direct combustion may be limited on a particular site or in a particular building, the use of electricity is also an important consideration. While the use of electricity does not directly involve the release of CO_2 by the end user, typically grid electricity is generated by burning fossil fuels. Also, grids are often connected to power stations burning coal (which is associated with particularly high carbon levels). Electricity grids also suffer from transmission inefficiencies which adversely affect CO_2 emission factors.

Organisations seeking to reduce their CO_2 emissions as a result of fossil fuel combustion should consider the options outlined in Table 4.2.7.

Option	Key features	Examples
Improve energy efficiency – sites, processes and buildings	This concerns using less energy for a desired outcome, eg to heat, cool or light a building, produce a product. This is part of process efficiency (see Chapter 4.4). Energy efficiency offers many opportunities for continual improvement in environmental performance.	Simple measures include: switching off unused equipment, resetting controls, installing simple controls, improving metering and monitoring of energy use, maintaining equipment, improved insulation, employee training. Capital measures include: purchasing efficient equipment, major insulation refurbishment of existing buildings, installing waste heat recovery systems (for heating or cooling), installing on-site micro-generation, introducing automatic energy management systems.
Improve energy efficiency – transport	This concerns using less energy for a desired outcome, eg to transport goods from A to B, conduct meetings. Again, this is part of process efficiency and techniques discussed in Chapter 4.4 are relevant.	This could involve the purchase, leasing or rental of highly fuel-efficient vehicles, regular servicing and maintenance, improved vehicle utilisation – payloads for goods, number of passengers for people, or effective route planning to avoid congestion or unnecessary mileage. Driver training to reduce unproductive energy use (eg optimal vehicle speed, gentle acceleration and braking) could be considered. Initiatives to reduce travel (eg improved meeting planning, telephone- or video-conferencing) may also be introduced.

Table 4.2.7
Options for reducing carbon dioxide emissions

Table 4.2.7
Options for
reducing carbon
dioxide emissions
continued

Option	Key features	Examples
Switch to lower carbon fossil fuels	Natural gas emits lower amounts of CO_2 than oil and coal because it has the lowest molecular carbon to hydrogen ratio of the fossil fuels (being composed mostly of methane). Grid-derived electricity is typically associated with higher CO_2 emissions because of transmission losses and the fact that it is often connected to generation by low-efficiency, coal-powered thermal plant.	Where appropriate, conversion from coal, oil or grid electricity to high efficiency natural gas applications. This should be based on careful technical (and financial) evaluation. There could be particular advantages in moving to on-site gas-generated combined heat and power (CHP), if feasible, which typically has high efficiency benefits. Emissions factors: kg CO_2 per kWh energy (net caloric value basis, includes all greenhouse gas emissions as units of CO_2 equivalent): • Natural gas 0.22554 • Petrol 0.29953 • Diesel 0.32021 • Fuel oil 0.33093 • Coal (industrial) 0.39465 • Purchased grid electricity 0.61707 (per kWh electricity consumed based on generation mix in 2008 and taking account of transmission losses). (UK factors – Source: Defra 2010) Switching to natural gas vehicles could be an option. However, payload implications through on-board storage of liquefied or compressed natural gas (LNG or CNG) and access to filling facilities should be factored in.

Option	Key features	Examples
Switch to 'low or no carbon' renewable energy	This involves using fuels and electricity derived from renewable sources (see Appendix 1). The economics and availability of these technologies can still be a limiting factor, although the feasibility is changing through technological development and supporting policy measures.	• On-site electricity generation from renewables, eg photovoltaics (solar) or biogas • Purchase of energy through dedicated (ideally accredited) 'green' energy tariffs where the electricity is generated from renewables, eg wind, small scale hydro, biogas • Possibly, purchase of natural gas, with high quality, accredited CO_2 offset through renewable energy and afforestation development projects • Possibly, use of biofuels as vehicle fuel
Consider high quality compensation/ offset projects	Since CO_2 impacts at the global level (as a greenhouse gas) and can otherwise be considered to be benign in terms of air quality, it is recognised that projects that compensate for (offset) an equivalent amount of CO_2 to that emitted may be acceptable. This is an emerging area – issues include the verification of the offset, the determination of baselines and the long term guarantee of the offset amount.	Offset projects might include: • renewable energy or energy efficiency projects in which the savings between the CO_2 emissions for that project compared to a fossil fuel/lower efficiency baseline provide the offset • reforestation or afforestation projects to allow the forests (biomass in the trees, undergrowth and soils) to absorb at least an equivalent amount of CO_2 to that emitted. Offsets might be especially useful for problematic carbon releases such as those associated with transport. However, such compensation should be undertaken as part of a wider carbon reduction strategy which includes reducing emissions at source (eg through resource efficiency) as a priority. Furthermore, the offsets should be those that have been approved through official certification schemes (eg the UK government's Quality Assurance Scheme for Carbon Offsetting).

Table 4.2.7
Options for reducing carbon dioxide emissions
continued

In the UK, extensive and impartial advice on energy efficiency, low carbon technology, micro-generation and other aspects of carbon and energy management is available from the Carbon Trust (see Appendix 3). In developing options to reduce CO_2 emissions, it can be important to ensure that the option does not lead to other concerns, eg through poor quality carbon offsets or other adverse impacts associated with the technology under consideration. Energy efficiency is therefore a particularly important starting point.

Also, while this section has concentrated on CO_2 from fossil fuel combustion, other processes lead to substantial CO_2 emissions (eg cement production from limestone) and to emissions of other greenhouse gases which are more powerful than CO_2 (see Table 2.4.2). Managing all greenhouse gas emissions through a comprehensive, co-ordinated carbon/greenhouse gas strategy (see section 5.2.9), supported by measurement and reporting as CO_2 equivalent (see section 5.1.5), is recommended.

d. Materials handling and storage incidents

Releases from materials handling and storage are usually associated with spills, leaks and (for powders or light materials) wind-blow. It is useful to conduct a risk assessment on storage and handling operations to help prioritise controls (see Chapters 3.5 and 4.1).

Common handling and storage issues to consider are shown in Table 4.2.8.

Table 4.2.8 Common handling and storage issues

Issue	Description
Underground storage tanks	These are particularly susceptible to corrosion and damage and, in general, it is not considered good practice to have such facilities. Where they are necessary, protective measures such as double-skinned tanks and piping, and leak detection should be considered.
Above ground storage facilities	These typically include tanks, drums and sacks. These facilities should be appropriate (eg in terms of construction, size and integrity) to the materials being stored and be regularly inspected to detect corrosion or damage. They should be sited on an impermeable base with bunding or kerbing to provide secondary containment in the event of a spill or leak, eg chemicals or oil. Stockpiles of material (eg on construction sites) capable of being blown by the wind may need appropriate fencing or damping down (noting that water is a key environmental resource) to reduce wind-blow. If materials are in containers, suitable covers should be used. Drip trays should be used when dealing with individual drums of chemical or oil.

Issue	Description
Site drainage	On most sites there are two types of drain: • surface water drains, which carry uncontaminated rainwater from surfaces such as roofs and clean yard areas to a watercourse or soakaway. These must not receive any contamination • foul drains, which carry contaminated water, effluent and sewage to the public sewer for subsequent treatment at a sewage works. Legal requirements will restrict what can be discharged to this route, including chemicals and oil. These drains should be clearly identified (eg through colour-coding such as blue for surface water, red for foul water) and appropriately protected (eg spill kits and drain protectors should be located in the vicinity of operations posing unacceptable risks). Oil–water separators should be sited so as to intercept any oil releases that may have entered drains.
Loading and unloading operations	Loading and unloading may need to be undertaken in kerbed or bunded areas (with ramp access) incorporating an impermeable yard surface. Regular checks should be made on hoses and connections to ensure they are in full working order and not corroded. Tank levels should be capable of being easily determined to avoid overflow – this may include visual methods and alarms. Automatic cut-off valves should be used to prevent overfill or stop transfer if the coupling becomes disconnected. Lockable couplings could be used to prevent unauthorised access. Spill kits should be available for materials such as chemicals and oil (including personal protective equipment for those cleaning up the spill).
General	Regular inspection and maintenance will help prevent incidents. Security may be a key issue requiring storage to be in fenced areas with lockable gates and/or lockable containers. A member of staff should be allocated overall responsibility for environmental protection associated with storage and handling activities. Simple procedures should be supported by employee training.

Table 4.2.8
Common handling
and storage issues
continued

e. Controlling releases from contaminated land

Much contaminated land exists because of low (or non-existent) standards regarding releases in the past, including the casual depositing of waste. However, contamination may still occur because of incidents such as spills or leaks.

Contaminated land is a parcel of land in which the contaminants pose an unacceptable risk to water resources, humans, animals, plants or property. The parcel of contaminated land becomes a problem when the land it occupies is developed but also if the contaminants are mobile and in the process of migrating along pathways towards at-risk receptors. Indeed, the process of developing the land may itself lead to the contaminants becoming mobilised.

Figure 4.2.3
Water resources at risk from contaminated land

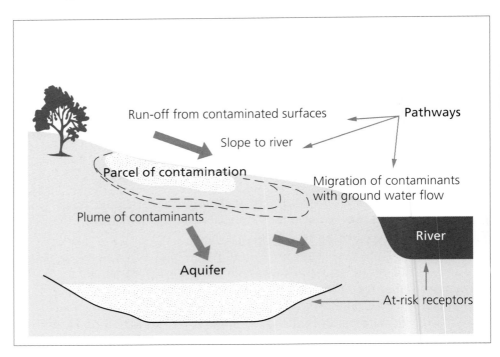

Sites that could have areas of contamination include those that have a history of past industrial activity, or that have experienced a major recent incident or an ongoing series of small incidents. Desktop reviews can often establish whether this is the case. Such a review should also establish the proximity and pathways to any at-risk receptors. If contamination is suspected, a detailed site investigation may be necessary to evaluate the extent of risk and what remediation is necessary if this risk is unacceptable. These investigations usually require a high degree of technical expertise.

When contamination is discovered and it is found to pose an unacceptable risk, remediation will be necessary. There are three main categories of remediation option. These are briefly summarised in Table 4.2.9.

Option	Description
Containment	This involves on-site engineering to contain the parcel of contamination – for example, it may include: • surface capping to create a barrier between the contamination and the surface, eg using tarmac, synthetic liner, imported soil • vertical barriers to prevent horizontal migration of the contaminants, eg using diaphragm walls, impermeable walls, sheet piling • horizontal barriers to prevent upward or downward migration of the contaminants, eg jet-grouting.
Removal	This involves excavating and disposing of the contaminated soil or sediment as waste in a licensed landfill. The landfill could be off site or it could involve creating an appropriately engineered and licensed landfill facility in a suitable area on site.
Treatment	Various techniques exist but need to be subject to rigorous economic and technical appraisal (including assessment of environmental impacts). They can take place on site (in situ) or off site depending on circumstances. Techniques include: soil washing, incineration, thermal stripping, biological action (eg microbes), chemical treatment, vapour extraction and vitrification.

Table 4.2.9
Remediation options for contaminated land

f. Controlling environmental noise

The release of noise can be something that annoys, disturbs or bothers neighbours, ie it can create a nuisance. The existence of nuisance depends on factors such as the timing of the noise (night-time noise can be particularly intrusive), the nature of the sound and how the recipient perceives it. Typical sources that can create a noise nuisance are road traffic, aircraft, loading and unloading operations, operation of industrial presses and hammers, street works, and demolition and construction sites.

It is usually cost-effective to deal with noise reduction when designing equipment or planning an activity. Later modifications or noise abatement may be more time-consuming and costly to install, and may not be as effective.

Cost-effective environmental noise management requires data on the level and type of noise that is reaching receptors, and how much these exceed an acceptable level of noise.

The hierarchy for noise control should be to:
1   prevent generation of noise at source, with good design and maintenance
2   minimise or contain noise at source by observing good operational techniques and management practice
3   use physical barriers or enclosures to prevent transmission
4   increase the distance between the source and receiver
5   sympathetic timing and control of unavoidably noisy operations.

Figure 4.2.4 illustrates some of the generic controls that might be used to alleviate the nuisance.

Figure 4.2.4
Overview of possible noise control options

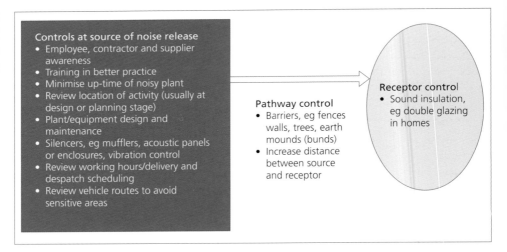

The impact of noise nuisance is linked to the actual level of noise at the receptor and how much of a nuisance the receptor considers it to be. Effective communication with local stakeholders (notably nearby residents) can be an effective management tool for reducing the perceived impact of environmental noise. Any complaints should be recorded and are best dealt with in a constructive manner.

4.2.4 Responsibilities, procedures and training

Key to the management of releases – as for all other environmental aspects – are the appropriate allocation of responsibilities, and the provision of effective documented procedures and training so that employees are aware of the issues and controls required. Checks should be carried out to ensure that the procedures are working and that they remain relevant.

4.3 Waste management

Broadly speaking, waste outputs include not only solid and liquid waste, but effluent discharges, atmospheric emissions and lost heat. However, this chapter will focus on good practice in the management of solids and contained liquids which are discarded by an organisation. These are usually removed from premises for recovery or disposal. However, it should be noted that certain waste streams in particular are being subject to 'producer responsibility' obligations which require a broader approach to product design and waste recovery. This is returned to in Chapter 5.1.

What constitutes waste is usually subject to legal definition. In the UK definition, the key concept is whether the substance or object is being discarded. In the UK, most discarded objects and materials from industrial and commercial premises are further defined as 'controlled wastes'. These controlled wastes are subject to a statutory duty of care. This duty is explained in a code of practice which sets out basic good practice in the storage, handling and transfer of controlled wastes. As controlled waste is subject to regulatory control this should mean that waste arisings from industrial and commercial activities are significant environmental aspects (see Chapter 2.2).

Furthermore, all wastes have the potential to cause environmental impacts if not correctly managed. For example, if waste material is spilled or leaks, it may contaminate land, pollute a watercourse or aquifer or cause nuisance. Proper containment of waste is therefore a fundamental management practice.

4.3.1 Typical wastes
Understanding why wastes arise and then investigating opportunities for preventive action is a key element in waste minimisation and improved process efficiency (see Chapter 4.4).

Typical wastes include:
- production residues, eg industrial slags, lathe turnings, material offcuts
- off-specification products
- goods and materials whose date for use has expired
- used (and unusable) parts, eg spent batteries and toner cartridges, exhausted catalysts
- objects or materials that have been damaged, eg broken equipment, damaged products or packaging, damaged paper
- residues from pollution abatement processes, eg scrubber sludges, baghouse dusts, spent filters, filter cake
- materials that have been spilled or leaked, and have been collected but can no longer be used
- adulterated materials, eg materials which have become contaminated as a result of a mishap or planned activity
- contaminated materials resulting from the remediation of contaminated land
- items for which the holder has no further use, eg obsolete equipment, fixtures and fittings or other articles
- materials resulting from maintenance and cleaning activities
- unwanted materials from buildings that are being demolished, or from facilities that are being decommissioned or refurbished.

It is important to bear in mind that waste is generated by a wide range of activities that go beyond production and manufacturing processes. For example, waste can be generated from various activities in offices, canteens, vehicle maintenance facilities, laboratories, warehousing and retail outlets.

4.3.2 Waste management hierarchy
Waste management should be subject to the waste management hierarchy shown in Figure 4.3.1.

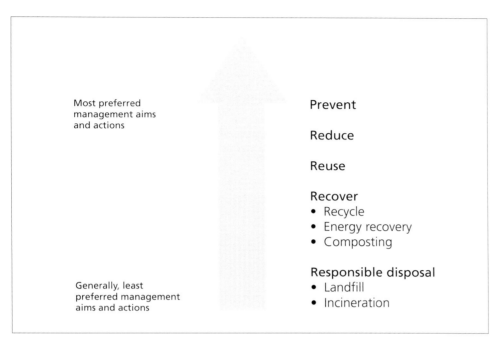

Most preferred
management aims
and actions

Prevent

Reduce

Reuse

Recover
- Recycle
- Energy recovery
- Composting

Generally, least
preferred management
aims and actions

Responsible disposal
- Landfill
- Incineration

Figure 4.3.1
Waste
management
hierarchy

As discussed in Chapter 4.1, this should be used as an indicative checklist. Importantly, the best practicable environmental option (BPEO) for certain waste streams will depend on:
- environmental aspects and impacts associated with transportation, reprocessing, treatment or disposal of the waste
- legal restrictions or requirements on the management of the waste, eg in the UK, certain types of waste can only be accepted by suitably licensed disposal facilities
- technical and economic feasibility of the option in question, eg there may be difficulties associated with recycling certain materials
- stakeholder views as to which options are acceptable and which are unacceptable, including recognised best practice.

Environmental issues associated with activities leading to the recovery or disposal of waste are outlined in Figure 4.3.2. These should form the basis for identifying the BPEO.

Figure 4.3.2
Key environmental
issues associated
with waste
management

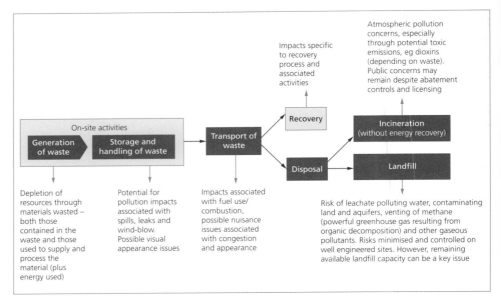

Figure 4.3.2 Key environmental issues associated with waste management

4.3.3 The waste management process

Waste management should incorporate the following steps:

a. identification of the principal waste streams
b. categorisation of the waste based on:
  • legal requirements
  • best waste management option (using the BPEO principle)
c. segregation of the waste according to the categories selected
d. implementation of controls to ensure the waste is dealt with responsibly throughout the entire chain of activities from its point of generation to reuse, recovery or disposal.

a. Identification of the principal waste streams

This is the starting point for waste management. It is also an important element in identifying process efficiency improvements (see Chapter 4.4) and in establishing a comprehensive list of environmental aspects (see Chapter 2.1). A site plan or process flow diagram to map out the use of key materials and the generation of wastes can help with this exercise. The following information should be obtained:

• quantity of waste (eg litres, kilograms, tonnes) over a suitable reference period (eg per day, week, month or year). The quantity may need to be estimated, eg based on the weight of an average skip containing the particular type of solid waste in question
• activity producing the waste
• composition of the waste, including physical properties (eg solid, sludge or liquid), chemical properties (eg flammable, corrosive, toxic) or other special considerations (eg putrescible).

b. Categorisation of the waste
There are numerous ways that waste can be categorised. However, the purpose of classifying waste should be to help achieve legal compliance and beneficial environmental and economic outcomes.

Factors which lead to various waste classifications are considered in Table 4.3.1.

Table 4.3.1
Factors affecting waste classification

Factor	Description
Compliance with regulatory controls on hazardous waste	In the UK and elsewhere, wastes that contain sufficient material with specified hazardous properties are classified as hazardous waste. Hazardous wastes are subject to particular controls and it is essential that these wastes are separated from non-hazardous wastes and that different categories of hazardous wastes are segregated from each other.
Implications of regulatory obligations on recovery	Producer responsibility laws place obligations on the producers of certain products to recover those products (or equivalent materials) when they reach their end of life and become waste. A key example is packaging in the UK, where regulations define the entire packaging chain as 'producers'. The law places obligations on those in the chain who handle above a certain level of packaging materials to recover calculated amounts of packaging waste from the national packaging waste streams. Businesses covered by the regulations may partially meet their obligations by recovering some of the packaging when unpacking supplied goods on site. Those organisations that are not covered by the requirements could find that their packaging waste may have recovery value to those businesses which have legal obligations.
Implications of economic instruments	Governments are increasingly using economic instruments to influence changes in behaviour. Waste disposal is an area where taxes are used to encourage practices further up the waste management hierarchy. For example, the UK has imposed a tax on waste for disposal in landfill so that this option becomes more costly and consequently less attractive. Different types of waste can attract different rates of taxation. In the UK, inert waste (as defined by law implementing the landfill tax) has a lower rate than other (non-inert) wastes.
BPEO	The waste should be categorised according to the different waste management options. This can include reuse, recovery (recycling, composting and/or energy recovery) and disposal (landfill or incineration). Wastes that are candidates for recovery include: waste oil, solvents, metal, paper, wood, glass, certain plastics and biodegradable material. Key considerations include: whether the waste is potentially recyclable, combustible, capable of being processed into a fuel or capable of being composted.

It is important to review the categorisation of waste regularly to take account of new regulatory regimes, changes to the scope and level of environmental taxation applied to waste, developments in recovery techniques and developments in markets for reused or recovered materials.

c. Segregation of the waste

Segregation is the practice of setting apart different waste streams and waste categories. This is best done as close as possible to the source of waste generation to avoid secondary handling (which may involve health and safety risks as well as extra operational costs). Clearly identified collection points should therefore be established for each of the categories of waste stream.

Ensuring that certain wastes are not mixed can be important for the following reasons:
- certain wastes may react with each other when mixed and lead to an environmental (or health and safety) incident
- the mixing of small quantities of hazardous waste with non-hazardous waste can make all the waste 'hazardous' under the law and thus subject to extra regulatory requirements
- the mixing of non-inert waste with inert waste will make all the waste non-inert and thus subject to extra landfill tax if (as in the UK) inert waste attracts a lower rate of tax.

Other benefits of segregation include:
- waste for different recovery or disposal routes can be easily identified, more effectively handled and efficiently despatched to the correct reprocessor or disposal facility
- data collection – including type and quantity of waste – is facilitated. This in turn can help with the completion of regulatory documentation, environmental performance monitoring and reporting, and the identification of waste minimisation/process efficiency opportunities.

d. On-site controls

Certain waste management activities may be subject to permitting. This may prescribe how these activities are managed, including the responsibilities, procedures, technical controls and training required to ensure that the conditions of the licence are met fully.

Table 4.3.2 outlines general good on-site practice.

Waste management practice	Description
Proper containers	The type of container should be suitable for its intended waste content so that the waste is properly contained. Containers typically include drums, tanks and skips. Proper covers and lids may also be required, particularly for chemical liquid wastes. Skips should have appropriate covers to prevent rainwater entering the waste to create leachate or to prevent windblow of loose wastes. Compaction may be appropriate for certain wastes so that the volumes of waste are reduced and the use of containers optimised.
Proper labelling	Clear labelling of waste containers and waste collection areas is important to ensure that proper segregation takes place. The labelling should state which wastes are to be placed in the container and may also indicate which wastes must not. Any particularly hazardous properties that would pose health, safety or environmental risks should also be clearly marked on the container and on adjacent signs. Notices should explain the level at which containers are to be considered full and who to inform to obtain an empty container/take the full container away. In particular, drummed liquid wastes require space to be left at the top of the drum (normally at least 15 per cent) to allow for expansion.
Security	To prevent the risk of vandalism or unauthorised deposit of waste (eg through public access) containers may need to be located in fenced areas and/or be capable of being locked.
Prevention of pollution	The main risks are from loss of containment – leaks from corroded, worn or damaged containers, or spills during handling. Pollution or littering may also occur from overflow of containers or windblow of loose material. This emphasises the need for appropriate primary containment (including covers and locks). If compactors are used, care should be taken to avoid the leakage of liquids. Secondary containment is also good practice so that any leaks and spills do not enter drains or watercourses or seep into the ground. Bunded or kerbed areas provide secondary containment.
Responsibility, procedures and training	A nominated individual should have overall responsibility for waste management for a given activity or area. Simple procedures should apply to waste management operations and all employees should receive training on segregation and relevant storage and handling controls to prevent pollution. Record-keeping is also important to help monitor compliance with legal requirements, monitor progress against targets and assist with the identification of waste minimisation opportunities. Periodic checks should be made to confirm that procedures are being followed and that they remain relevant.

Table 4.3.2
Waste management practices

The practices outlined in Table 4.3.2, for example, are incorporated into the duty of care code of practice that applies to waste storage and handling in the UK.

e. Transferring waste to off-site facilities

Legal requirements usually control how waste is transferred to third parties and transported to reprocessing or disposal facilities. In the UK, this is also covered by the duty of care for waste, and waste carriers (with some exceptions) must be registered. The transfer of the waste must be accompanied by a note which describes the nature of the waste in a way that subsequent holders can rely on, eg the type of waste, how it is contained, its quantity and a description of any special handling considerations. Furthermore, disposal and recovery facilities must be licensed to take the waste in question.

More stringent requirements apply to hazardous wastes. In the UK, the regulatory authorities must be notified of the movement of hazardous waste and a detailed description of its hazardous properties should be shown on transfer documentation. Only facilities with a regulatory permit to take the hazardous waste in question can accept that waste. Importantly, those transferring the waste also need to be sure that it will not escape containment en route to its destination.

An essential principle is that there should be an 'audit trail' for waste. The audit trail allows the organisation and others (such as enforcers) to know where the waste has gone and what has happened to it. The audit trail also helps ensure that those involved are discharging their own duty of care for waste.

Again, there should be a nominated person with overall responsibility for waste transfer. Procedures, communication and training should ensure that the relevant waste is being transferred to a registered carrier, securely contained, with appropriate documentation correctly completed, and that it is destined to go to a properly permitted facility. Transfer documents should be filed in accordance with regulatory requirements and be readily accessible for inspection. Periodic checks should be made to ensure the procedures are being followed and that they remain relevant.

It is good practice for representatives of an organisation to visit recovery and disposal facilities which deal with its waste to help exercise a duty of care. The frequency of these visits should depend on factors such as the extent of any issues or historic problems encountered, and the nature and quantity of the waste material.

4.4 Process efficiency

Process efficiency aims to achieve greater resource productivity from organisational or business activities. This has environmental and economic benefits for the organisation and is often referred to as the 'win win' scenario. Process efficiency is about using fewer resource inputs (materials and energy) and generating less waste (in all its forms) for a given level of production or service. It therefore incorporates waste minimisation, energy efficiency and material productivity. In particular, process efficiency (including energy efficiency and the avoidance of leaks of methane and refrigerants) should be an important element in any greenhouse gas reduction strategy (see also section 5.2.9).

4.4.1 Benefits
How process efficiency improves environmental performance depends on which environmental aspects are addressed. However, process efficiency can generally be considered to deliver the benefits listed in Table 4.4.1.

Environmental benefits	Business benefits
• Contributes to resource conservation • Helps reduce environmental impacts associated with specific emissions, effluent and other waste streams	• Savings through avoided material and energy/utility wastage • Savings through avoided waste handling and disposal costs, emission abatement or effluent treatment and discharge costs • Reduced exposure to environmental taxes such as landfill tax, energy levy, discharge or emission charges • Avoidance of wasted effort, and more productive use of plant, equipment and storage space contribute to reduced operating costs

Table 4.4.1
The benefits of resource efficiency

4.4.2 Overview
Production processes transform raw materials or assemble components into products. A 'process', however, can also be an activity (or set of activities) that delivers a service – for example, a transportation process that moves people or goods from A to B, or a process that stores and packages goods.

In this chapter, the emphasis is on the role of process efficiency in the production of goods, but it is important to recognise that the principles also apply to the provision of services.

Figure 4.4.1
Generic inputs
and outputs of the
manufacturing
process

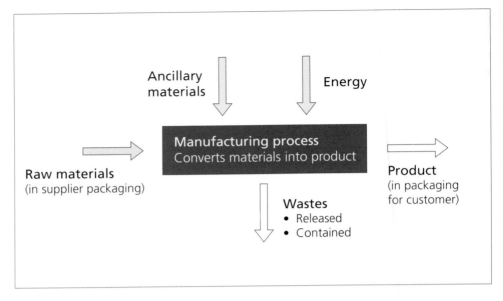

Figure 4.4.1 above identifies the main inputs and outputs of a manufacturing process. It is useful to distinguish between the different categories of inputs (see Table 4.4.2).

Table 4.4.2
Inputs to a
manufacturing
process

Category	Description	Examples
Raw materials	Those essential materials that end up in the product, as well as those which are used to pack the product before its despatch/distribution (customer packaging)	• Steel in appliance products • Clay in ceramic products • Water in drink products • Packaging materials, eg wooden pallets, cardboard boxes and filler, glass or plastic bottles
'Ancillary' materials	Materials used indirectly for production but which do not form part of the final product	• Lubrication oil in manufacturing equipment • Water for cooling or cleaning • Solvents for cleaning
Energy	Provides a range of process services, including motive power, equipment power, light, heating or cooling	• Fuel – gas, oil or coal • Electricity
Supplier packaging	Packaging used in the delivery and storage of the raw and ancillary materials (from suppliers)	• Wooden pallets • Metal or plastic drums • Cardboard boxes • Plastic sacks

Process efficiency aims to optimise useful outputs and minimise unwanted outputs so that inputs are not wasted and, as a result, less resource input is required. Fundamental to this process is the systematic reduction of waste at source (see Figure 4.4.2).

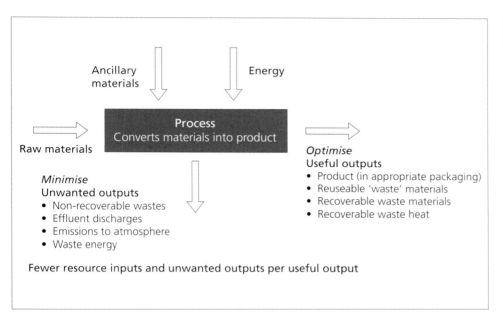

Figure 4.4.2
Process efficiency

Reducing waste at source requires the prevention of waste during the production process. For example, this might include ensuring that:
- raw materials, work in progress or finished products are not lost through damage, spillage (if powder or liquid) or degradation (if subject to shelf life)
- the production process avoids the manufacture of reject products
- energy and/or material inputs used are the correct amount for the job so that excess use (eg packaging, power or heat) and superfluous off-cuts (wasting raw material) are avoided.

Waste minimisation also includes finding uses for otherwise waste outputs (these outputs effectively become by-products). Such uses can be either in the process in question, in other processes on the site or elsewhere in the organisation, or in other processes external to the organisation. Possible initiatives could include those outlined in Table 4.4.3.

Opportunity	On-site example	Off-site examples
Reuse of materials	Use of supplier packaging for own packaging purposes, eg storage of work in progress or despatching products to customers	Return packaging to suppliers or deliver to other external users so that it can be reused
Recovery of waste materials through recycling	Return waste to start of process, eg cullet (broken or off-cut glass) for remelting in glassworks or bottling factory	Collect metal waste to send for resmelting (via scrap metal merchant or direct)
Energy recovery from waste materials	Anaerobic digestion of organic wastes to generate biogas. This is then used as a fuel in a furnace or reciprocating engine	Collect oil waste to deliver waste-to-energy facility (via waste oil contractor or direct)
Recovery of heat	Use of waste process heat to help heat air or water used elsewhere in the process or help meet other site heat requirements	Use of waste heat as part of district heating scheme

The feasibility of these initiatives will depend on technical, economic and market factors and they may need to be subject to a detailed investment appraisal (this is vital if they involve capital projects). The initiatives may also have negative environmental impacts from material transportation or reprocessing. In these situations, the organisation will need to consider any environmental 'trade-offs' due to the various positive and negative impacts. Other factors, such as legislative or financial implications, may also be central to making a decision. Generally, on-site reuse or recovery of materials is preferred as this avoids transport-related impacts. Also, housekeeping measures tend to provide environmental benefits which are low cost and have rapid payback.

4.4.3 Approach and techniques
Process efficiency involves the following steps:
1 map the various process stages to show how raw materials flow through the process to become product (a process flow chart is a useful tool for this purpose)
2 identify the principal inputs (raw and ancillary materials, energy) and outputs (product, by-products and wastes) at each process stage
3 quantify the amount of product created by the process, the material and energy used and the by-products and wastes generated, at each process stage, together with their associated costs

4 prioritise areas for improving efficiency or reducing waste based on cost and environmental concerns (linkage to assessment of significance would be sensible – see Chapter 2.2)
5 generate improvement options
6 assess the technical and economic feasibility of the options identified – where possible, guided by BPEO considerations
7 agree action and build into environmental target-setting process (see Chapter 3.3) and environmental management programme (see Chapter 3.4).

4.4.4 Mapping the process/identifying inputs and outputs
Figure 4.4.3 provides an example of the stages in a simple business process. It also identifies the main inputs and outputs.

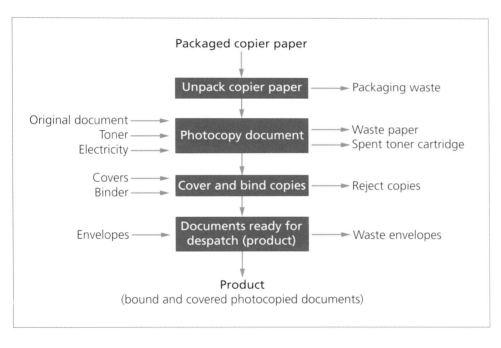

Figure 4.4.3
Process flow chart example: producing bound and covered photocopied documents

4.4.5 Generating options for improvement
The mapping and quantification processes can help pinpoint opportunities for improvement by identifying what happens, and where. Quantification of the material and waste volumes and associated costs indicates the priority areas for reducing waste. Diagrammatic representation of the findings, perhaps through simple histograms or pie charts, can help in spotting opportunities. Two particularly useful techniques for illustrating the production process can be scattergrams of production against a key input or waste output, or Sankey diagrams to provide a pictorial analysis of 'mass balance'.

In the scattergram (see Figure 4.4.4), production has been plotted against a key resource input or waste output. This approach is particularly useful for batch processes. By plotting each batch on the graph, relative performance (efficient and inefficient) can be established. In the diagram, two obvious 'flyers' ('A' and 'B') have tended to use more resource (or generate more waste) per unit output, while other batches have clustered together in a way that allows a line of good practice to be drawn. Investigating why A and B show relatively poor performance can lead to conclusions which suggest action to improve the situation and identify opportunities for performance improvements.

Using the example of a photocopied document, each batch could be a particular document run, with the number of copies produced plotted against waste pages. The two flyers A and B might be ascribed to an individual who had not had sufficient training on the copier, or to the fact that a particular paper causes an upset in the copier run. There may be other reasons but the key point is that the analysis helps home in on poor performance so that solutions can be identified.

Figure 4.4.4
Scattergram –
production against
resource
input/waste
output

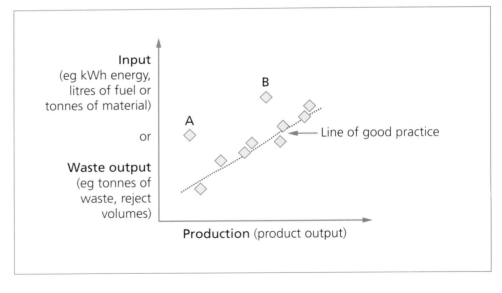

For certain materials (eg water, solvent), a 'mass balance' exercise is useful to allow all the inputs and outputs of a material in a given process or operation to be established. A perfect mass balance exercise would find that the inputs to a process match the outputs (since material does not disappear). However, in reality a proportion of the outputs is often difficult to account for and may require further detailed investigation. Indeed, the further investigation of substantial outputs which cannot initially be accounted for often yields opportunities for improved process efficiency.

The Sankey diagram is a useful technique for representing mass balances. The example in Figure 4.4.5 considers the destination of process water. The 11 per cent that cannot be accounted for could be due to a combination of leaks and steam losses. Process efficiency measures could seek to reduce these losses as well as consider reduction, reuse and recovery options to avoid discharge as effluent and disposal in sludge.

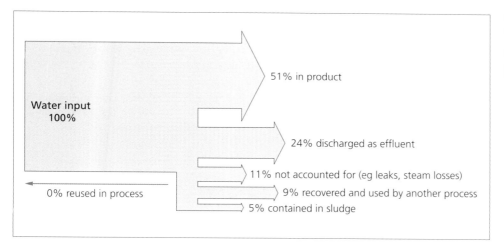

Figure 4.4.5
The mass balance of water for a production process

A key part of generating options for improved process efficiency is to identify the reasons why poor performance occurs or why waste arises. A useful technique is cause–effect analysis. This involves bringing together a small group of people who have knowledge of the process being analysed. A particular problem ('effect') is specified, eg why a particular waste is generated or material losses occur. The 'effect' is placed at the head of the 'fish' in a fishbone diagram (see Figure 4.4.6) and members of the group generate ideas as to why the problem occurs.

Figure 4.4.6
Fishbone or
cause–effect
diagram

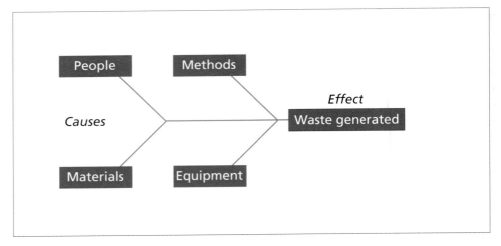

The causes are recorded on the 'bones' of the fish. To help with this process, typical 'cause' categories are 'people', 'methods', 'materials' and 'equipment' and these can label separate fish bones to prompt ideas. The causes should be recorded under each category, with any additional categories (eg 'communication') added as a new bone.

Figure 4.4.7 shows how this has been developed for the waste paper 'effect' from the document production example.

Figure 4.4.7
Cause–effect
diagram for waste
paper from a
document
production process

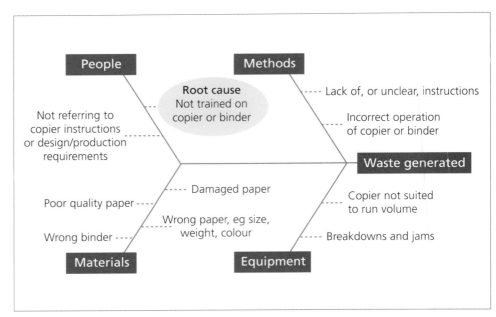

The aim of the technique is to identify and agree the root causes of the 'effect'. A check needs to be made that causes are not in fact symptoms. For example, 'breakdowns and jams' are a symptom rather than a cause, so reasons why such events occur should be established, eg lack of maintenance, operator error. In the example, training of the copier operator is suggested as the main root cause. It is useful to record all ideas before assessing whether they are true causes or in fact symptoms.

Having generated options for improving process efficiency, it is necessary to assess their technical and economic feasibility. Use of the benefit/ease of action grid may help with this (see Chapter 3.3). Opportunities may range from simple housekeeping or improved maintenance and behavioural changes, through to small technical changes or to large capital projects, eg the installation of combined heat and power plant. All projects (other than low cost projects) should be subject to an appropriate level of investment appraisal in line with an organisation's policy and procedures.

When action is agreed, process efficiency initiatives should be incorporated into improvement targets and environmental management programmes (see Chapters 3.3 and 3.4).

Appendix 3 includes details of organisations that provide free and impartial advice on process efficiency, waste minimisation and energy efficiency.

5: Moving forward

5.1 Beyond operational control

5.1.1 Looking beyond the 'perimeter fence'

An organisation's 'perimeter fence' can provide a clear and practical boundary when first developing an environmental management system (EMS). However, many organisations find that to get the most out of environmental management, they need to extend the scope of their environmental management considerations into areas beyond on-site activity. Indeed, there is increased pressure through regulatory developments and other initiatives to do so.

The reasons for extending the scope of environmental management more widely than the site boundary include:

- an organisation's environmental footprint is wider than its immediate operations and includes the indirect environmental aspects and impacts associated with, for example, the use of supplier and contractor transport, product use and recovery/disposal, and other supply chain factors
- the main life cycle environmental impacts of a product may not be under the direct operational control of the organisation, but at another stage – upstream (eg in terms of suppliers) and/or downstream (eg in terms of customer use or disposal), as explained in the chapter on life cycle assessment (Chapter 2.4). 'Life cycle thinking' helps to address this issue
- the ISO 14001 standard requires an organisation to identify the environmental aspects of its activities, products and services that it can control and those that it can influence, and to ensure that the aspects related to significant impacts are considered in setting its environmental objectives
- ensuring that suppliers and contractors are managing their operations responsibly helps to reduce the risk of disrupted supplies and any consequent commercial impact on the organisation
- extending environmental management to cover a wider scope of activities can be considered to be part of continual improvement of the EMS (see also Chapter 2.1).

This chapter therefore considers environmental management action beyond direct operations, with a focus on partnerships involving suppliers, contractors, customers, employees and the local community. It also considers some issues that might be overlooked both within and outside the site, including biodiversity, geodiversity and the historic environment. Important elements are represented in Figure 5.1.1. Those 'outside the fence' are often typically in the area of influence rather than direct control, eg employees' commuter travel, suppliers' environmental performance and customers' use of a product.

Figure 5.1.1
Elements to
consider beyond
immediate site
operations

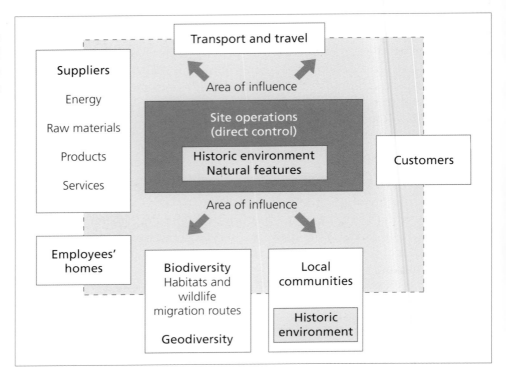

5.1.2 Suppliers

Overview
There are good business reasons for working with suppliers, both in terms of general environmental management and specific environmental issues.

For example, requiring suppliers to exercise effective environmental management can help to ensure continuity of supply or service by reducing the risk of an incident that could disrupt business, eg through the supplier closing key operations for clean-up, or through regulatory action. In addition, process efficiency measures in the supplier's or contractor's operations should improve their cost base and efficiency of service and therefore help them remain competitive. Reputational issues may also be at stake, particularly if the aim of the organisation is to achieve and maintain a high reputation with key stakeholders. Such status requires working with responsible suppliers and contractors and avoiding those with poor credentials and no commitment to improve.

Importantly, there are also good environmental reasons for co-operation, since the supplier or contractor's own operations may be the source of significant environmental impacts and represent significant indirect aspects for the organisation being supplied or serviced. The choice of supplier may also be important in helping to manage direct aspects, such as selecting suppliers of low carbon energy or of products that are easy to reuse, recycle or otherwise recover.

This section is concerned with suppliers, including contractors who are not directly employed in the organisation's operations. Table 5.1.1 considers the different types of supplier.

Category	Description
Suppliers	Manufacturers, distributors and other external entities that predominantly supply goods and products to the organisation.
Contractors	Typically, external providers of services to the organisation. This provision may be largely on site (eg construction work, maintenance, facilities management or catering), in which case they should be directly subject to site operational standards and procedures. It may also be predominantly or wholly off site, eg hauliers contracted by the organisation to transport goods and products, or vehicle servicing firms that maintain the organisation's car, van or lorry fleet at an external service centre.
Preferred suppliers/ contractors	Suppliers or contractors that the organisation has selected (shortlisted) as (potential) preferred partners for supplying goods or services.

Table 5.1.1
Categories of supplier

Although this chapter focuses on areas beyond the direct operational control of the organisation, the operational control of contractors and suppliers on (or near) the organisation's premises should not be forgotten. They could be the source of particular environmental problems. Some examples of environmental issues and typical management mechanisms are provided in Table 5.1.2. Interface documents can be particularly important in such situations.

Table 5.1.2
On-site
management
issues relevant to
suppliers

Issue	Detail
Possible environmental problems	Suppliers may, for example: • not segregate waste on site in accordance with site policy and procedures • not be switching off equipment to reduce energy use and carbon emissions • create impacts such as noise nuisance from vehicles or unloading • cause an incident such as a spill.

Typical management mechanism	Might include:
	• contractor pre-qualification arrangements
	• contract details
	• proper induction, updates and instructions
	  ○ briefing on operational standards and procedures for specific activities and aspects
	  ○ other appropriate communication techniques (see Chapter 3.7).

	A concise and clear environmental management interface document is often important. This should:
	• be agreed by all parties – especially where a contractor is involved in ongoing or critical work
	  ○ include relevant environmental targets, standards and contingency plans that affect the contract
	  ○ set out allocated actions, responsibilities, timescales and reporting mechanisms
	  ○ provide a clear statement of prime responsibility, ie contractor, subcontractor or client.
	
	The interface document can stand separate from the contract, but it should be related to it.

Purchasing and supply

When managing a supply chain, an organisation is faced with the following inter-related issues:

- selecting suppliers to meet their various business needs – in terms of key products and services, this is often through a shortlist of preferred suppliers and the use of a tendering process for the award of specific contracts (see Figure 5.1.2)
- working with their suppliers to deliver required standards of performance
- integrating environmental factors, along with price, delivery, safety, quality and other considerations into the selection process, performance standards and improvement targets.

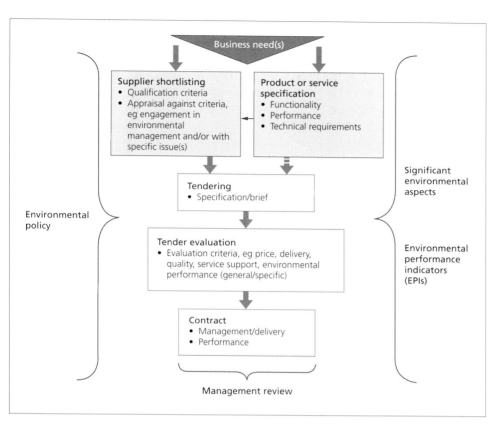

Figure 5.1.2
Key elements in purchasing and supply, and the interface with environmental management

Deciding how to deal with suppliers on environmental issues should be based on identified business and environmental priorities. Figure 5.1.3 suggests one approach by categorising suppliers according to:
• the level of dependence the business has on them (actual if an existing supplier, or potential if a prospective supplier)
• the environmental significance of the supplier.

It is highly likely that preferred suppliers and those commissioned for major contracts will have high dependency scores.

The environmental significance of the supplier could be determined by considering whether the product or service being provided (or tendered for) directly affects the environmental performance of the client organisation. This would be the case if the client has identified the material or energy input being supplied as a direct significant aspect. The supplier becomes particularly significant if an improvement objective or target has been set or is being considered (see Chapter 3.3) to improve the environmental performance of that aspect and direct assistance from the supplier is required to achieve it.

Figure 5.1.3
Prioritising
suppliers in terms
of environmental
management

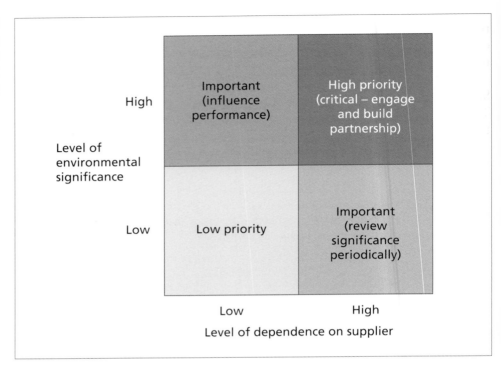

Suppliers can also be categorised according to the actual or potential significance of environmental issues affecting the supplier's organisation and operations. While this normally requires an assessment of on-site practices to have first taken place, a provisional category could be allocated based on a general understanding of the types of issue expected. Life cycle thinking (as discussed in Chapter 2.4) could be used to highlight key issues.

In Figure 5.1.3, high priority (critical) suppliers are those who fall into the high dependency/high environmental significance area of the matrix. Suppliers who score high on environmental significance but low on dependence should still be considered as important and appropriate measures used to influence improved supplier performance.

It is useful to record a short description of why a supplier is allocated into a particular category, and the process should be reviewed periodically, or if there are significant developments, eg in terms of environmental laws or supplier circumstances. A subsequent supplier assessment (eg a more detailed assessment) may mean that a supplier who is initially allocated to a particular environmental significance category may need to be reallocated, eg from low to high. It may be particularly relevant for high dependency suppliers, who have previously been regarded as having relatively low environmental significance, to be reviewed regularly, eg to consider the effect of changing government policy or potential changes in the production of relevant products.

Supplier assessment
To be manageable and effective, supplier assessment should be based on the prioritisation process outlined above.

One criticism of assessing suppliers on environmental (and other) matters has been the practice of sending lengthy questionnaires to existing or prospective suppliers. Although common, this can be particularly inefficient if it is part of a general approach to all suppliers, irrespective of what they supply, or when the objectives are unclear and when no feedback on the supplier's information is provided. Sending out blanket questionnaires can create burdensome paperwork for both the supplier and the procurer. It can also give a negative impression of environmental management, suggesting it adds cost and becomes a bureaucratic exercise. Excessive information is unlikely to translate into appropriate or relevant environmental management actions and could lead to confusion. Key to working with the supply chain on environmental (and other) matters is that the process must add value.

The type and level of information required should not be the same for low priority suppliers as for high priority (critical) suppliers. Indeed, for low priority suppliers it may simply be appropriate to ask for a copy of the supplier's environmental policy, and some evidence that it is being implemented. For critical suppliers, a targeted questionnaire may be appropriate, seeking information relevant to the client's environmental policy and objectives. This might focus on the key environmental considerations to be addressed as part of a contract – stating which targets/standards of performance are required and asking for clear explanations of how these will be met or exceeded.

The type and level of information might also depend on the stage in the procurement process. A typical process is set out in Figure 5.1.2. Usually, more generic environmental management information is required in pre-tender shortlisting. Specific environmental qualification criteria in the supplier filtering process should depend on the environmental significance of the prospective contract and on relevant factors in the product and service specification, eg performance requirements. However, in the tendering phase greater emphasis may be put on how specific environmental performance requirements will be achieved (and how performance will be monitored and reported) if the contract is awarded.

The degree of assessment should also depend on factors such as risk and the size and nature of the contract. The assessment should also consider the resources available to small and medium-sized enterprises (SMEs) and, in particular, micro-businesses (avoiding unnecessary bureaucracy).

The organisation should be clear about what information it wants and how it will be used from different suppliers, for different contracts and at different stages in the procurement process. This might include both generic information and specific information depending on the category of supplier. Generally, more specific information should be required from critical and important suppliers (as categorised in Figure 5.1.3) where the level of environmental significance of the supplier, their services or products is considered to be high.

Table 5.1.3
Types of environmental information from suppliers

Type of information	Examples
Generic Emphasis on general environmental management	• The supplier's environmental policy • Outline of the supplier's significant environmental aspects • Information on how these aspects are managed, eg system arrangements, personnel, training • Evidence of general performance to date • Explanation of how any incidents or complaints have been dealt with and the lessons learned • Willingness to engage with environmental issues and to commit to continual improvement
Specific Emphasis on specific issues, aspects or impacts, and/or on management processes	• The supplier's environmental policy and practices regarding the required products or services • How the supplier will demonstrate their performance in specific areas (eg aspects and impacts) relevant to the supply of the required products or services • How a product or service meets or exceeds any environmental performance/functionality requirements • Factors that help the client meet their own specific objectives or targets in particular areas, eg low carbon, minimising packaging • Mechanisms for monitoring and reporting on environmental performance (either generally or in terms of the contract)

Note: The information sought will vary. It should be appropriate to the supplier, the nature of the contract and the stage in the procurement process.

Table 5.1.3 gives examples of requirements for generic and specific information, while Table 5.1.4 considers example questions to illustrate how they can be developed. A key point is to think about why a question is being asked/why that information is being sought, ie the purpose of the question.

Example question	Purpose	Information expected	How assessed	
Does your organisation have a documented environmental policy? If so, please provide a copy.	Helps establish the extent to which the supplier is committed to environmental management.	Confirmation that a policy exists, plus a copy of the current policy statement (signed and dated).	The policy should be appropriate to the contract. Best practice would be for a policy signed by a sufficiently senior person, eg managing director. It should have commitments that cover key issues and management arrangements, including regular reviews.	Table 5.1.4 Example questions for suppliers and their rationale
Does your organisation have access to environmental advice or assistance (internally and/or externally)? If so, please outline the arrangements.*	Helps establish the supplier's capability to manage environmental issues and improve performance.	A description of any environmental management post or posts and any consultants employed.	The resources should be appropriate to the organisation and be capable of meeting policy commitments. If specific aspects are of concern to the client, then the question may also ask about expertise regarding that aspect. This information may also be useful to identify a potential contact if the client wishes to develop a partnership or joint environmental initiative.	
Specifically, does your organisation have arrangements for supplying timber from sustainable sources? If so, please provide details.*	Helps establish what is being done by the supplier for an aspect of particular relevance to the client (ie a significant aspect) that will help their performance in this area.	A description of requirements set by the supplier, including reference to commitments, objectives, checking arrangements, plus any product certification schemes signed up to, eg Forest Stewardship Council.	The arrangements should be aligned to the needs of the client and show how they can meet their policy commitments, performance standards and any improvement goals or communication needs on, in this case, sustainable timber. As a cross-check, the supplier's response to such a question should also fit with the information supplied for other questions. For example, if a policy statement has been requested (as would be typical in most situations), this should have a commitment that covers this aspect in an appropriate way.	

* The client may also ask for specific information to support such questions, eg organisational structure charts, professional qualifications or evidence concerning a relevant product certification scheme.

While the information sought from potential suppliers will typically be obtained via a questionnaire, where possible other techniques might also be considered. It is worth noting that using the scoring of responses to a supplier questionnaire as the sole contract-awarding technique might miss improvement opportunities, and that scoring should be used as an indicator, rather than the decisive factor.

Other methods might include interviews, site visits and/or product/ equipment demonstrations, depending on the supplier and the product or service being offered. An assessment of a supplier's organisational culture can be important and therefore will benefit from face-to-face meetings. For critical suppliers and major contracts, the assessment could be undertaken through a mix of approaches. Critical suppliers, in particular, should also be entitled to expect feedback and follow-up. The aim should be to set the scene for building an effective partnership on environmental management, especially to address significant aspects.

Some suppliers may be keen to engage with environmental issues but lack the capacity. This situation can offer opportunities for the client to assist with the 'greening' of its supply chain by providing knowledge – and perhaps resources and support – to help build supplier capacity for effective environmental management.

Suppliers occupy various positions in the 'spectrum of engagement' set out in Figure 5.1.4. The stages in the spectrum (as a hierarchy of environmental engagement) are also set out in more detail in Table 5.2.7 in Chapter 5.2.

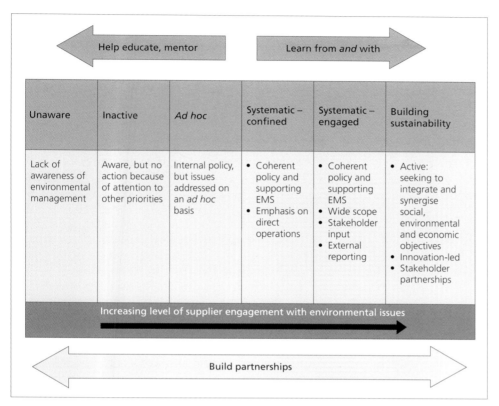

Figure 5.1.4
The spectrum of supplier engagement with environmental issues

Furthermore, a client organisation with a comprehensive policy and systematic approach to environmental management that sets about working with its supply chain can normally be considered to be, at least, entering the 'systematic – engaged' stage.

Ongoing supplier relationship and interface
Determining the stage their suppliers are at on the engagement spectrum (see Figure 5.1.4) can help clients define initiatives to help build, maintain or enhance supplier relationships.

This could include:
- education of 'unaware' suppliers
- resources and support to help develop an effective EMS for the 'inactive' and 'ad hoc'. This might include mentoring
- a variety of partnerships to deal with specific issues, aspects and impacts, especially for those engaged in 'systematic' environmental management and those 'building sustainability'. Successful partnerships at this end of the spectrum are likely to involve two-way learning, ie learning for both the client and supplier (both from each other and with each other).

Table 5.1.5 sets out some specific mechanisms to engage with suppliers on environmental issues.

Table 5.1.5
Possible
mechanisms to
engage with
suppliers

Aim	Emphasis	Possible methods
To stimulate overall environmental improvements	• Raising general awareness of the benefits of effective environmental management • Helping suppliers to conduct environmental reviews • Encouraging process efficiency initiatives	• Sponsoring, hosting or running seminars, workshops, working groups • Publicising success • Sharing best practice
To target improvements on specific issues	• Selecting the key issue, aspect, or impact relevant to the supply chain/client organisation, including any challenging environmental goals • Giving advice on meeting performance requirements	• Organising workshops, brainstorming sessions, site visits and/or demonstrations • Setting up an inter-organisational task group to explore technical and commercially sound solutions • Producing an interface document with actions, timescales and responsibilities designed to achieve targets (see also Table 5.1.2)

Areas for specific initiatives might include:
• supplier packaging, eg opportunities for minimisation, increasing recyclate content, design for reuse or recovery
• travel and transportation, eg opportunities for improved payload, reduced trips, use of more efficient vehicles, use or piloting of alternative fuels
• substances and materials, eg opportunities for alternatives or substitutes that are less toxic, or switched sourcing to sustainable renewable sources or to materials containing enhanced recyclate content
• energy supply, eg energy efficiency initiatives, electricity or heat from renewable sources, developing (high quality and accredited) carbon offset projects.

Implications for client organisation's EMS
When undertaking supply chain initiatives, it is important that environmental aspects being managed along the supply chain are aligned with the assessment of significance under the client's EMS.

It is also important that the client's environmental policy includes a clear statement of the degree to which the client intends to engage with their suppliers. For some organisations a separate environmental purchasing policy might be used. This might include a commitment to:

- encourage suppliers to develop effective environmental management appropriate to their size and sector
- educate suppliers on how to develop effective environmental management in their organisation
- include appropriate environmental criteria in procurement procedures along with other criteria, including financial, safety, quality and delivery parameters
- develop appropriate initiatives with suppliers, including education, support and partnership working (depending on their level of engagement with environmental issues)
- ensure suppliers are given clear environmental performance requirements through relevant contract conditions, product and service specifications, and appropriate communication and feedback mechanisms
- encourage the development and use of materials, products and energy supplies with improved environment performance.

Any policy statements relevant to suppliers must link to objectives, targets and related actions; monitoring (eg performance indicators); auditing and management review processes. Key contracts should be incorporated into these processes, including the management review (see Figure 5.1.2).

5.1.3 Considering customers
Customers may be other organisations or individual consumers.

If the customer is another organisation, then the supplier could be proactive and seek to understand how it can help its key customers meet their environmental objectives; in particular, how they can manage the indirect upstream aspects and impacts for which they are responsible. For example, if supplying timber from sustainable sources is an issue for the customer, then the supplier needs arrangements in place to make sure that they can supply such timber and that the customer is confident with their approach.

If customers are individual consumers, it might be appropriate to establish consumer opinion on environmental features and the environmental performance of products and services, for example, through market research with target market segments, such as through focus groups.

Figure 5.1.5 suggests a means of categorising customers in terms of environmental management. Those customers, or market segments, on which the organisation is highly dependent (or is targeting) for business and which have a high degree of interest in environmental issues should be those which are the priority for the organisation.

Figure 5.1.5
Categorising
customers in
terms of
environmental
management

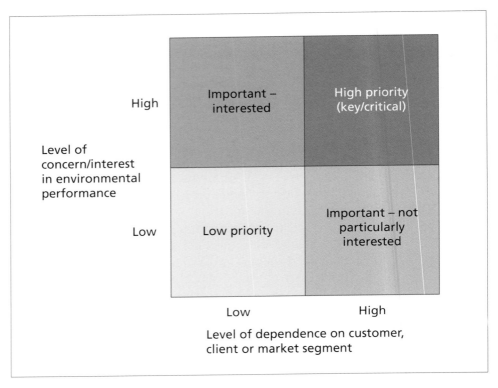

It is particularly important for the organisation to understand the requirements and issues of these key/critical customers and to actively address them. For those who have a low interest in the environment but on whom the organisation is highly dependent, there could be an opportunity to inform and raise awareness about relevant environmental issues. For those customers who are highly interested in environmental issues but on whom the organisation is not highly dependent, then the organisation should seek, at least, to satisfy their needs and also monitor their views. The organisation should also have regular reviews to establish the likelihood of these customers becoming more significant.

5.1.4 Products and producer responsibility

Some of the key pressures on producers to manufacture more environmentally beneficial products, and to address the performance of products during their use and at the end of their life, are set out in Figure 5.1.6. This includes government policy measures such as producer responsibility obligations, eco-labelling (including energy labelling) and eco-taxes. For example, taxes on electricity will encourage producers to make electronic equipment more energy efficient and increases in fuel duty puts pressure on manufacturers to produce more fuel-efficient vehicles.

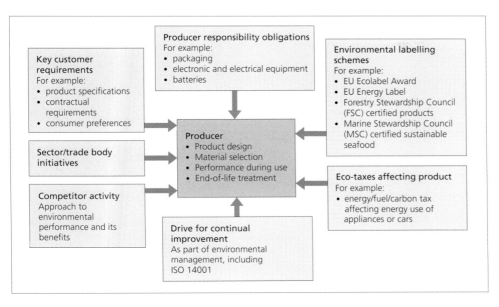

Figure 5.1.6
Pressures on
producers to be
more responsible

Such pressures increasingly require producers to design, manufacture and market products which:

- avoid or minimise the use of hazardous substances in the product
- maximise the use of sustainably produced renewable material (eg wood from sustainable forests) or recycled material in the make up of the product
- consume fewer resources (materials and energy) during use
- produce less waste (emissions, liquid and solid waste) during use
- can be reused or recovered when they reach their end of life – technically (eg ability to be recycled), through organisational arrangements (eg take-back mechanisms) and in ways that minimise other impacts (eg impacts associated with collection, transportation and reprocessing).

It is also important that customers are properly informed about what to do with the product. Producers and distributors should therefore consider:

- how customers are made aware of the best ways to minimise environmental impacts of the product during use
- how customers are made aware of what to do with the product at the end of its life.

This could be through various point-of-sale and after-care communication methods. A combination of the following may be used:

- information leaflets
- demonstrations
- websites
- helplines.

Again, prioritisation will help the process to be manageable – particularly for businesses with a large product range, eg wholesale or retail outlets. Factors such as the level of dependency of the business on the product (eg volume sold, market share), new product launch or branding plans, specific stakeholder concerns and the existence of producer responsibility and other product or supply-related legislation should be used to identify priority products.

The EU has pursued a 'producer responsibility' policy for priority product and waste streams, including packaging, electronic and electrical equipment, and batteries. For example, producer responsibility packaging obligations in the UK require organisations to meet specific recovery and recycling targets (individually or as part of a compliance scheme) based on their role in the supply chain (ie as manufacturer, converter, packer/filler, seller, importer of packaging) and the type of packaging material in question (paper, plastics, glass, metal, wood). Some of the generic considerations of producer responsibility are set out in Figure 5.1.7.

Figure 5.1.7
Generic elements
of producer
responsibility

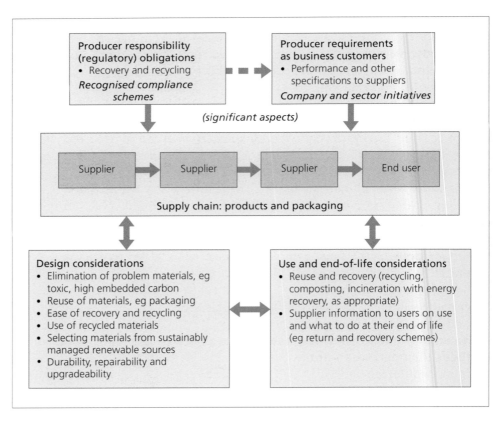

Organisations should not only respond to producer responsibility legislation but actively monitor policy developments and other pressures (as set out in Figure 5.1.6) as part of their strategic environmental management processes, eg the management review. Also, it is important that organisations include factors that affect products (and services) in their assessment of significance. This is particularly important for those seeking certification to ISO 14001. Producer responsibility obligations applying to an organisation's products or packaging (eg end-of-life recovery requirements) should make these 'significant' aspects in any EMS (see Figures 2.2.2 and 2.2.3).

5.1.5 Carbon footprint and related issues

Greenhouse gases and related issues are dealt with in various chapters of this book. This section seeks to draw together some of the key issues in identifying an organisation's carbon footprint, especially as key aspects can be beyond the immediate operations of most organisations and requires life cycle thinking.

As will be discussed in Chapter 5.2, over the past decade or so, carbon and climate change have, arguably, moved to the forefront of the environmental and sustainability agenda (see, for example, Table 5.2.3). Increasingly, measures such as energy taxes, tradeable permits, energy labelling and greenhouse gas reporting initiatives are used to try to control emissions of carbon dioxide (see also Chapter 1.4).

For most organisations, carbon (ie carbon dioxide) is associated with energy use and therefore energy supply choices and energy efficiency (see, for example, Table 4.2.7). However, it can also be associated with specific processes (eg CO_2 released during the processing of limestone to manufacture cement) or other types of greenhouse gas (eg methane leaks from gas supply systems, refrigerant leaks from air conditioning and other equipment, or venting methane from landfill sites). Indeed, some greenhouse gases – molecule for molecule – are much more powerful than CO_2 (see Table 2.4.2). For example, methane has a global warming potential (GWP) of 21, while CO_2 has a GWP of 1.

Since there is a close association between carbon emissions and energy use, and given the need for energy in virtually all activities, all organisations will need to map areas of energy consumption in order to establish their carbon footprint.

To establish a carbon footprint most organisations should begin by reviewing site energy use for all activities, such as heating, lighting, power, process heat and on-site transport, including consumption of:

- electricity
- natural gas
- fuel oil
- coal.

For certain organisations the purchase of heat, steam and cooling might also be relevant. It will also be necessary to identify and quantify any greenhouse gas releases (including CO_2, CH_4 and refrigerants) from on-site processes or through fugitive releases arising from leaking pipes and equipment.

Energy consumption figures must then be multiplied by appropriate emission factors to give a CO_2 equivalent. Any direct releases of other greenhouse gases from fugitive or process emissions should also be expressed as CO_2 equivalents (so that potential global warming effects are factored in). Detailed information on emission factors and the consistent reporting of greenhouse gases as CO_2 equivalents is available from official sources (eg at the time of writing, Defra in the UK – see Appendix 3).

As shown in Figure 5.1.8, transport is essential for getting employees to and from home and work, goods and services to customers, and supplies to the site. There is also the issue of business travel to visit customers, suppliers and for various other business reasons, including meetings in other parts of the organisation, to attend a conference or trade fair, or for off-site training. Here, it should be noted that travel and transport by road and air tend to be particularly reliant on the burning of oil-based fuels (ie petrol, diesel or jet fuel).

It is good practice to measure, manage and report emissions from an organisation's owned transport as part of the scope. This might include lorries, vans, cars and, where relevant (and especially for transport-related businesses), motorbikes, trains, ships and aircraft.

For wider business travel and commuting, developing travel and commuting plans (see also section 5.1.6) are important in managing such travel. Note that managing travel can have other environmental benefits, as well as helping to manage CO_2 emissions (again, see section 5.1.6).

In establishing a carbon footprint, it is particularly important to define the scope of the system being considered and, when reporting, make it transparent which activities are included (and perhaps those that have

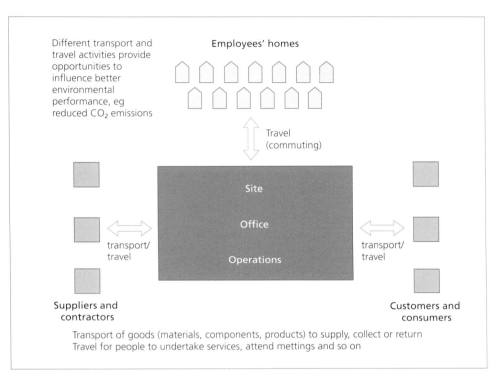

Figure 5.1.8
Transport as a key
activity beyond
site operations

been excluded). Stating the period covered is also crucial, as is ensuring that there is a common unit of reporting, ie in terms of CO_2 equivalent.

UK government guidance (see Appendix 3 – selected publications) on greenhouse gas measurement recommends that organisations include in their scope all direct operational emissions from fuel combustion, relevant processes, fugitive releases and related energy use. Also recommended are releases from all owned transport. Other releases such as those from commuting, business travel and distribution are currently discretionary. UK organisations should refer to such guidance and keep abreast of any changes and related developments as part of their management review processes. Furthermore, the International Organization for Standardization (ISO) is developing guidance on measuring, reporting and verifying greenhouse gas emissions (see Appendix 2).

When an organisation seeks to understand its wider greenhouse gas releases, the size of its reported footprint can be expected to increase, possibly dramatically (see Figure 5.1.9). This has implications, for example, for improvement targets. Therefore, it can be useful to define targets for specific areas where like-for-like or year-on-year comparisons can be made. This could be for office emissions (eg CO_2 per unit floor space), specific processes (eg CO_2 per unit output) or transport (eg CO_2

Figure 5.1.9
The relationship
between reported
carbon footprint
and the scope of
activities measured

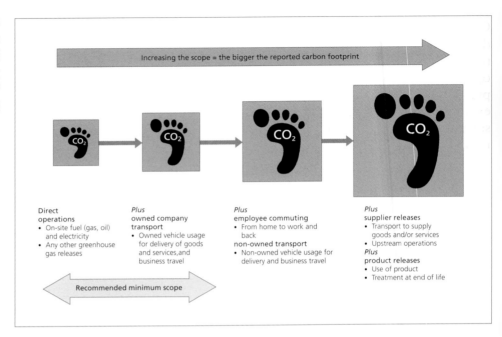

Figure 5.1.9 The relationship between reported carbon footprint and the scope of activities measured

per vehicle or per delivery drop). Establishing off-site emissions for an activity (eg for commuting) might lend itself to an investigation target at first (see also Chapter 3.3). Also, as the scope increases to cover non-owned activities and assets, organisations may be measuring emissions that are also counted by others. However, as the objective is to build a sense of which greenhouse gas emissions the organisation controls and which it might influence, such 'double counting' should not normally be a concern, especially as such data are not the basis of national emission inventories. However, if the organisation is covered by regulatory requirements on greenhouse gas emissions, then ensuring those covered by such requirements are clearly identified (and ring-fenced) will be important. Data management and communication (including clear statements about scope and calculation methods, especially any assumptions made and the time period covered) are important considerations in establishing and reporting a carbon footprint.

Because energy use (currently predominantly based on burning hydrocarbon fossil fuels) is fundamental to human society and the industrial system (see also Chapter 1.1), CO_2 emissions occur from primary extraction through to end-of-life treatment. Key factors associated with such emissions are shown in Figure 5.1.10. Energy efficiency and renewable energy (either used directly or via a high quality 'green tariff') can help to contain or reduce emissions, while approved offsets (and tradeable permits) might also have a role (see also Table 4.2.7 and Chapter 1.4).

Controlling transport emissions can often be challenging, but the development of green transport plans should be considered for business travel and vehicle fleets. This can include consideration of route planning, optimal payloads, vehicle type, fuel type, mileage allowance incentives, public transport alternatives and the avoidance of travel through, for example, teleconferencing. This can be fertile ground for employee suggestion schemes. Employee commuting is another consideration and is returned to in section 5.1.6.

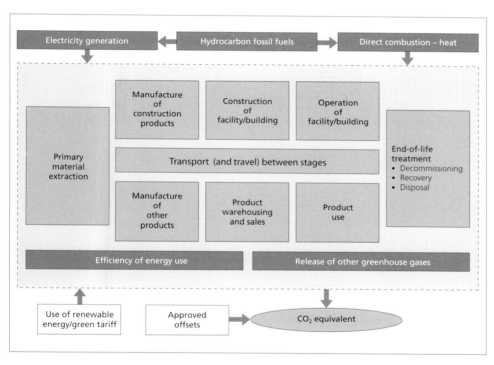

Figure 5.1.10
Key factors in determining carbon emissions

Greenhouse gas emission measurement and reporting requires attention to detail. It is recommended that organisations consult detailed guidance, including emission factors (eg for various types of fuel and electricity) and ensuring units are reported as CO_2 equivalent, which is available from official sources, such as Defra in the UK (see Appendix 3). ISO is another source of guidance (see Appendix 2).

Chapter 5.2 considers how managing greenhouse gas emissions should be part of a strategic approach. Scoping and then calculating the carbon footprint is a key starting point (see Figure 5.2.7).

5.1.6 Employee commuting

The involvement and participation of employees in all on-site environmental management processes is vital. However, initiatives to enable employees to address environmental issues beyond working hours can help build awareness and motivation.

When extending environmental initiatives beyond immediate operations, one area usually associated with the significant indirect aspects of the organisation is employee commuting. The principal concern is the use of cars and the associated environmental impacts, including congestion and nuisance, emission of pollutants that contribute to poor air quality, and the release of CO_2 contributing to climate change.

Employee participation in the design and development of a greener commuting scheme is therefore strongly recommended. Furthermore, because the local or regional transport infrastructure is provided by a variety of players and modes of transport, a wider community partnership may be required. This could include bus manufacturers, lease-hire firms, private bus companies, rail operators, local authorities and the police. To improve viability, it could also include representatives from other employers in the neighbourhood. It might also include innovative partnerships, such as bus manufacturers or vehicle-leasing companies working with fuel suppliers to consider alternative fuel buses using liquefied or compressed natural gas, or possibly hydrogen.

Elements to consider in a greener commuting scheme include those set out in Table 5.1.6.

Beyond commuting, organisations may find it appropriate to encourage employees to take simple and pragmatic actions to help reduce environmental impacts caused by activities at home and in their personal life, for example, through energy efficiency, reduced water consumption, waste recycling and personal travel choices.

Option	Typical issues
Cycling	Provision of: • shower and changing facilities at work • secure bicycle racks or sheds at work • dedicated, safe and protected cycle lanes • provision of high visibility vests and safety clothing • promoting additional health benefits
Walking	• Distance to work • Safety issues concerning the route • Availability of pool cars if need to go out on business and public transport is not suitable or available • Promoting additional health benefits
Car sharing	• Matching drivers with passengers, including consideration of home and work locations and working hours issues (possibly addressed through use of intranet or notice board) • Ensuring passengers can find an alternative if a driver is unavailable at the designated time • Provision of on-site pool cars (perhaps using alternative fuels or piloting new technology) for business travel if commuters leave their own car at home • Highlighting relative fuel efficiency of different cars (eg as demonstrated by energy labels) and advice on fuel efficiency (eg different vehicles, fuel choices, driving methods)
Bus transport	• Timetable match with working hours (and punctuality) • Bus routes to link home to work locations • Viability of dedicated express bus routes • Opportunities for alternative fuel pilots with bus operators • Information about routes, timetables, fares and so on, eg on notice boards or intranet
Rail transport	• Timetable match with working hours (and punctuality) • Availability of stations and connecting train routes between home and work locations • Integration with bus service (public or dedicated) • Provision of station car parking • Information about routes, timetables, fares, parking and so on, eg on notice boards or intranet
General	• Cost and tax issues (for example 'congestion charging', road tolls, parking charges) • Incentives to encourage non-car use

Table 5.1.6 Elements to consider in developing greener commuting

5.1.7 Considering natural and historic environments

In their environmental management programmes, many organisations may focus on aspects such as energy use, emissions, effluent and waste, but not consider explicitly the natural or historic environment.

Certainly, organisations such as extractive industries or property developers involved in land-take in one form or another are likely to have considered such aspects – especially if they have conducted environmental impact assessments (EIAs) required by planning legislation. This section seeks to introduce some considerations concerning the natural and historic environment to organisations that might typically overlook them.

An organisation's site may be next to a designated site of either natural or historic importance (in some cases these may be on site). Such a designation might be statutory or non-statutory. For example, in the UK a designated site might be a habitat designated as a Site of Special Scientific Interest (SSSI) or Special Area of Conservation (SAC) – both of which are statutory. An example of a non-statutory natural site is a Local Geological Site (England), which deals with important rock outcrops, landforms and soils. In the UK, sites of historic importance are designated as listed buildings or scheduled monuments. An organisation's site may contain these or alternatively it might be located in a conservation area which has a specific historical character or provides a special architectural environment.

An organisation should consider such designations as part of their environmental review and management review processes – building factors such as these into their assessment of significant aspects.

Furthermore, the local community and employees (including former employees) may be interested in conserving or enhancing natural and historic features. Again, as discussed in Chapter 2.2, building these stakeholder views into the assessment of significance may be highly appropriate. For example, in old industrial areas, existing factories, offices, retail outlets, catering establishments and so on may occupy historic industrial premises or contain historic industrial structures which are considered by both the local community and its employees to be part of the area's important cultural heritage. Preserving key features could therefore be important for retaining tangible evidence of that heritage.

Figure 5.1.11 summarises some key elements to consider. Specific action would depend on the nature of the designated site or community interest. It could include preservation of key features, managing access to prevent damage (eg breeding periods for wildlife or wear and tear on historic structures) and considering protection from incidents (eg spills or fire – see also Chapter 3.5). It might also involve enhancing the natural or historic environment. This might include the creation of a wildlife area, especially if this helps overcome local problems of habitat disruption (eg through fragmentation) or loss. Also, historic structures and geological outcrops could be incorporated into building and landscape design. For some organisations, it might simply be to create small-scale wildlife enhancements, such as bird boxes to encourage nesting or planting flowers that attract bees.

If a site has a community interest or an educational value, an organisation could consider allowing access to its natural or historic features, or help improve appropriate access to nearby sites. This might, for example, only be at certain times (such as on open days), taking into account the sensitivity of the site and organisational practicalities. This could be supported by interpretation – a term used for communication about what is important about the feature or site through media such as guided tours, leaflets, panels, exhibits or electronic formats.

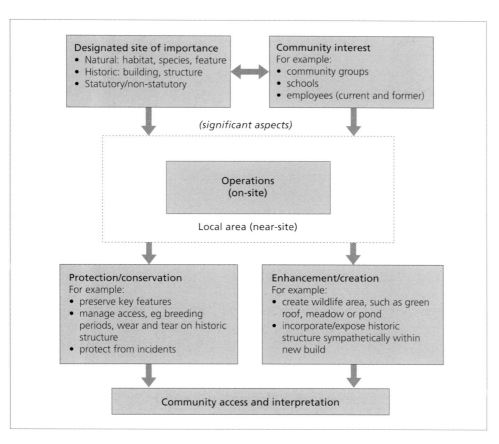

Figure 5.1.11
Consideration of natural and historic aspects

Supply chain considerations could be particularly important in terms of the natural environment. This might, for example, include the choice of food (eg Marine Stewardship Council-certified seafood for a restaurant or canteen) or material supplies to ensure purchasing from more sustainable source (eg preference for Forestry Stewardship Council-certified timber products). Life cycle thinking, supplier initiatives, strategic thinking (see Chapter 5.2) and corporate social responsibility (CSR) processes (see Chapter 5.3) can help highlight issues along the supply chain that could be highly relevant to biodiversity and heritage.

5.1.8 Local community initiatives

Residents, schools, hospitals and various businesses (including small and micro-businesses) are key elements of the local community. They may also be neighbours. In addition, while some may have no direct links to an organisation, others will have important connections – as employees, suppliers, contractors and local customers.

Selecting local environmental initiatives that are connected to the organisation in some way can be particularly appropriate, particularly schemes that are linked to a significant aspect, eg a community tree-planting scheme to overcome a visual intrusion impact.

A partnership approach – perhaps including regulators, local authority, conservation groups, neighbours, local schools, suppliers and customers – can enhance relations between all parties. For example, following on from section 5.1.7, an organisation might choose to develop an area on its site into a nature area with agreed access to the public, or sponsor habitat improvement in a local wood or park, along a local river or on nearby derelict land. It might decide to use income from an on-site recycling scheme to help fund off-site recycling initiatives, or develop a waste 'brokerage' where waste outputs from local organisations are used as inputs by others. A community initiative may include a 'buy local' scheme, which could also benefit in terms of carbon footprints. Such initiatives could become 'virtuous circles'.

Initiatives may include nature conservation or biodiversity projects, and the preservation or improvement of local cultural heritage or amenity. Encouraging employees to participate in biodiversity, or other nature, heritage or amenity projects, could be particularly worthwhile. This could, for example, be linked to environmental quizzes and team-building exercises as part of the internal awareness and motivation process.

Organisations may find that such initiatives can be part of their CSR work, where they help address material issues (see Chapter 5.3).

5.2 Environmental management and sustainable development

5.2.1 Background

The most commonly accepted definition of sustainable development was devised by the UN-sponsored World Commission on Environment and Development (WCED) chaired by Gro Harlem Brundtland (then Prime Minister of Norway). The definition was published in its 'Our common future' report in 1987 and is usually referred to as the 'Brundtland definition'. It is: "Development that meets the needs of the present without compromising the ability of future generations to meet their own needs."

An essential interpretation of this definition is that continued economic and social development is vital, but this development must avoid the degradation of natural resources, particularly as human activity and further development depend on the quality of these resources.

It is vital to note that sustainable development is a process, not a goal. This is a crucially important distinction because it means that sustainable development should, wherever possible, occur now, not just in the future. The ultimate goal is sustainability, and achieving this goal requires contributions from all sectors of society, as well as action across the globe.

There have been a number of UK Sustainable Development Strategies. In 2005, 'Securing the future' was published, which set out the following as guiding principles:
• living within environmental limits
• ensuring a strong, healthy and just society
• achieving a sustainable economy
• promoting good governance
• using sound science responsibly.

It also set out the following priorities for action:
• sustainable consumption and production (achieving more with less)
• climate change and energy (for example, requiring a profound change in how energy is generated and used)
• natural resource protection and environmental enhancement (for example, understanding environmental limits and addressing degraded environments)
• sustainable communities (ensuring that sustainable development principles apply at the local level).

Organisations should monitor developments in sustainable development policy relevant to all the countries where they operate.

In this chapter, the focus is on environmental sustainability, but it should be remembered that sustainable development requires the delivery of the so-called 'triple bottom line' of economic, environmental and social performance.

While 'sustainable development' is increasingly understood as a concept, and is generally accepted as intrinsically desirable and even essential, it is often unclear to organisations what it means for them in practice.

Environmental sustainability will need a reduction in the various pressures on the earth's natural systems. These pressures may mean that the earth's carrying capacity is exceeded so that it will no longer be able to support future human populations fully or provide the required quality of life. Such a scenario may already be occurring in parts of the world. This fundamental concern was introduced briefly in Chapter 1.3.

The sum of man-made environmental impacts affecting the earth's systems can be thought of as a function of:
- the total human population
- the average consumption level of each person
- the technologies servicing that consumption.

The world's population was estimated to be around 2.5 billion in 1950, and by 2000 it had exceeded 6 billion. By 2025, it is estimated that it will approach 9 billion. Per capita consumption, including demands on food and raw materials, is also expected to rise substantially, particularly as living standards and expectations rise in industrially developing countries. Table 5.2.1 shows how consumption accelerated during the second half of the 20th century. Population growth and the industrialisation of the developing world mean that such trends are likely to continue apace in the first half of the 21st century.

Selected global indicators	Table 5.2.1
• Global fossil fuel use increased by a factor of 4.5 from 1950 to 1999 (from 1,666 million tonnes of oil equivalent (mtoe) to 7,647 mtoe)	Global indicators for the second half of the 20th century
• World per capita paper and board consumption doubled between 1960 and 1998 (from 25 kg to 50 kg per person)	*Source: Worldwatch Institute (2000)*
• The global automobile fleet increased almost tenfold between 1950 and 1999 (from 53 million vehicles to 520 million)	
• In 1999, world per capita fertiliser use was four times as great as it was in 1950 (5.5 kg per person in 1950 to 22.3 kg per person in 1999)	
• In 1999, atmospheric concentrations of carbon dioxide reached 368.4 parts per million (ppm) from 316.7 ppm in 1965	

These and other factors put hugely increased demands on the earth's resources. In Chapters 1.1 and 1.3, it was noted that the earth is the source of land, raw materials and our fossil fuel-derived energy, and is also the sink for the disposal of gaseous, liquid and solid wastes. Pressure on some of these sinks is already a cause for concern. For example, most scientists believe that the atmosphere is assimilating CO_2 and other greenhouse gases to such an extent that we are beginning to witness the impacts of global climate change, and that countries and businesses should be planning to deal with the impacts of that change, not only in terms of controlling emissions but also adapting to the impacts. In other words, it is thought that this vitally important sink might already be too full.

An international panel of leading scientists set up by the UN to monitor and assess the implications of climate change (the Intergovernmental Panel on Climate Change – IPCC) considers that worldwide greenhouse gas emissions must be reduced substantially (by 60 to 80 per cent) below existing levels if adverse impacts are to be avoided by the end of this century. UN action is taking place under the United Nations Framework Convention on Climate Change (UNFCCC). Under the Convention, the Kyoto Protocol targeted a reduction in greenhouse emissions below 1990 levels of 5.2 per cent across developed countries by 2008–12 (for the UK, this is 12.5 per cent). Negotiations on developing this Protocol are ongoing through the United Nations Conference of the Parties (or COP) process (essentially the parties being the different countries covered by the UNFCCC). Despite uncertainties and disagreements at the international level, pressure for action is set to continue. In the UK, energy and climate change has become a top priority for government action. Table 5.2.3 sets out some of the key developments over the past two decades.

Meeting an accelerating level of global consumption while controlling environmental impacts will require a substantial improvement in the productivity of technology (in its widest sense) and resource use. Many authorities suggest that this improvement needs to be of a factor of 10 well before the end of the 21st century. This degree of performance improvement is often referred to as a paradigm shift (see Table 5.2.5). Some environmental specialists believe that proven technology could deliver a change in resource efficiency of a factor of four. However, implementing these, or even bigger, improvements in overall resource efficiency represents a huge challenge for society, including government and business.

5.2.2 Sustainability – a strategic issue for organisations

Sustainability is a strategic issue. Understanding the developing sustainability agenda and both contributing and responding to sustainability issues is central to the strategy of an increasing number of organisations.

Businesses have two basic goals – survival and success. The sustainability agenda can have a major bearing on both these goals. Some organisations have already experienced the direct effects of major sustainability-related issues such as the ban on the manufacture of ozone-depleting chemicals, or depleting fish stocks through over-fishing. Sustainability measures, such as energy taxes and producer responsibility obligations to recover waste materials, are also affecting an increasingly wide range of businesses and other organisations.

The importance of sustainability becomes obvious when the implications of unsustainable activity are considered. Essentially, an organisation that has unsustainable needs, or which is operating unsustainably, will need to modify its behaviour if it is to survive, let alone prosper. In an environmental context, this points to the need to use sustainable resources, and to have sustainable products and services.

Governments, businesses and other organisations are actively investigating how best to modify behaviour to achieve sustainable development. Organisations that understand sustainability issues and their implications can modify their practices not only to survive, but also to become better placed in the market. They may even change beyond all recognition. Organisations which focus solely on managing their risk of incidents (spills, leaks and non-compliance) and that have set their strategic aim as, for example, certification to ISO 14001, will be making some progress toward reducing environmental impacts. However, to engage in sustainability they will need to build processes into their environmental management that address resource productivity and incorporate true strategic thinking.

5.2.3 Strategic thinking

The trends and developments associated with sustainable development present both challenges and opportunities, and it is important that organisations understand, monitor and address the issues. Strategic thinking can be incorporated into environmental management, whether an organisation is certified to ISO 14001 or not. In particular, organisations should build strategic environmental thinking into the identification and evaluation of significant environmental aspects, the formulation of policy goals and corporate objectives, and into regular management reviews.

The management review (see Chapter 2.3), in particular, should be used to help develop strategic thinking to incorporate a move to greater sustainability. This key management process should consider not only the environmental performance of the organisation and the adequacy of existing arrangements, but external developments, including new laws and economic instruments, and opportunities for building innovative partnerships, adopting best practice and demonstrating or deploying technology, as well as emerging market opportunities.

Strategic environmental thinking has two fundamental dimensions:
- a view to the future – incorporating a thoroughly proactive approach so that emerging issues are understood and assessed in terms of opportunities and threats
- life cycle thinking – providing a broad view of the scope of environmental management so that the implications of emerging issues and developments are understood, not only in terms of immediate operations but, importantly, in terms of the supply chain and future markets.

Sustainable development is the framework that will define the future operating space of an organisation – determining what it can do and, for commercial organisations, what it can sell.

Role of business in sustainable development
Business has a pivotal role in moving society towards production and consumption practices that are more sustainable, especially as it is responsible for: • research, development, design, demonstration and production of new technology, products and services   • initiating change and innovation   • influencing customer choice and developing new markets   • creating wealth and employment, and therefore livelihood opportunities   • selecting and using natural resources – materials and energy   • generating waste (in all its forms) and devising more efficient processes and products to minimise the waste of resources and the burden on sinks, including that on the atmosphere as an increasingly problematic carbon sink.

Table 5.2.2
Business and sustainable development

5.2.4 Innovation as a key factor in sustainable development

A central feature of building sustainability should be innovation. Importantly, innovation can occur at many levels and it should not just be seen as research and development (R&D) or adopting novel technology, eg renewable energy. Innovation is about doing things better, thinking about which changes can improve matters and, crucially, putting them into practice. It can include applying existing technologies in new ways or it might involve applying a new technology or service for the first time.

Innovation may be part of gradual change (leading to progressively improved processes, products, partnerships or procedures) or be part of something more radical (leading to fundamentally different products, processes, working methods, organisations or business models). Increasingly, sustainability will require radical changes (notably to achieve improvements in resource efficiency of a factor of 10 or more). Even so, gradual improvements may also contribute to sustainable development, especially for those seeking actionable first steps. Furthermore, gradual improvements by many organisations or helping many individuals (especially consumers' use or disposal of products) can be part of significant improvement in reducing aggregated impacts across society and economies.

Some of the factors affecting innovation and the tools that might help to achieve it at the organisational level are set out in Figure 5.2.1. Importantly, innovation can be helped by effective management processes, including awareness of wider and external developments and practices, opportunities to share experience and ideas, and establishing a problem-solving culture. These processes are consistent with those for effective environmental management. Some of the strategic tools, eg SWOT (strengths, weaknesses, opportunities, threats) analysis and scenario-building, are considered further in this chapter, while cause–effect mapping (diagrams) is covered in Chapter 4.4 and life cycle thinking in Chapter 2.4. Knowledge exchange can include communication methods, such as partnership working, interdepartmental and interdisciplinary workshops and seminars, conferences and exhibitions (including professional development and cross-sector events), as well as general networking.

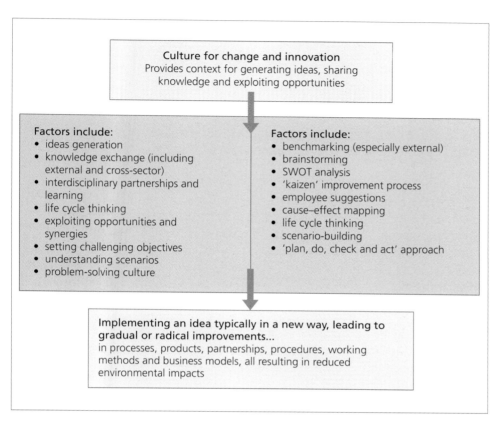

Figure 5.2.1
Factors affecting innovation

5.2.5 Understanding the developing sustainability agenda

To determine the strategic situation in relation to sustainability, an organisation needs to monitor and assess external environmental developments and trends.

Key questions revolve around the availability of, and access to, resources (see Figure 5.2.2) as sources of raw materials and energy, or as sinks for wastes.

Resources may become increasingly constrained through:
- depletion, eg non-renewable resources
- degradation, eg polluted resources
- over-exploitation, eg renewable resources
- regulation, eg bans and restrictions
- stakeholder concerns, eg customer avoidance of products associated with certain resources, public protests at the construction of new facilities in certain locations
- economics, eg increased costs due to diminishing access to resources or through the imposition of eco-taxes.

Alternatively, other resources may become more attractive, eg renewable energy, recycled materials.

It is notable that in recent years reliance on oil has become an increasing concern, not only in relation to climate change and other environmental impacts (including spills and other process accidents) but to the economics resulting from so-called 'peak oil'. Peak oil is the term used for the point in time when the rate of global extraction of petroleum reaches its maximum. Because of the huge dependency of society on oil for transport, agriculture and industry – both as a source of energy and a raw material (eg for the petrochemical industry, including fertilisers and plastics) – once 'peak oil' has been passed then prices can be expected to increase, possibly severely, since demand is not expected to fall. This means there could be disruptive shortages in energy and raw material supply unless economic alternatives are in place. Peak oil may be reached within the next decade.

Figure 5.2.2
Key strategic questions for business

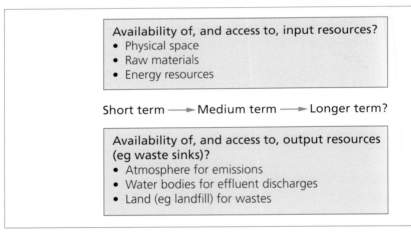

Ideally, all organisations should be aware of the current and emerging sustainability agenda so that they can make informed decisions about the future and plan for it. A major contributor to this agenda is governmental policy. Figure 5.2.3 provides a simple model of how issues evolve into policy instruments. Proactive organisations are alert to emerging issues and policy proposals. They are well placed for a constructive role in the policy debate and so can help shape their future operating space.

Governments have increasingly introduced policy measures based on the 'precautionary principle'. This was defined in Principle 15 of the 1992 UN Rio Declaration on the Environment and Development, which stated: "In order to protect the environment, the precautionary approach shall be widely applied by States according to their capabilities. Where there are threats of serious or irreversible damage, lack of full scientific certainty shall not be used as a reason for postponing cost-effective measures to prevent environmental degradation." This emphasises that absolute scientific certainty is not required for policy measures to be developed.

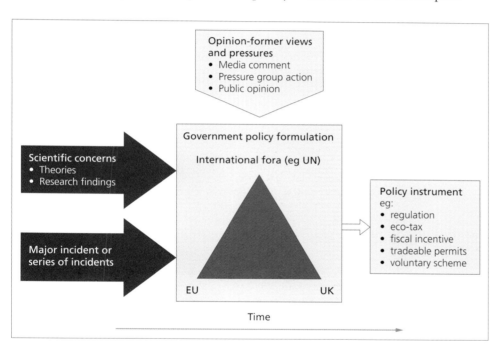

Figure 5.2.3
Evolution of issues into policy instruments affecting organisations

Organisations may perceive that scientific findings in relation to the environment are remote from operational reality. The rapid evolution of the climate change agenda illustrates that this is not so. Table 5.2.3 provides a timeline of some (by no means all) indicative developments affecting UK organisations in relation to energy and greenhouse gas emissions policy and initiatives. It might come as a surprise that, in the early 1990s, many UK businesses thought it very unlikely that there would be a carbon-related tax. Yet in 1999, legislation was in place to introduce the climate change levy. Table 5.2.3 also shows that organisations need to monitor developments in policy thinking and not just react to laws once they are passed or other policy instruments once launched. Again, this requires a strategic approach.

Year	Key events
1988	Intergovernmental Panel on Climate Change formed to assess the problem of global warming.
1990	First Intergovernmental Panel on Climate Change scientific report published, predicting that global average temperatures could rise by 2.5° C by 2100 based on a 'business as usual' model. Note: subsequent reports have refined scientific concerns and provided the impetus for policy development.
1992	UN Earth Summit held in Rio. One of the conventions signed was the UN Framework Convention on Climate Change (UNFCCC). Under the Framework, certain countries, including the UK, made a commitment to return emissions of carbon dioxide back to 1990 levels by 2000.
1994	UK published 'Climate change – the UK programme'. This included promotion of free best practice advice to industry through the (already existing) Energy Efficiency Best Practice Programme.
1997	Kyoto Protocol to the UN Framework Convention on Climate Change agreed. This committed developed countries (Annex 1 countries) to reduce a basket of six greenhouse gases, including carbon dioxide and methane, by 5.2 per cent on 1990 levels by 2008–12. It introduced a requirement for national inventories of ghg emissions for Annex 1 countries, set out the concept of emissions trading and fostered the 'clean development mechanism', whereby Annex 1 countries can resource carbon reduction projects in less developed countries (subject to these meeting certain rules and the savings being validated and verified), which then can be used as carbon credits.
1998	EU members signed the Kyoto Protocol. Agreement reached within the EU on how target of 8 per cent reduction should be shared between member states. UK agreed to a 12.5 per cent reduction.
1998	Marshall Report on 'Economic instruments and the business use of energy' issued. This explored the use of energy taxes and tradeable permits to reduce carbon dioxide emissions in the UK.
1999	UK government announced introduction of the climate change levy (CCL) on energy use for businesses.
2000	UK published revised 'Climate change – the UK programme'. This set out measures to reduce greenhouse gas emissions. It also confirmed the commitment to the Kyoto target and stated the domestic goal of reducing carbon dioxide by 20 per cent on 1990 levels by 2010. It set the scene for reductions beyond 2010.

Year	Key events
2000	UK published guidelines for (voluntary) company reporting greenhouse gas emissions after piloting the methodology.
2001	CCL introduced – it applies to energy used by businesses throughout the UK. Good quality combined heat and power (CHP) and renewable energy is exempt. Many large energy users secure reductions in the levy in exchange for audited reductions in energy use based on sector-level agreements.
2001	Carbon Trust established (part funded by the CCL) to help organisations reduce carbon emissions. The Trust offers advice and incentives on energy efficiency, carbon management and investment in low carbon technologies.
2002	Launch of the first UK greenhouse gas emission tradeable permit scheme for large energy users (see Chapter 1.4).
2003	UK government's Energy White Paper set an aspiration for the UK to reduce carbon emissions by 60 per cent by 2050 (with plans for significant progress by 2020).
2005	UK published 'Transition to a low carbon society' – its national strategy for climate and energy. It set the target to cut greenhouse gas emissions by 18 per cent on 2008 levels by 2020, in the context of an objective of an 80 per cent reduction on 1990 levels by 2050. The plan also set other targets, eg to produce around 30 per cent of electricity from renewable sources by 2020.
2007	UK introduced the Climate Change Bill with the aim of introducing a long-term legally binding framework to tackle climate change, including legally binding reduction targets.
2008	UK passed the Climate Change Act, requiring a reduction in greenhouse gas by at least 80 per cent on 1990 levels by 2050 and a 34 per cent reduction against the 1990 baseline by 2020. Among its many provisions were powers to set up a carbon trading scheme and the requirement for new guidance for companies on greenhouse gas reporting.
2008	Carbon Trust introduced the Carbon Trust Standard, which allows organisations to demonstrate that they are measuring, managing and reducing their carbon footprint through independent verification and the use of the Standard's logo.
2009	UK issued detailed guidance for organisations to measure and report greenhouse gas emissions, as well as set targets to reduce them. A separate guide for small businesses was also issued.

Table 5.2.3
Evolution of the climate change/ carbon agenda since 1988
continued

Table 5.2.3
Evolution of the
climate change/
carbon agenda
since 1988
continued

Year	Key events
2010	Feed-In Tariff (Clean Energy Cashback) Scheme was introduced in the UK, under which energy suppliers make guaranteed regular payments to householders and communities who generate their own electricity from renewable and low carbon sources. One aim is to help increase demand for micro-generation (and therefore help establish the market for such suppliers).
2010	UK's Carbon Reduction Commitment (CRC) Energy Efficiency Scheme officially began for organisations consuming 6,000 MWh of half-hourly metered electricity in the baseline year of 2008. This introduced the UK's first mandatory carbon allowance scheme.

Organisations can monitor external developments through a wide range of methods. These include conferences and workshops, trade associations, industry bodies, stakeholder dialogue sessions, stakeholder surveys, trade press, environmental journals, government and agency publications (including official websites) and professional institution networking.

5.2.6 Strategic analysis

A useful technique to assess the implications of external developments is to conduct a SWOT analysis. The opportunities and threats element stems largely from external developments, while strengths and weaknesses concern internal capabilities. This is illustrated in Figure 5.2.4.

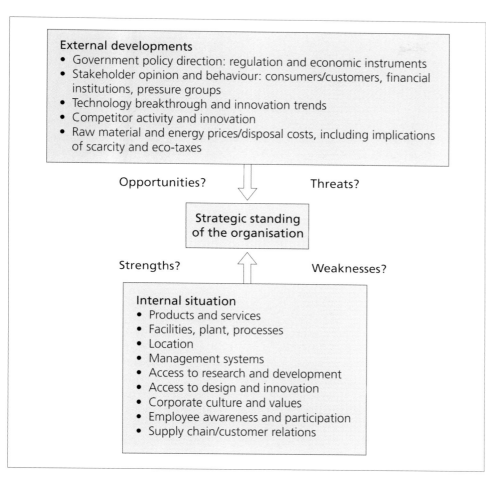

Figure 5.2.4
Elements in
strategic
assessment

The analysis is used to generate options that build on strengths, exploit opportunities, overcome weaknesses and avoid threats. It can also be used to identify key survival issues, ie those that must be successfully addressed if the business is to survive and prosper.

Table 5.2.4 provides a simple example of a SWOT analysis (for a single issue – energy). It is for a hypothetical UK company that had been alerted to the possibility of an energy tax by the Marshall Report in 1998. The company not only uses energy in its operations, but its product uses electricity and is sold to industrial customers.

Table 5.2.4
An example SWOT
analysis for a
company with
respect to energy
use (if conducted
in 1998)

Strengths	Weaknesses
• Environmental management initiatives have been successful in areas of waste, effluent and avoidance of incidents • Workforce is aware and motivated to improve efficiency of operations • Senior management is committed to continual improvement in performance • Budgets exist for major refurbishment of offices and investment in new boiler • Design team has been investigating improved energy efficiency in use of the product; incremental improvements will be introduced in next model	• Energy use (grid electricity and gas) represents significant controllable cost • No comprehensive energy management programme in place within operations; focus of environmental management to date has been on waste, effluent and spills • Use of old, inefficient boiler to provide heat in key and costly production area • Products are for business customers and electricity use is a key factor in their operation
Opportunities	Threats
• Information from official sources (eg UK's Energy Efficiency Best Practice Programme in 1998) suggests a combination of low cost and capital cost measures (eg CHP) may be feasible for some organisations • Energy services company literature suggests CHP may be technically feasible instead of separate new gas boiler and grid electricity. Possibility that CHP may be exempt from future energy tax provides additional factor • Major business customer has identified its life cycle carbon dioxide emissions as a major issue it plans to manage • Competitors understood not yet to be concerned over energy use in equivalent product	• High probability that energy tax will be applied to business use of energy and will significantly increase energy costs for own operations and customers' use of products • Scientific findings, international agreements and government policy commitments suggest that further measures will be implemented to reduce greenhouse gas emissions; there is every likelihood that any tax would be progressively increased over the longer term

The outcome from the SWOT analysis suggests the options to be explored. In the above example, a full energy survey, a technical and economic evaluation of on-site CHP and an employee awareness programme might be the outcome. Developing programmes to improve the energy efficiency of the product further is also an option, together with responsible marketing to industrial customers and promoting the energy efficiency benefits of the new model. If the SWOT analysis had been updated in 2008, it would have a different set of strengths and weaknesses and, especially, opportunities and threats. The rapidly developing climate change agenda, with the increasing range of government policy instruments and advances in technologies, suggests that such an analysis should be undertaken regularly. It would also be good practice for such an analysis to form part of an organisation's management review process.

5.2.7 Scenario-building

Some organisations have found it useful to build scenarios – plausible but varying pictures of what the future could look like. Traditionally used by larger businesses, they can be just as useful for smaller organisations. They are attempts to make sense of the increasing complexity and dynamic changes facing organisations, and the implications of the sustainability agenda are therefore particularly relevant to scenario development. The technique helps organisations consider alternative futures and can be applied at various levels, from local to global, or over different timescales (short, medium or longer term), as required.

Scenarios can be developed from brainstorming sessions. The inclusion of key stakeholders can be advantageous to generate different views. A simple technique involves identifying the external factors affecting the organisation, such as: technology and competitor innovation, policy and legislation, resource availability and costs, customer preferences, financial institution practices or social and economic issues. For each of the factors, possible outcomes are considered for a given timescale and incorporating different rates of change (see Table 5.2.5 for three key types of change). These are then developed into a number of alternative (plausible but different) scenarios.

Type of change	Incremental change	Step change	Paradigm shift
Nature	Small gradual changes	Sudden change from one level to another	Major change from one system or model to another
Example	Small but regular (eg annual) rises in eco-tax (eg landfill or energy) increase the price of using the environment incrementally	Introduction of new regulatory regime, eg producer responsibility, requiring stringent recovery targets for end-of-life products	Major breakthrough in new technology, eg rapid uptake of photovoltaics leading to widespread deployment of solar power and a shift to hydrogen as a fuel, displacing hydrocarbons

Figure 5.2.6
Building and using
scenarios

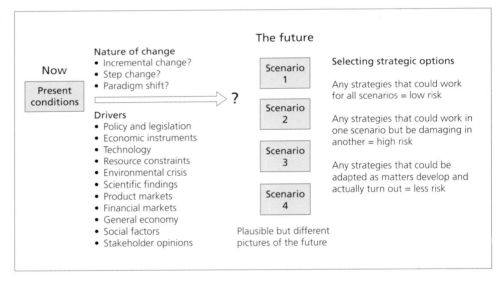

As illustrated in Figure 5.2.6, four scenarios are recommended, although even two can be informative. It should be noted that those organisations that develop three may find that there is often a tendency to treat the middle scenario as the most likely. It is good practice to keep an open mind about all future possibilities, while also acknowledging that reality is likely to be somewhat different from any of the individual scenarios developed. Scenario-planning allows a mix of common and different themes and key survival issues to be identified. This should help an organisation make informed decisions about future business planning and investment.

Strategic options that would work under different scenarios are likely to represent low risk options. Those that might work for one scenario but damage the business under another are likely to be higher risk. Strategies that can be adapted to fit the situation as it actually develops would represent a lower business risk.

General scenarios are also developed by industry, government or independent 'think tanks' and may provide a ready resource for organisations that have limited capability to develop their own.

5.2.8 Actionable first steps

Environmental management and sustainable development are both 'change processes'. In common with all change processes, success requires the following four elements to be in place:
- an understanding of the pressure for change
- a clear shared vision
- resources to implement the change
- a forward plan with actionable first steps.

The actionable first steps will depend on where the organisation currently stands in terms of environmental management and the implementation of more sustainable practices. To be actionable, the first (and subsequent) steps need to be suitable, acceptable and feasible. To be of value, they should also have measurable outcomes and be linked to key performance indicators and, preferably, key survival issues.

Possible actions that would be consistent with building sustainability include those in Table 5.2.6.

Resource/supply-related options	Operational options	Market-related options
• Substitution of materials or energy from non-renewable resources with sustainable renewable resources, eg from accredited sources • Substitution of materials and products with lower embodied energy/carbon • Substitution of virgin materials with reused or recycled materials • Procurement of products awarded recognised eco-labels • Selection of materials with less eco-toxicity • Consideration of distance from source and associated transport impacts, eg local sourcing • Goods supplied with the minimal amount of packaging needed, preferably with the packaging being reusable or recyclable • Assistance with supplier performance • Selection of brownfield rather than greenfield sites for premises • Avoidance of building on (or affecting) sites such as floodplains (eg helping to reduce the likelihood of flooding and of disrupting important habitats)	• Enhanced process efficiency • Enhanced resource productivity (reduced use of water, materials and energy per unit output of product or service) • Waste minimisation through reuse and recovery (on site or off site) • Selection of best practicable environmental options to minimise pollution transfer • Shift from end-of-pipe solutions to intrinsically cleaner technology • Improved use of transport, alternative communication methods, green commuting schemes, alternative fuel vehicles • On-site electricity generation using low or no carbon technology • Rainwater collection and grey water recycling	• New or improved products or services • Products designed for reuse or recyclability, eg through reduced material mix, design for disassembly, parts common to different equipment, material identification • Products designed for durability or repair, eg minimal wear, ease of disassembly, standard parts, service arrangements • Product take-back and recovery schemes • Efficiency of delivery of service • Products more efficient in use – energy and materials • Products based on low energy use, or on low or no carbon emissions during use • Products with lower embodied energy or carbon

Cross-cutting practices	• Life cycle thinking to 'design out' main areas of impact • Research, development and demonstration of new technology, eg pilot projects • Investment appraisal systems that actively incorporate 'intangible benefits' and future developments • Training and participation of employees to encourage innovative thinking • Partnerships with suppliers, contractors, customers and other interested parties	
Success factors	Suitability	Options should exploit strengths and opportunities, and avoid or remedy weaknesses or threats
	Acceptability	Impact on performance – financial (profitability, financial risk) and environmental. Internal and external stakeholder views
	Feasibility	Availability of technology, materials and skills at acceptable levels of price and cost; readiness of marketplace; availability of funds

Table 5.2.6
Possible actions to help build sustainability
continued

5.2.9 Addressing carbon

Perhaps one of the most important issues affecting all organisations is that of greenhouse gas emissions and climate change, especially given the world's current dependency on fossil fuels and consequent emissions of CO_2. It is now widely regarded as the most pressing global environmental problem.

This issue has been dealt with in a number of chapters in this book, including 1.3, 1.4, 2.4, 4.2 and 5.1. With the rapidly developing agenda on climate change (see Table 5.2.3), it will become increasingly important for all organisations to have a greenhouse gas management strategy (addressing CO_2 equivalent) as part of their environmental management policy.

Figure 5.2.7
Key elements of a
greenhouse gas
management
strategy

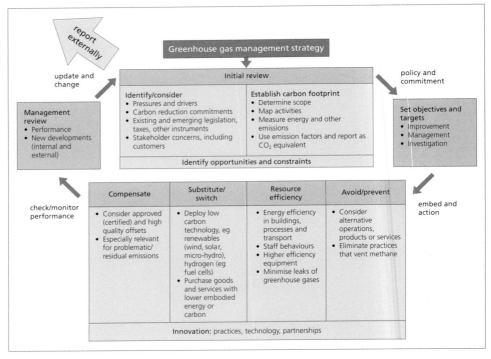

Figure 5.2.7
Key elements of a
greenhouse gas
management
strategy

Figure 5.2.7 sets out some of the key elements of a greenhouse gas management strategy. Essentially, the approach follows that of the 'plan, do, check and act' cycle, which is the basis of an EMS. However, important in this approach is an understanding of the organisation's carbon footprint (see Chapter 5.1) as a basis for action. External reporting on the strategy and performance (including constraints encountered in its implementation) can also be an important element.

Actions may differ between different types and sizes of organisation, or between different parts of the same organisation. In some areas it might be possible to prevent emissions through changing a process, eg to avoid venting methane. In other areas the focus might be to reduce emissions through a range of energy reduction or efficiency measures – both behavioural (ie how people use and waste energy) and technological (eg controls that ensure only the right amount of energy is used for a job, or high efficiency equipment). In others, it might be appropriate to install 'low to no carbon' renewable technologies, eg solar electricity or solar heating. Furthermore, some actions may need to be investigatory – for example, to properly understand a source of emissions, to explore the feasibility of different technologies, or to identify sources of products with lower embodied carbon.

Generally, organisations should seek to avoid and reduce emissions through considering alternative behaviour, processes or products; through resource efficiency; and through substitution with lower carbon technology. Only then should they consider compensation. Compensation is best employed for problematic emissions, such as emissions from transport after all practical avoidance, efficiency and substitution options have been implemented. Furthermore, it is important that compensation is from high quality offset schemes that have been officially approved and certified. Under the Kyoto Protocol there are strict rules as to what can constitute a carbon credit and any organisation seeking to report an offset as a credit in terms of their greenhouse gas emissions accounting needs to take particular care with respect to this. It is best practice to reduce emissions at source whenever possible.

5.2.10 Towards sustainability

Organisations can be at different stages in environmental management. Those at an early stage may be particularly daunted by the process of sustainable development. Table 5.2.7 and Figure 5.2.8 set out a 'hierarchy (or spectrum) of engagement' that can be used to determine the stage at which an organisation is engaged with environmental sustainability. There are increasingly fewer organisations in the 'unaware' and 'inactive' stages, not least because of the breadth of government policy measures on environmental issues.

The hierarchy provides an indicative benchmark against which an organisation can determine where it stands. The table does not state what a totally sustainable enterprise might look like – such an organisation would be expected to have neutral or even positive environmental impacts overall, and be achieving high levels of economic and social performance. This ideal situation may seldom be possible, but it is a valid goal. All individual organisations, however, can make a valuable contribution to the process of sustainable development and, in doing so, improve their competitive position.

Table 5.2.7
The different levels
of environmental
engagement
leading to building
sustainability

Stages in environmental management	
Building sustainability	• Actively seeking to integrate and 'synergise' economic, environmental and social objectives. Environmental factors fully incorporated into corporate strategy, including the development of key survival issues. Environmental considerations integrated into business development as well as operational decision-making processes. • Forward-looking policy and corporate objectives supported by key sustainability performance indicators. Life cycle thinking is the norm. Whole organisation is urged to seek viable business opportunities/competitive edge from the developing agenda, which is constantly monitored and regularly reviewed. Technical and commercial innovation pursued. • Process efficiency embedded into culture and practice, not only in operations, but also in all other areas, especially product design, marketing and sales, procurement and finance. • Emphasis is on the search for enhanced resource productivity. Active participation of fully trained employees at all levels. Partnerships with suppliers, customers and others to find profitable solutions, research, pilot or deploy new intrinsically cleaner technology, develop new products and services, and create new markets. • Fully engaged with stakeholders. Comprehensive, verified reporting on plans and performance.
Systematic – engaged	• Coherent policy and management system in place, including widespread use of SMART objectives and targets. Evaluation of the significance of environmental aspects includes criteria based on stakeholder concerns. Employees at all levels encouraged to participate in the improvement process. Engaging with key external stakeholders, including suppliers and customers, to improve environmental performance on a continual basis. Public reporting on environmental performance and plans. Regular monitoring and assessment of developments in legislation and best practice across a range of activities, products and services. • Sharing best practice throughout the organisation and along the supply chain. Focus on best practicable environmental option to minimise pollution transfer. Full understanding of the implications of economic instruments.
Systematic – confined	• Coherent, publicly available environmental policy, objectives and targets, plans and assigned responsibilities addressing issues of direct operational significance. Effectiveness audited and reviewed. Employees trained and aware. Developments in legislation and good/best practice reviewed on annual basis. Regularly seeking site-based opportunities for continual improvement and cost savings, but there may be a prevalence of end-of-pipe technical solutions in many situations.

Stages in environmental management	
Ad hoc	• Internal policy statement exists but remains largely a stand-alone document. Issues are addressed on an *ad hoc* basis and are predominantly reactive/compliance-based. Some improvement initiatives exist but tend to be independent and isolated. Employees are aware of the need to reduce the risk of incidents in specific situations (eg chemical handling), but overall environmental management knowledge is limited.
Inactive	• Awareness of pressures to adopt environmental management exists, but no action to date. Either general belief that there are more important priorities and that environmental management may be a temporary phenomenon, or uncertainty about how to become involved in a cost-effective way. Widespread belief that environmental management is a paperwork exercise, and that it costs money.
Unaware	• Lack of awareness of the environmental agenda and its relevance to business.

Table 5.2.7
The different levels of environmental engagement leading to building sustainability *continued*

Effective environmental management requires a systematic approach – this is a key theme throughout this book. A key tool to achieve this is a thorough initial environmental review (see Chapter 2.3), which considers all key activities, products and services and their environmental aspects. For organisations to move towards sustainability, the focus of this chapter, they need to be proactive and external facing, and, importantly, build environmental issues into their strategic processes so that environmental management is increasingly comprehensive, embedded and innovative. This includes greater life cycle thinking both up and down the supply chain (see Chapter 5.1) and the desire and capacity to build stakeholder partnerships (ideally in line with their CSR processes – see Chapter 5.3).

British Standard BS 8900 was introduced to help organisations develop an approach to sustainable development. It recognises that organisations need to evolve and adapt to meet new and continuing challenges and demands. BS 8900 provides a framework for a structured approach to sustainability and is designed to help organisations connect the various environmental, social and technical standards (eg the ISO 14000 environmental series and AA 1000 concerning social accountability – see Chapter 5.3) in addressing environmental, social and economic issues.

Figure 5.2.8
Hierarchy/
spectrum of
environmental
engagement

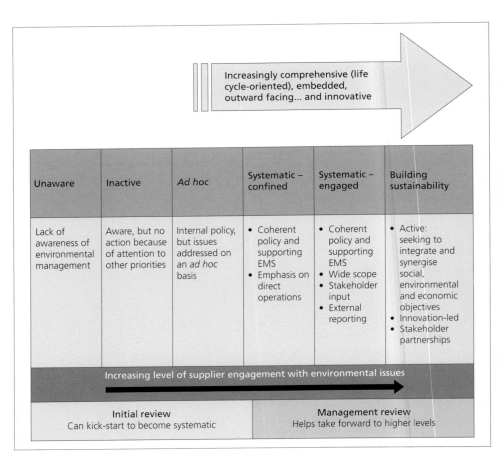

Unaware	Inactive	*Ad hoc*	Systematic – confined	Systematic – engaged	Building sustainability
Lack of awareness of environmental management	Aware, but no action because of attention to other priorities	Internal policy, but issues addressed on an *ad hoc* basis	• Coherent policy and supporting EMS • Emphasis on direct operations	• Coherent policy and supporting EMS • Wide scope • Stakeholder input • External reporting	• Active: seeking to integrate and synergise social, environmental and economic objectives • Innovation-led • Stakeholder partnerships

Increasingly comprehensive (life cycle-oriented), embedded, outward facing... and innovative

Increasing level of supplier engagement with environmental issues

Initial review	Management review
Can kick-start to become systematic	Helps take forward to higher levels

5.3 Corporate social responsibility and environmental management

Corporate social responsibility (CSR) is a term that has been used over the past decade or so, although the term corporate responsibility may be steadily replacing it. This chapter provides an introduction to CSR and explains its links to environmental management. While often thought to apply mainly to big multinational companies, CSR is relevant to all organisations in that no organisation can operate in isolation of its social context, including customers, suppliers, employees and local community. However, the scope of CSR will be influenced by factors such as the organisation's operations, products and services; its geographical spread in terms of suppliers, operations and markets; and, crucially, its key stakeholders. Stakeholders are the people, communities or organisations that have an interest in an organisation or are affected by its plans, activities and impacts.

5.3.1 Stakeholder issues
CSR should be driven by stakeholder issues. Its key management processes require meaningful stakeholder engagement. CSR requires an organisation to commit to understanding the expectations and needs of key stakeholders to operate in a socially and environmentally responsible manner. Strategically, this is about ensuring that the organisation has 'space' to operate (see also Chapter 1.4).

Many of the issues raised by CSR are social and therefore beyond the immediate scope of this book. However, typical generic CSR issues include:
- full and active compliance with legal obligations and regulatory requirements
- responsible marketing (promotion, pricing and distribution) of products and services to customers and consumers
- responsible sourcing of products and services from suppliers with acceptable working practices, including human rights and fair contractual arrangements
- responsible investment practices in activities, products and services and across different geographic areas, including addressing corruption
- fair remuneration and decent working conditions, including protection of health and safety
- equal opportunities for existing and prospective employees
- good relationships with local communities.

However, environmental concerns may play a major, and in some cases predominant, role in the CSR agenda. Examples of environmental issues that might be particularly relevant to CSR are set out in Table 5.3.1.

Table 5.3.1
Examples of
environmental
issues relevant to
CSR

Issue	Typical stakeholders
Compliance with environmental laws and regulatory requirements	• Government • Regulators • Green groups
Conformance with an industry environmental code of practice	• Trade or sector body • Chamber of commerce
Green marketing claims	• Business customers and/or domestic consumers (depending on product or service) • Green groups
Effective management of nuisance	• Local communities/neighbours • Local government
Land take or water extraction	• Regulators • Local communities/neighbours • Green groups • Social NGOs
Effective and transparent response to pollution incidents	• Government • Regulators • Local communities/neighbours • Green groups • Social NGOs
Support for dissemination of environmental management best practice, particularly to SMEs or organisations in developing economies	• Suppliers • Business customers
Depletion of sensitive resource, eg sensitive ecosystem or rare habitat	• Government • Local communities/neighbours • Green groups • Social NGOs • Customers and consumers
Management of energy and other aspects relevant to climate change, ie carbon footprint	The high profile of this issue attracts a wide range of stakeholders, including: • General public as part of civil society • Government • Regulators • Local communities/neighbours • Green groups • Social NGOs • Customers and consumers
Responsible procurement of materials	• Regulators • Green groups • Customers and consumers

5.3.2 Key management processes in CSR

The key management processes in CSR are:

- governance arrangements from top management down, to ensure a CSR strategy is developed and implemented
- stakeholder engagement
- identifying the significant or 'material' issues
- policies, goal setting and actions to implement and embed the strategy
- monitoring and checking performance
- open disclosure of performance to stakeholders, including the wider public
- independent assurance of processes, performance and claims
- review of CSR management processes and performance to ensure that they are suitable, adequate and effective.

These processes are set out in Figure 5.3.1.

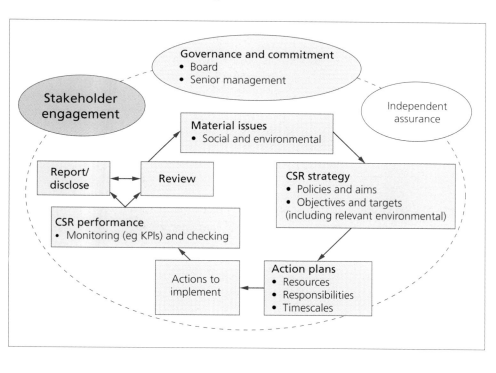

Figure 5.3.1
Key CSR management processes

Disclosure of material issues (see section 5.3.3), the goals and arrangements that address them, and how the organisation has performed are key elements of CSR. An established way of doing this is through a CSR report (eg produced annually) that is posted on the internet and/or emailed to key stakeholders. Typically, the report is also available in printed format. Guidance on reporting is available through the Global Reporting Initiative (GRI) and through the AA 1000 series of standards (on organisations becoming accountable, responsible and sustainable) produced by AccountAbility (see Appendix 3).

While transparency is vital for building and maintaining stakeholder confidence, another key factor is independent assurance. This should be not only of the CSR report but also the CSR processes behind the performance data, including the degree to which stakeholder concerns are addressed. Best practice is to include key stakeholders in the assurance arrangements, as well as independent assurance specialists. Guidance on assurance is available in AA 1000AS (Assurance).

Another useful standard for CSR is SA8000 (developed by Social Accountability International – see Appendix 3), which provides a framework for companies and their supply chain to incorporate human rights issues and ethical practices throughout their activities.

5.3.3 Establishing material issues

This should start with an initial review to identify as many as possible of the existing and potential social and environmental issues (ie a long starting list) relevant to the organisation, together with the stakeholders that they are of particular concern to. This should be followed by an assessment of which issues are of material importance to the organisation.

Establishing what these issue are is essentially a prioritisation/filtering process. It is therefore similar to establishing which environmental aspects are significant in environmental management. However, it requires the issues to be assessed from a stakeholder and strategic perspective. One way is to allocate issues to a grid based on the impact on the organisation's 'operating space' and the degree of key stakeholders' concern (see Figure 5.3.2). A set of criteria can be developed to help with the assessment – for example, to show different degrees of impact on operating space.

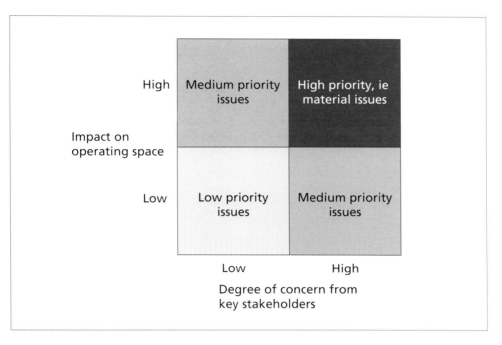

Figure 5.3.2
Establishing
material issues

Significant environmental aspects identified as part of environmental management should help to identify the environmental topics among the long list of CSR issues. Conversely, designating any CSR issue with an environmental component as 'material' should mean that the associated environmental aspects are 'significant' in any EMS (Figure 5.3.3). For example, if green marketing claims arise as a CSR material issue, the EMS should also address this and its relevant aspects (eg energy use, using more sustainable materials, recyclability and so on for the product(s) in question), through its environmental policy and procedures. In short, the CSR strategy and environmental management processes should be aligned.

Figure 5.3.3
The relationship
between material
CSR issues and
significant
environmental
aspects

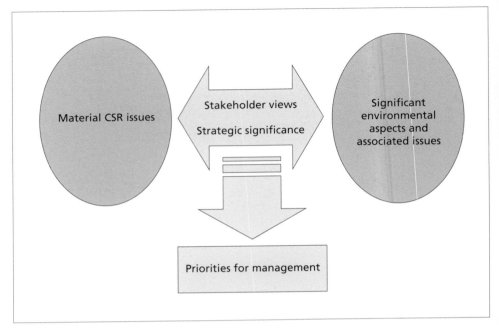

5.3.4 Stakeholder engagement

It has been emphasised that stakeholder engagement is a vital part of CSR. However, a potentially large number and diverse range of stakeholders interact with an organisation. This means it is usually necessary to prioritise stakeholders. As suggested in Chapter 3.7 on targeting audiences for external (environmental) reporting, one method is to allocate stakeholders to a grid based on influence on the organisation's operating space and the degree of interest in the organisation's activities, products or services and/or associated issues.

This should help identify 'high priority' stakeholders who need to be fully engaged with; the 'important' stakeholders who need to have expectations and needs satisfied and whose views should be regularly monitored; and the 'interested' stakeholders who should be mainly kept informed, eg through receiving the CSR report and other pertinent information.

Full engagement requires two-way dialogue ('communication', not just 'dissemination'). The organisation should draw on a range of

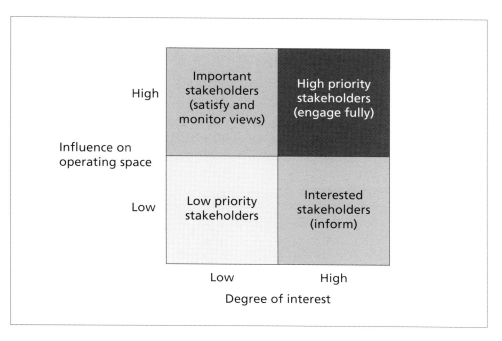

Figure 5.3.4
Categories of
stakeholder

communication and engagement methods depending on the nature of the stakeholder, experience with existing methods and practical issues (eg the ability to access key stakeholders), as well as opportunities to link to sector initiatives. Importantly, engagement needs to be planned effectively. Engagement sessions, such as workshops, may benefit from professional independent facilitation, especially if conflicts of interest are anticipated.

As set out in Figure 5.3.5, there is a need to regularly review the engagement process, including the range of stakeholders, their priority categorisation and the effectiveness of engagement mechanisms and communication methods – making changes as appropriate. Key (high priority) stakeholders might be included in the assurance process to establish views on material issues and to input on the methods (eg criteria) for assessing them.

Guidance on stakeholder engagement is provided in the AccountAbility standard AA 1000SES (Stakeholder Engagement).

Figure 5.3.5
Stakeholder
engagement
overview

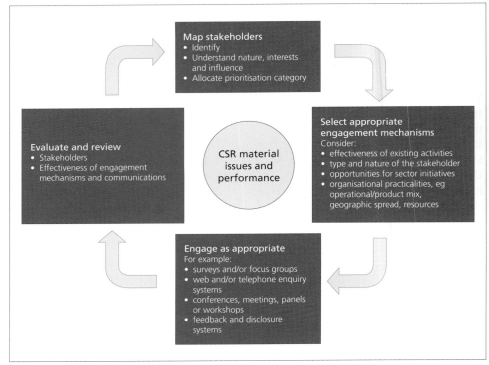

5.3.5 EMS–CSR links

Some of the links between EMS and CSR processes are set out in Table 5.3.2. It is important that both approaches are aligned in the organisation – the same is true of other processes, including health and safety and quality.

An EMS, including one based on (or certified to) ISO 14001, should be a subset of arrangements to help deliver a CSR strategy. The overall CSR approach set out in Figure 5.3.1 also conforms to the 'plan, do, check and act' cycle that underpins effective environmental management (see Chapter 3.1).

CSR processes	Supporting environmental management system processes	Comments	See also Chapter...
Governance arrangements from the board down to ensure that a CSR strategy is developed and implemented	Environmental policy stemming from top-level management. Reports back to board. Allocating relevant responsibilities from the board down – in all sections and at all levels. The management review should help ensure that the environmental issues are relevant and that system components remain suitable, adequate and effective.	There should be a mission statement that covers CSR (including environmental) issues. Such commitment and arrangements are essential for all policies, including environmental.	3.6 2.3
Stakeholder engagement	Building stakeholder concerns into the assessment of significant environmental aspects and responding appropriately through meaningful communication on relevant environmental issues.	By engaging key stakeholders the environmental policy commitments and priorities for management are likely to be better defined.	2.2 3.7
Identifying the significant or 'material' issues	Interface between material issues and significant environmental aspects. Building stakeholder concerns into the assessment.	This should help better define priorities for the organisation.	2.2
Policies, goal setting and actions to implement and embed the strategy	The environmental policy and its aims should align with the CSR strategy, including material issues and the CSR goals. The alignment process may be iterative and require regular reviews and fine-tuning. The EMS should help deliver appropriate action on material environmental issues.	This should also help improve the efficiency of delivering and reporting performance across the organisation. Agreement with key stakeholders in goal setting may be important in CSR, ie the 'A' in SMART (see Chapter 3.3).	3.2 3.3 3.4

Table 5.3.2
Interface between CSR and EMS processes

Table 5.3.2
Interface between
CSR and EMS
processes
continued

CSR processes	Supporting environmental management system processes	Comments	See also Chapter...
Monitoring and checking performance	Environmental issues which are identified as material should have EPIs that become strategic KPIs for the organisation. Data collection, reporting and auditing of the EMS should support this.	The EMS should help to deliver appropriate action on material environmental issues.	2.3 3.3 3.4 5.2
Open disclosure of performance to stakeholders and to the public	An effective EMS will have robust data collection on significant environmental aspects which can feed into the CSR report. The organisation may already have useful experience with a CER (corporate environmental report).	Many of the considerations in producing a CSR report are similar to those in producing a CER report.	3.7
Independent assurance of processes, performance and claims	Certification to ISO 14001 should help, in part, with this. Also, the organisation may have further experience with assurance if a CER is produced and it has been independently verified.	A comprehensive and planned assurance programme is required for CSR to be meaningfully addressed. This might include key stakeholder involvement.	3.1

Concluding thoughts

Environmental management is assuming an increasingly important, and sometimes crucial, role in organisations of all sizes and types.

At the very basic level, environmental management helps organisations to understand key environmental issues, to comply with environmental legislation and to reduce operational risks. Increasingly, however, it is also seen as a route to increasing resource and operational efficiency through better procurement, and reducing waste, energy and materials (ranging from manufactured substances to basic essentials such as water).

Even so, organisations need to ensure that environmental management is part of core business practice, from the formulation of strategy to detailed operational performance. By applying the 'plan, do, check and act' model, environmental management processes can be linked to strategy and everyday operations. This also supports continual improvement.

While third party certification to an environmental management standard such as ISO 14001 may not be essential, it can help build confidence both internally (with employees) and externally (with other stakeholders). However, using the systematic framework of an environmental management system (EMS) will help ensure that organisational arrangements and practices are properly targeted and prioritised, and that they remain suitable, adequate and effective.

Overall, the environmental agenda is complex, growing in importance and in a continual state of flux. Perhaps no other issue exemplifies this better than that encompassing energy, greenhouse gas emissions and climate change. Over the past two decades climate change has moved to the forefront of environmental and sustainability agendas. It is now a mainstream societal concern, with important stakeholder issues for many organisations. It is therefore very likely to be a material issue in an organisation's corporate social responsibility (CSR) considerations. Indeed, environmental managers can expect to be increasingly involved in measures to address the impacts of climate change on their organisation, in addition to managing aspects of their organisation that contribute to climate change. The need to understand and respond to key stakeholders and consider supply chain issues are other major developments.

With new laws, economic instruments and other pressures for change – and with the interface between environmental management and the wider sustainability and CSR agendas, it is important that environmental management is used to help an organisation look forward and align their environmentally driven actions with their other core strategies and practices.

This overriding goals of this book are to provide a comprehensive introduction to environmental impacts, the business case for effective environmental management, the essential strategic and operational processes required for continual improvement, and to set the scene for addressing wider issues and developing challenges. The appendices provide insights into relevant and related vocabulary. The appendices also signpost other key resources, such as helpful standards, useful organisations and sources of further information, including case studies.

We trust that understanding the issues and processes set out in *Essentials* will help readers to ensure that their organisations are proactive and effective in managing environmental issues. We also hope that *Essentials* helps to facilitate continual improvement and innovation to address both the challenges and opportunities ahead.

Appendix 1: Glossary of environmental management terms

The following provides a brief description of terms commonly encountered in environmental management and associated areas.

Term	Meaning
AA 1000 series	Series of standards building on the AA 1000 framework – an accountability standard designed to improve accountability and performance by learning through stakeholder engagement/integrating stakeholder engagement processes into the activities of an organisation. The AA 1000 series is an ongoing programme of specialised standards. More details are available from AccountAbility (see Appendix 3).
abatement	Control, reduction or lessening of pollution or removal of a nuisance by technical (eg plant, equipment or procedure) or regulatory means (eg permit, order or duty), or both.
accredited certification body	An organisation that has been assessed as meeting certification criteria set out by a government agency or other impartial organisation. Accredited certification bodies can undertake certification, eg certification of another organisation's environmental management system to ISO 14001.
acid rain	Certain gases (eg nitrogen oxides and sulphur dioxide) react with atmospheric moisture, increasing its acidity. These return to the earth's surface as acid rain or other forms of precipitation (eg snow, fog), resulting in the acidification of receiving waters and soil.
ambient pollution	Pollution in the surrounding environment – the sum of pollution resulting from background concentrations and the various sources of the pollution in question (including the contribution from a specific organisation's activities).
aquifer	Underground geological formation containing water which has typically accumulated over thousands of years. Can be a key source of drinking water.

audit

An objective (typically independent) check or assessment on the performance or standing of an organisation. An environmental audit checks the environmental performance or standing of the organisation. There are different types of environmental audit.

benchmarking

Comparison of performance against other organisations, typically peer operators or competitors (external benchmarking). It can also be undertaken between units in the same organisation (internal benchmarking). This helps the organisation (or unit) understand where it stands in terms of best practice.

best available techniques (BAT)

Central requirement of the EU's Integrated Pollution Prevention and Control Directive. This requires emission (release) limit values for installations covered by the Directive to be based on best available techniques. 'Best' refers to the most effective techniques in achieving a high level of overall environmental protection; 'available' means those techniques developed on a scale which allows implementation in the relevant sector under economically and technically viable conditions; 'techniques' refers to both the technology used and the way in which the installation is designed, built, maintained, operated and decommissioned.

best practicable environmental option (BPEO)

The option which, for a given set of objectives, provides the most benefit (or least damage) to the environment as a whole, at acceptable costs, in the long as well as the short term. The concept recognises that in abating pollution there are often environmental 'trade-offs' (eg combating air emissions may create other wastes), which need to be considered when establishing the most appropriate option to implement.

bioaccumulation

Biological process that concentrates toxic substances in certain organisms. Toxins can be passed to humans and other higher predators via the food chain.

biodegradation

Natural process of decomposition in which complex organic compounds are broken down into their constituent simple molecules, including carbon dioxide and water.

biodiversity	The variety of life on earth as reflected in the diversity of habitats, species of plants and animals, and other genetic diversity. Linked to the earth's ecology.
biological oxygen demand (BOD)	Measure of the oxygen required by microbes to reduce waste to simple compounds, and an indicator of the biodegradable organic pollution present in either a body of water or an effluent stream.
brainstorming	A technique to help solve problems or identify opportunities. Members of a group are actively encouraged to share any idea they have in relation to the issue in question, no matter how strange or unfeasible this may at first seem. All ideas are recorded, eg on flip charts. In the early stage, no evaluation of the ideas takes place and the emphasis is on producing a quantity of ideas, some of which may be different and often radical. Having obtained as many ideas as possible, the group then considers each one in more detail, evaluating its value in relation to the issue, and its feasibility. Brainstorming can be useful both within an organisation and, for example, in stakeholder focus groups.
bund	A type of 'secondary containment' in the form of an impervious wall around a tank or other primary container. Should there be a spill or leak from the primary container, a suitable bund prevents the substances (eg chemicals, oil, liquid waste) from escaping into the environment and causing pollution.
BS 8555	A British Standard 'Guide to the phased implementation of an environmental management system, including the use of environmental performance evaluation'. It was first published in 2003 and encompasses a six-phase approach to environmental management. BS 8555 provides guidance on how to implement a generic EMS, which can also be used as a route towards ISO 14001 and EMAS.
carbon dioxide equivalent (CO_2 e)	The accepted standard unit (typically in tonnes) of reporting emissions of greenhouse gases which takes into account the different potential of each greenhouse gas to contribute to global warming, allowing trends and comparisons to be determined.

carbon footprint	The measure of all the greenhouse gas emissions reported as carbon (typically CO_2 equivalent) resulting from an organisation, product, service, activity, event, individual or other entity. In practical environmental management terms the scope of the measurement needs to be clearly defined. Increasingly the footprint goes beyond calculating direct emissions (eg from an organisation's site-based activities) but also establishes indirect/life cycle emissions within its scope (eg including transport and, increasingly, embodied carbon in products).
carbon offset	Because climate change is a global issue, greenhouse gas savings in one part of the globe can be used to compensate more difficult to achieve savings elsewhere. For example, achieving additional reductions of transport emissions after measures to avoid travel and to maximise efficiency have been implemented may be a problem. In these circumstances compensating through others making an equivalent greenhouse gas saving elsewhere could be beneficial. However, there are important issues involved in such compensation and such offsets should only be acquired through officially approved sources, eg offset providers approved by the UK government's Quality Assurance Scheme (QAS) for Carbon Offsetting.
carcinogen	Class of substance or preparation that may induce cancer in the human body through skin, inhalation or ingestion exposure.
certification	Process of independent assessment to ascertain whether an organisation or product meets a specified environmental standard, eg certification of an organisation's environmental management system to ISO 14001.
chemical oxygen demand (COD)	The measure of the oxygen consumed in the chemical oxidation of organic and inorganic matter in water or effluent. It provides an indication of the impact of effluent on dissolved oxygen levels. A standard test uses potassium dichromate in a sample of the water or effluent.

combined heat and power (CHP)	Highly efficient energy technology in which electricity is generated and where heat is not wasted but used, eg for heating buildings, or for hot water. The technology can use fossil fuels efficiently – especially natural gas – but also fuels from renewable sources, eg woodchip and organic waste.
combustion	Rapid chemical reaction in which hydrocarbon fuels combine with oxygen to produce new molecules (notably CO_2 and water) and heat and light.
continual improvement	Enhancing an environmental management system to achieve improvements in overall performance in line with an organisation's environmental policy. It is a central requirement of ISO 14001. It need not take place in all areas of activity simultaneously.
corporate environmental report (CER)	A publicly available report (printed copy or in electronic format, eg web document) which sets out an organisation's environmental policy and environmental performance for a given period (typically annually) and outlines plans for future performance. Best practice reports include an overview of governance arrangements, performance against corporate objectives and an independent verification statement concerning the data and claims reported.
corporate social responsibility (CSR)	Concerns an organisation's commitment to operating in an economically, socially and environmentally responsible manner, through engagement with stakeholders. A key aspect is the recognition of stakeholders' various interests with a view to resolving problems and thereby helping to ensure business continuity and success. Essentially, CSR is about responsible business practice, in support of sustainable development. Increasingly, the term is being replaced by corporate responsibility (CR).

Deming cycle	Developed in the 1980s by Deming and Walton, the cycle identifies the sequence 'plan, do, check and act' as a logical approach to continual improvement. The 'act' component is about adapting aims and objectives to ensure the overall improvement process continues. The model is the basis of environmental, safety and quality management systems, including ISO 14001 (environment), OHSAS 18001 (occupational health and safety) and ISO 9001 (quality).
discharge	Process of releasing substances – typically effluent – into a drain or body of water.
discharge limit	Limit on discharge parameter, eg prohibition of certain substances at certain times, limit on concentration of certain substance released. Limit may be set by a regulatory requirement (eg permit condition), a best practice standard or an improvement target.
dispersion modelling	Modelling of the dispersion mechanisms of pollutants following their release into either air or water, eg from a stack or discharge pipe. This is used to predict the spread, dilution and reduction of the concentration of the pollutants, and the risk to sensitive receptors.
dissolved oxygen (DO)	The oxygen dissolved in a body of water and available to marine life, eg fish. It provides an indication of the health of the water body and its ability to support balanced aquatic life. The level of dissolved oxygen can rapidly fall with the onset of pollution, eg through the introduction of effluent with high biological oxygen demand (enhanced microbial activity consumes oxygen), materials which hinder re-oxygenation by preventing transfer of oxygen from the atmosphere (eg surface films of oil or detergents) or heated discharges (higher temperatures reduce the ability of water to hold dissolved oxygen).

duty of care	Legal requirement which places a duty on prescribed persons to take certain steps and assume certain responsibilities. In the UK, a duty is imposed by legislation on those holding (eg storing, treating or disposing of) controlled waste to prevent its escape, document its transfer, ensure its transfer is only to authorised persons (eg registered carriers) and ensure that it is disposed of at appropriately licensed facilities
ecosystem	A community of interdependent organisms and the physical and chemical environment they inhabit.
eco-tax	A tax which aims to encourage organisations to change behaviour to that which is more beneficial to the environment, or otherwise incur the financial impact of the tax. For example, an energy tax encourages energy efficiency, a carbon tax encourages a switch to lower carbon technologies and non-fossil fuels, a landfill tax encourages waste minimisation.
effluent	Liquid waste stream that is released (discharged) into a drain or body of water.
EMAS	The EU Eco-Management and Audit Scheme is a management tool for companies and other organisations to evaluate, report and improve their environmental performance. The scheme was first open to industrial companies in 1995 but in 2001 it was opened to all economic sectors, including public and private service organisations. ISO 14001 is an accepted EMS under the standard. A key additional element of EMAS is the requirement for public reporting.
embodied carbon	A sub-set of life cycle assessment. Embodied carbon refers to a measure of the carbon dioxide generated during the life cycle, or selected parts of the life cycle, of a product, installation or service, eg manufacture of a product in addition to its use. The scope of the life cycle subject to measurement must be defined and transparent.
emission	The term can be applied to the release of any waste substance. More specifically, it is used for referring to waste streams that are released to atmosphere. It can also include noise.

emission limit	Limit on an emission parameter, eg prohibition of certain substances at certain times, limit on concentration of certain substance released. Limit may be set by a regulatory requirement (eg permit condition), a best practice standard or an improvement target.
endocrine disruptors	Chemicals that have the capacity to interfere with hormones (endocrines) in the body. Hormones regulate the functions of the body and its development. Certain substances are implicated with mimicking female hormones, with adverse effects on male sexual development and fertility.
end-of-pipe abatement	Treatment of a waste stream so that the pollutant is either removed before its release or its level is reduced to a required level. This typically means that the waste stream (or a proportion of it) is transformed to another form of waste. This may require further treatment or special disposal arrangements and may lead to other environmental impacts. The treatment process will typically involve the consumption of energy and, possibly, other materials.
environment	Surroundings in which an organisation operates, including air, water, land, natural resources, flora, fauna, humans and their inter-relation. These can extend from within the organisation to the global system (ISO 14001 definition).
environmental aspect	Element of an organisation's activities, products and services which can interact with the environment (ISO 14001 definition).
environmental impact	Any change in the environment, whether adverse or beneficial, wholly or partially resulting from an organisation's activities, products or services (ISO 14001 definition).
environmental management system (EMS)	Part of an organisation's overall management system that includes organisational structure, planning activities, responsibilities, practices, procedures, processes and resources for developing, implementing, achieving, reviewing and maintaining the organisation's environmental policy (based on ISO 14001).

environmental performance indicator (EPI)	Specific parameters that provide information about an organisation's environmental performance. These may be aspect performance indicators (eg quantity of carbon dioxide emitted per unit output) or management performance indicators (eg number of major, moderate and minor corrective actions identified by environmental management audit findings).
environmental quality standard (EQS)	A standard typically established by legislation or a regulatory authority that specifies the quality of the ambient environment, eg the maximum concentration of a pollutant in the air or a body of water. Releases from an installation may be required to comply with such standards.
eutrophication	Natural process in which algae proliferate in water because of high availability of nutrients, eg. through fertiliser or effluent rich in rapidly decomposable organic matter reaching the water body.
fishbone diagram	A visual analytical technique that facilitates the exploration of the causes of a problem, eg waste generation, pollution incident. Having identified the causes, the solutions to the problem can be established, eg waste minimisation opportunities, risk management practices or innovation.
fuel cells	Technology that employs electrochemistry (electrodes and electrolyte) to convert hydrogen gas mixed with oxygen to generate electricity. A key issue is the source of the hydrogen, since most is derived from fossil fuels – typically natural gas. However, any developments in renewable generation that might lead to large-scale hydrogen production (eg using off-peak electricity to convert water into hydrogen) could significantly affect the prospects for this technology especially in terms of greenhouse gas emissions and conservation of fossil fuel reserves.
fugitive emission	The many and varied *ad hoc* releases that can occur in a process or around a site, eg leaks from pipe joints and glands, evaporative losses from storage tanks. Such releases are particularly relevant for volatile organic compounds.

geodiversity	The range or diversity of rocks, landforms, deposits and soils, including their features, assemblages, systems and processes across the earth or in a defined area. Geodiversity is linked, for example, to landscape value, resources (such as aggregates) and the abiotic basis of ecosystems.
greenhouse gas (GHG)	Any gas that contributes to the earth's greenhouse effect by trapping long wave radiation and thereby increasing the likelihood of global climate change. Gases include carbon dioxide, methane, nitrous oxide, hydrofluorocarbons, perfluorocarbons and sulphur hexafluoride (gases included in the Kyoto Protocol). Each of these gases has different global warming potentials (GWPs). For example, carbon dioxide has a GWP of 1, methane of 21, and sulphur hexafluoride of 23,900.
ground-level ozone	The creation of ozone near the surface (in the troposphere) through the complex reaction of nitrogen oxides and certain volatile organic compounds in the presence of sunlight. At ground level, ozone can be harmful to organisms.
habitat	The specific environment in which an organism lives. This is shared with other organisms in a complex set of inter-relationships.
innovation	Typically involves either applying an existing technology or techniques in new ways or applying a new technology or techniques for the first time for a project or situation. Innovation should be part of continual improvement and has a key role in building sustainability in an organisation.
Integrated Pollution Prevention and Control (IPPC) Directive	An EU Directive that requires member states to issue permits to a range of prescribed installations. Permit conditions seek to protect the environment taken as a whole and include: compliance with emission limit values (based on BAT and any relevant environmental quality standards), avoidance of waste production, the efficient use of energy, noise control, measures to prevent incidents and limit their consequences, requirements to avoid pollution risks, and eventual return of the site to a satisfactory state.

International Panel on Climate Change (IPCC)	A body of over 300 international scientists set up by the UN to examine the threat of global climate change.
interpretation	The term used for an approach to communicating ideas and feelings which help people understand more about their environment, especially its cultural and natural heritage. It is especially relevant to sites which have any particular historic, biodiversity or geodiversity interest – this could include industrial or commercial sites as well as parks, nature reserves and historic attractions. Methods include guided walks, talks, displays, signs, brochures and electronic media, which are typically developed to reach target audiences and communicate important themes. The approach could also apply to explaining an environmental technology being deployed on a site, eg composting, recycling, solar energy or pollution abatement. It could be particularly useful for industrial sites to use to communicate environmental initiatives during 'open days'.
ISO 14001	The international environmental management standard. It specifies the requirements for an environmental management system. ISO 14001 applies to those environmental aspects which the organisation has control and over which it can be expected to have an influence. It was first published in 1996 and has since been revised and updated.
kaizen	Literally 'change to become good or better'. A management model originating in Japan that seeks to embed continual improvement in an organisation's culture through teamwork, personal discipline, improved morale, quality circles and suggestions for improvement. The approach is key to quality management and a fundamental goal is that of eliminating waste and inefficiency. The philosophy therefore resonates well with environmental management and can be a means to help harness innovation.

key performance indicator	A parameter that measures the level of achievement in an area determined to be of particular (possibly critical) importance to the organisation. This should normally be in relation to a high priority significant aspect. KPIs may be set at both strategic (corporate) and operational levels. They should be linked to objective- and target-setting.
key survival issue (KSI)	An issue that an organisation will need to address if it is to survive in the longer term. These issues can be established through strategic SWOT analysis and/or scenario-planning. KSIs should be determined as part of an organisation's approach to sustainability.
landfill	Essentially, disposal of waste in a hole in the ground. Landfills must now be properly engineered and licensed facilities. Restrictions on the type of waste accepted and the types of site available take account of the potential for the anaerobic decomposition of organic waste and the generation of methane gas (collected and vented, or used to generate electricity) or leachate (a liquid which contains dissolved substances or suspended solids present in the waste).
life cycle assessment (LCA)	A specific environmental management technique that attempts to identify and, where possible, aggregate the various material, energy and waste flows to evaluate the environmental impacts associated with the provision of a product or service over its entire life cycle. It is often referred to as 'cradle to grave', but as reuse or recovery is preferred to disposal, it is increasingly referred to as 'cradle to cradle'.
life cycle thinking	An environmental management technique that considers impacts over the wider life cycle of a product or service to minimise overall impact. This tends to be less rigorous than LCA (although it may also involve LCA studies) but supports a move 'cradle to grave' or 'cradle to cradle' thinking and can be an important part of an organisation's approach to sustainability.
mutagen	Class of substance or preparation that may induce non-hereditary genetic defects in the human body through skin, inhalation or ingestion exposure.

nuisance	Interference with another's use and enjoyment of the environment (including loss of amenity) through something that annoys, bothers or causes damage to that person or their property. Includes noise, odour and visual intrusion.
ozone depletion	The breakdown of ozone in the upper atmosphere (stratosphere) by manufactured chemicals containing bromine and chlorine, eg CFCs and halon. This layer of ozone helps protect life on earth from damaging ultraviolet radiation.
ozone precursor	A substance that can lead to ground-level ozone creation in the lower atmosphere (troposphere) in the presence of sunlight. Nitrogen oxides and many volatile organic compounds are ozone precursors.
pathway	The route which is available to a pollutant from its source to a receptor where an adverse impact can occur, eg oil spill via drain to river, chemical spill via permeable ground to aquifer, odorous air emission via prevailing wind to local community, toxic substance via food chain to humans.
'payback' period	Traditionally a simple method of investment appraisal that estimates the length of time it will take to recoup the money invested. It can be used, for example, to assess the length of time before savings resulting from process efficiency improvements will equal the amount invested in the improvement. The term, however, is also being used as part of life cycle thinking in which the 'energy' or 'carbon payback' of technology such as renewable energy systems are considered. In this sense the payback is calculated in terms of the time taken for the technology to either generate enough energy or to save sufficient carbon compared to that expended or emitted (respectively) during its production, installation, maintenance and decommissioning. Also relates to 'embodied carbon'.

permit

A regulatory document which sets out the environmental conditions under which an installation, activity or process can operate. Other names that have been used, or can apply (eg depending on country), include licence, consent or authorisation. Permits typically include restrictions on what can be released into the environment, eg limits on discharges to sewer or watercourse, limits on emissions to atmosphere. It may set monitoring requirements to ensure releases remain within the prescribed limits. The permit may also request other good management practices (eg training and maintenance) and specify how compliance/ performance is reported to the regulatory authority.

photosynthesis

The means by which certain organisms containing chlorophyll – eg phytoplankton (sea) and green plants (land) – use energy from sunlight to convert carbon dioxide and hydrogen (from water) into organic matter (carbohydrates).

plankton

Free-floating life-forms in the sea or other body of water consisting of minute plants (phytoplankton) and animals (zooplankton).

pollution

The direct or indirect introduction (as a result of human activity) of substances, vibration, heat or noise into the air, water or land which may be harmful to human health or the quality of the environment, result in damage to material property, or impair or interfere with amenities or other legitimate uses of the environment (EU IPPC Directive definition).

process efficiency

Use of fewer resource inputs (materials and energy) and generation of less waste (in all its forms, eg solid and liquid wastes, waste heat, emissions and effluent) for a given level of production or service. It incorporates waste minimisation and energy efficiency.

producer responsibility	Can be viewed as a 'life cycle' extension of the 'polluter pays principle'. It is aimed at ensuring that organisations that place products on the market take (increasing) responsibility for the environmental impact of those products beyond their immediate operations. In particular, that they take responsibility for the environmental fate of products when they reach the end of their useful life.
receptor	Entity that receives contaminant or pollutant and which can be subject to an environmental impact. It can be a body of water or air; parcel of land; ecosystem, habitat, particular species or individual organism; human being, local community or property. Some receptors are particularly sensitive to certain pollutants.
recovery	Can refer to either: reprocessing of waste so that value can be obtained from it either through recycling, composting or energy recovery; or recovery of spilled oil or chemicals so that they are removed from the environment. Depending on the condition of the recovered oil and chemicals (eg degree to which they are adulterated), they may be either responsibly disposed of, or reused or recycled.
renewable energy	Energy that is derived from resources that can be replaced within an immediate or short timescale, typically directly from the sun or via planetary cycles powered by solar radiation. Examples include passive solar (building design to maximise heating), active solar heating (through collectors such as plates or tubes), photovoltaics (panels that convert sunlight directly into electricity), wind power (via turbines either as farms offshore or onshore and typically connected to the grid, or onshore turbines, including micro-turbines on a particular site), hydroelectricity (large-scale turbines connected to the grid or on-site generation, including the use of micro-turbines) and biofuels (using organic waste, timber or energy crops). Renewable energy technology also includes geothermal energy which uses underground sources of heat and includes the use of heat pumps to exploit temperature differentials and thereby provide heat in winter and cooling in summer. These technologies are at different stages of development and feasibility tends to be site-specific.

resource

In general terms, something that is useful to humankind. It can include land/soil, water, air, minerals, biomass and landscape. It can also include the ability to use the atmosphere, body of water or piece of land as sink for disposing of waste. There are two important types of resource – renewable and non-renewable (or stock). Renewable resources are replaced within immediate or short timescales (eg solar energy) while stock resources tend to have been created over a geological timespan (eg oil).

SA 8000

International voluntary workplace standard developed by Social Accountability International (SAI). The standard promotes management systems that upgrade working conditions. It is based on International Labour Organization and other human rights conventions and approaches used by ISO. More details are available from SAI (see Appendix 3).

Special Areas of Conservation (SAC)

These are areas which have been given special protection under the EU Habitats Directive. SACs provide increased protection to a variety of animals, plants and habitats with the aim of conserving biodiversity.

scenario-planning

Strategic business process in which pictures or stories of alternative – but plausible – futures are established by mapping out various pressures, developments and outcomes. The process helps managers consider the longer term and, indeed, think the unthinkable. It enables managers to generate strategic options to position their organisation for survival and success.

significance assessment

Systematic evaluation of the importance of the environmental aspects (interactions) of an organisation and their environmental impact. This can occur at the strategic or operational level. It should include the assessment of each aspect in terms of regulatory requirement and stakeholder concern. It is a first order prioritisation process in which the organisation decides which environmental interactions need to be managed.

sink	A receptor for disposal of waste, eg atmosphere for emissions, body of water for effluent discharges, and landfill for solid and contained liquid wastes. Sinks represent a type of resource – a resource for disposal of unwanted materials and waste heat.
SMART environmental target	An environmental performance goal that is specific, measureable, agreed, realistic and timebound. It should be linked to a key performance indicator.
stakeholders	Individuals, communities or organisations that have an interest in the organisation or are affected by its policy, practices and performance. They include shareholders, employees, customers, suppliers, local communities, neighbours, regulators, pressure groups and the media. They can influence the organisation's operating space – what it can and cannot do in terms of the environmental interaction of its activities, products and services.
suspended solid (SS)	Particulate matter in suspension in a body of water or effluent stream. Sometimes referred to as total suspended solids (TSSs).
SWOT analysis	Assessment of an organisation, activity, product or service in terms of (largely internal) strengths and weaknesses, and (largely external) opportunities and threats.
teratogen	Class of substance or preparation that may induce foetal malformations if it enters the human body through skin, inhalation or ingestion exposure.
toxic	A property of a substance or preparation that can cause death or harm to an organism. Depending on factors such as the dose of the substance and sensitivity of the receptor organism, the effect can be acute (immediate or short-term adverse effect following exposure – typically clear cut, rarely reversible, possibly fatal) or chronic (adverse effect occurs over the longer term – less clear cut, possibly reversible, possibly fatal if not addressed). Alternatively, it may be determined to have no predicted effect at the concentrations in question.

tradeable permit   A permit which provides flexibility to an operator as to how the quota set by the permit (eg a certain amount of emissions or discharge, or volume of waste recovered) can be met through the ability to buy and sell permission via a trading facility. The operator can choose to meet the quota. Alternatively, the operator can fail to meet the quota and buy extra permission – or better the quota and sell the surplus permission to others.

transpiration   Process by which water drawn from the soil is returned to the atmosphere from the leaves of plants. Together with other evaporation from land and water surfaces, it forms an important component of the hydrological cycle. The combined term 'evapo-transpiration' is commonly used.

unburnt hydrocarbons (UBHCs)   Compounds in hydrocarbon fuels which are not oxidised in the combustion process and which are emitted in the exhaust or flue gas. Many are ozone precursors. The term can be synonymous with volatile organic compounds. Includes methane, but when explicitly excluded, the other unburnt hydrocarbons are termed non-methane unburnt hydrocarbons.

volatile organic compounds (VOCs)   Organic compounds which evaporate readily (ie are volatile). There is a wide range of VOCs, including ethylene, propylene, benzene and solvent preparations. VOCs contribute to a number of air quality issues depending on the properties of the compound in question (eg benzene is carcinogenic). Many are ground-level ozone precursors. Methane can be included as a VOC, but when explicitly excluded, the other VOCs are termed non-methane VOCs.

waste   In its widest sense, waste is anything that is discarded. It includes effluent discharges and atmospheric emissions, as well as solid waste and contained liquid waste. National law usually defines the materials and articles that constitute waste and which are therefore subject to legal controls. Furthermore, legislation also tends to recognise that certain wastes exhibit hazardous properties and therefore should be subject to additional regulatory controls. This is the case in the EU.

waste
minimisation

The practice of reducing the amount of waste destined for disposal through prevention or reduction of waste at source, or the reuse or recovery of the waste that is produced. Reuse and recovery can occur either on or off site. Waste recovery involves reprocessing waste outputs so that value can be obtained from them, either through recycling, composting (if suitable biodegradable waste) or energy recovery (if combustible waste).

Appendix 2: ISO 14000 series and related standards

The International Organization for Standardization (ISO) has produced a series of standards on environmental management and supporting techniques. These are grouped together under the ISO 14000 series. The environmental management standards have been produced by ISO Technical Committee (TC) 207, which was set up shortly after the 1992 United Nations Summit in Rio on meeting the challenge of sustainable development. The ISO Strategic Advisory Group on Environment (SAGE) was established in 1991.

The ISO 14000 series has been developed to interface with ISO quality management standards (9000 series) developed by ISO TC 176. The BS OHSAS 18001 health and safety management systems standard has been similarly developed, since the introduction of ISO 14001. A common standard ISO 19011 sets out guidelines for auditing environmental and/or quality management systems (EMS/QMSs), and is expected to incorporate health and safety management systems in due course.

In addition to ISO 14001 (the EMS standard), the additional guidelines on environmental management in ISO 14004 and the guidance on evaluating environmental performance (ISO 14031) key subgroups include:

- ISO 14020 subgroup: environmental labels and declarations
- ISO 14040 subgroup: life cycle assessment
- ISO 14064-9 subgroup: greenhouse gas measurement, reporting and verification.

A list of individual environmental standards, related standards and technical reports is provided below. Importantly, the published standards are often subject to revisions and additional standards are added to the series so that this list should be treated as indicative only. Updated information (including draft standards and forthcoming revisions in the ISO 14000 and related series) can be obtained from the British Standards Institution (BSI) or the ISO – see Appendix 3 for contact details. It is advisable for organisations to be aware of draft standards, particularly in their strategic thinking. The development of such standards should be included in the management review processes.

ISO Standard/Draft Standard/Guide	Date	Title
ISO 14001	2004	Environmental management systems – requirements with guidance for use
ISO 14004	2004	Environmental management systems – general guidelines on principles, systems and supporting techniques
ISO/DIS 14005	–	Environmental management systems – guidelines for the phased implementation of an environmental management system, including the use of environmental performance evaluation
ISO/CD 14006	–	Environmental management systems – Guidelines on eco-design
ISO 14015	2001	Environmental management – Environmental assessment of sites and organisations (EASO)
ISO 14020	2000	Environmental labels and declarations – general principles
ISO 14021	1999	Environmental labels and declarations – self-declared environmental claims (type II environmental labelling)
ISO 14024	1999	Environmental labels and declarations – type I environmental labelling – principles and procedures
ISO 14025	2006	Environmental labels and declarations – type III environmental declarations – principles and procedures
ISO 14031	1999	Environmental management – Environmental performance evaluation (EPE) – guidelines
ISO 14032	1999	Examples of environmental performance evaluation (EPE)
ISO/AWI 14033	–	Environmental management – quantitative environmental information – guidelines and examples
ISO 14040	2006	Environmental management – life cycle assessment (LCA) – principles and framework
ISO 14044	2006	Environmental management – life cycle assessment (LCA) – requirements and guidelines
ISO/WD 14045	–	Eco-efficiency assessment – principles and requirements

ISO Standard/Draft Standard/Guide	Date	Title
ISO/TR 14047	2003	Environmental management – life cycle impact assessment (LCA) – examples of application of ISO 14042
ISO/TS 14048	2002	Environmental management – life cycle assessment – Data documentation format
ISO 14049/TR	2000	Environmental management – life cycle assessment – Examples of application of ISO 14041 to goal and scope definition and inventory analysis
ISO 14050	2002	Environmental management – vocabulary
ISO/CD 14051	–	Environmental management – material flow cost accounting – general principles and framework
ISO/TR 14062	2002	Environmental management – integrating environmental aspects into product design and development
ISO 14063	2006	Environmental management – environmental communication: guidelines and examples
ISO 14064-1	2006	Greenhouse gases – part 1: specification with guidance at the organisation level for quantification and reporting of greenhouse gas emissions and removals
ISO 14064-2	2006	Greenhouse gases – part 2: specification with guidance at the project level for quantification, monitoring and reporting of greenhouse gas emission reductions or removal enhancements
ISO 14064-3	2006	Greenhouse gases – part 3: specification with guidance for the validation and verification of greenhouse gas assertions
ISO 14065	2007	Greenhouse gases – requirements for greenhouse gas validation and verification bodies for use in accreditation or other forms of recognition
ISO/CD 14066	–	Greenhouse gases – competency requirements for greenhouse gas validators and verifiers document
ISO/WD 14067-1	–	Carbon footprint of products – part 1: quantification

ISO Standard/Draft Standard/Guide	Date	Title
ISO/WD 14067-2	–	Carbon footprint of products – part 2: communication
ISO/AWI 14069	–	GHG – quantification and reporting of GHG emissions for organisations (carbon footprint of organisation) – guidance for application of ISO 14064-1
ISO Guide 64	2008	Guide for addressing environmental issues in products

Notes

1 ISO prefix – denotes that the publication is an ISO international standard.
2 Additional prefixes denote either the publication has been developed specifically as a joint international standard (with another national standards body) or it indicates the type of document, eg TR denotes a technical report, TS a technical specification. Alternatively, it may denote the stage of development of the standard, ie DIS denotes a draft international standard.
3 Guides are informative documents.
4 When sourcing from the British Standards Institution (BSI), these standards will also display the BS prefix. This includes BS OHSAS 18001, which is not an ISO standard.

Notable environmental and sustainability management standards outside the ISO 14000 series include British (BS) and European (EN) standards:

- BS EN ISO 19011:2002 Guidelines for quality and/or environmental management systems auditing
- BS 8555:2003 Environmental management systems – Guide to the phased implementation of an environmental management system including the use of environmental performance evaluation (a useful step-by-step guide to the implementation of ISO 14001)*
- BS 8900:2006 Guidance for managing sustainable development (applies a management systems approach to the economic, environmental and social aspects of an organisation's activities)
- BS EN 16001:2009 Energy management systems – Requirements with guidance for use.

* Once adopted, ISO/DIS 14005 is expected to introduce a phased approach to environmental management as an international standard.

Appendix 3: Selected sources of further information

The following is a selection of sources of further information and publications on environmental management and related issues. There is an emphasis on sources relevant to the UK.

Useful organisations

The following list of organisations, which includes UK and international bodies, is indicative only, as the situation is in constant flux as new organisations emerge and others disappear. For example, UK government departments and agencies may be subject to change through political restructuring and other considerations. In 2010, for instance, Envirowise was incorporated into WRAP (and had itself been created out of the Environmental Technology Best Practice Programme of the 1990s). Contact details are also subject to change.

Organisation	Description	Contact details
AccountAbility	A global, not-for-profit organisation founded in 1995. At the core of its work is the AA1000 series of standards. It seeks to encourage: • inclusivity – people should have a say in the decisions that affect them • materiality – decision-makers should identify and be clear about the issues that matter • responsiveness – organisations should be transparent about their actions.	www.accountability.org t +44 (0)20 7549 0400
British Standards Institution (BSI)	BSI is the UK's national standards body (NSB) and was the world's first. BSI develops, publishes and markets standards and related information products. As the UK NSB, it works with governments, businesses and consumers to represent UK interests and facilitate the production of European and international standards. This includes the ISO 14000 series.	www.bsigroup.com t +44 (0)20 8996 9001

Organisation	Description	Contact details
Business in the Community (BITC)	An independent UK-based charity. BITC works with business to build a sustainable future for people and planet. BITC offers a framework to support and challenge business to improve its performance and benefit society through four key areas – community, environment, workplace and marketplace.	www.bitc.org.uk t +44 (0)20 7566 8650
Cadw	The historic environment service of the Welsh Assembly Government. Cadw is a Welsh word for 'to keep'. It is responsible for protecting historic buildings, ancient monuments, historic parks, gardens and landscapes, and underwater archaeology.	www.cadw.wales.gov.uk t +44 (0)1443 336000
Carbon Trust	A not-for-profit UK company with the mission to accelerate the move to a low carbon economy. Provides specialist support to business and the public sector to help cut carbon emissions, save energy and commercialise low carbon technologies.	www.carbontrust.co.uk t +44 (0)800 085 2005
Commission for Architecture and the Built Environment (CABE)	CABE provides independent design advice to improve the quality of the built environment and open spaces in England, including design incorporating sustainability, particularly through its sustainable cities initiative. CABE issues publications and case studies.	www.cabe.org.uk t +44 (0)20 7070 6700
Countryside Council for Wales	The UK government's statutory adviser on sustaining natural beauty, wildlife and the opportunity for outdoor enjoyment in Wales and its inshore waters. This includes important biodiversity and geodiversity sites.	www.ccw.gov.uk t +44 (0)845 130 6229
Department for Environment, Food and Rural Affairs (Defra)	The UK government department responsible for environmental policy and sustainable development. Its policy is implemented via a wide variety of government agencies (eg Environment Agency) and other bodies (eg WRAP).	ww2.defra.gov.uk t +44 (0)20 7238 6951/ +44 (0)845 933 5577

Organisation	Description	Contact details
Department of Energy and Climate Change (DECC)	The UK government department responsible for all aspects of UK energy policy, and for tackling global climate change on behalf of the UK. A key role at DECC is to help the UK move to a low carbon economy. For example, it provides information on market instruments, carbon offsetting, valuation and neutrality, and the UK's Carbon Reduction Commitment (CRC) Energy Efficiency Scheme.	www.decc.gov.uk t +44 (0)20 7979 7777/ t +44 (0)30 0060 4000
Energy Institute (EI)	The UK-based professional body for the energy industries. It is licensed by the Society for the Environment to award Chartered Environmentalist status. It publishes codes, industry standards, guidelines, manuals and other material that address all aspects of the energy industry, including environmental best practice.	www.energyinst.org.uk t +44 (0)20 7467 7100
English Heritage	Responsible for protecting the historic environment in England, including listed buildings, scheduled monuments, registered parks and gardens, registered battlefields and protected wreck sites. It also provides guidance and information on conservation areas.	www.english-heritage.org.uk/protecting/heritage-protection t +44 (0)870 333 1181
Environment Agency (EA)	Responsible for environmental protection in England and Wales. It provides a wide range of information on regulatory requirements (including pollution and waste controls) and on best practice (including resource efficiency).	www.environment-agency.gov.uk t + 44 (0)1709 389201/ +44 (0)870 850 6506
Environment Council	An independent UK charity that brings together people from all sectors of business, NGOs, government and the community to develop long term solutions to environmental issues and sustainability. Advice includes principles and techniques for effective stakeholder dialogue and engagement.	www.the-environment-council.org.uk t +44 (0)20 8144 8380

Organisation	Description	Contact details
Envirowise (part of WRAP)	Envirowise offers free and independent support to organisations across the UK to help them to become more resource efficient and to save money. Advice is also provided on supply chain and other initiatives. Envirowise has a comprehensive range of publications on environmental best practice. In 2010, Envirowise was incorporated into WRAP.	http://envirowise.wrap.org.uk t +44 (0)800 585794
Europa	Europa is the portal site of the European Union (EU). It provides up-to-date coverage of EU affairs, including environmental policy. It all provides access to all legislation and associated measures currently in force or under discussion, links to the websites of each of the EU institutions.	http://europa.eu Europe Direct: t 00 800 6789 10 11
Foresight	A UK government-sponsored programme, Foresight produces challenging visions of the future to help develop effective strategies for leaders in government, science and business. This includes sustainability factors and issues, eg sustainable energy and the built environment.	www.bis.gov.uk/foresight
Forum for the Future	Founded in 1996, Forum for the Future is a UK-based independent, non-profit organisation which seeks to promote sustainable development. It works with businesses and public service providers to understand and manage the risks and new opportunities of global challenges and to implement social and environmental responsibility. It also shares knowledge with others to work towards a more sustainable society.	www.forumforthefuture.org t +44 (0)20 7324 3630

Organisation	Description	Contact details
Global Reporting Initiative (GRI)	A network-based organisation that has pioneered the development of sustainability reporting. Its framework sets out the principles and indicators that organisations can use to measure and report their economic, environmental, and social performance. It has published free Sustainability Reporting Guidelines (G3 Guidelines, 2006). Other components of the framework include Sector Supplements (unique indicators for industry sectors) and National Annexes (unique country-level information).	www.globalreporting.org t +31 (0)20 531 0000 (The Netherlands)
GoodCorporation	A UK-based consultancy that has developed the GoodCorporation Standard (launched 2001) with the Institute of Business Ethics. The standard underwent a broad consultation with businesses, NGOs, trade unions, CSR organisations and others. The standard aims to address the increasing demands on businesses and organisations to behave in a transparent, responsible way.	www.goodcorporation.com t +44 (0)20 7736 7379
Historic Scotland	The Scottish government agency responsible for protecting Scotland's historic environment, including historic buildings, ancient monuments, historic parks, gardens and landscapes, and underwater archaeology.	www.historic-scotland.gov.uk t +44 (0)131 668 8600
Institute of Business Ethics (IBE)	A UK-based charity working to develop and promote ethical policies and practices in business.	www.ibe.org.uk t +44 (0)20 7798 6040

Organisation	Description	Contact details
Institute of Environmental Management and Assessment (IEMA)	The UK-based professional membership body for promoting best practice standards in environmental management, auditing and assessment for all industry sectors. The Institute offers ongoing support to environmental professionals and aims to promote sustainability through improved environmental practice and performance. IEMA is also the 'competent body' in the UK for EMAS and offers the Acorn Scheme, which provides a phased approach to environmental management conforming to BS 8555. It is licensed by the Society for the Environment to award Chartered Environmentalist status. It has a wide range of publications on environmental management and associated topics.	www.iema.net t +44 (0)1522 540069
Institution of Environmental Sciences (IES)	A UK-based charitable organisation which promotes and raises public awareness of environmental science and provides support to professional scientists and others working on the environmental issues. It is a provider of Professional Partnership for Sustainable Development (PP4SD) and it is licensed by the Society for the Environment to award Chartered Environmentalist status.	www.ies-uk.org.uk t +44 (0)20 7730 5516
Institution of Occupational Safety and Health (IOSH)	The UK-based chartered body for health and safety professionals and practitioners. IOSH has a range of up-to-date, authoritative material on a wide range of health, safety and environmental issues. Help and advice is available through IOSH's Information Helpline and its Environmental and Waste Management and other sector-specific groups.	www.iosh.co.uk t +44 (0)116 257 3100 Information helpline: t +44 (0)116 257 3199

Organisation	Description	Contact details
International Organization for Standardization (ISO)	ISO is the developer and publisher of International Standards and supporting information. It is a non-governmental organisation and a network of the national standards institutes of 163 countries, including Britain (BSI). The environmental management standards (ISO 14000 series) have been produced by ISO Technical Committee (TC) 207, which was set up in 1993. A full list of standards is available in the ISO catalogue.	www.iso.org www.iso.org/iso/ iso_catalogue t +41 22 749 01 11 (Switzerland)
Joint Nature Conservation Committee (JNCC)	The public body that advises the UK government and devolved administrations on UK-wide and international nature conservation. It provides information on a variety of species, habitats, geoconservation issues and the range of protected sites, including Special Areas of Conservation (SACs) and Special Protection Areas (SPAs).	www.jncc.gov.uk t +44 (0)1733 562626
Natural England	An independent public body whose purpose is to protect and improve England's natural environment and encourage people to enjoy and get involved in their surroundings. This includes important biodiversity and geodiversity sites. For example, it is responsible for enforcement policy for Sites of Special Scientific Interest (SSSIs).The website includes locations and details concerning SSSIs and a range of publications on a variety of environmental issues.	www.naturalengland. org.uk t +44 (0)845 600 3078

Organisation	Description	Contact details
Netregs	NetRegs provides free environmental guidance for small and medium-sized businesses in the UK. It helps organisations to understand what they need to do to comply with environmental law and protect the environment, including advice on using resources more efficiently. It is sponsored by the EA, SEPA and NIEA.	www.environment-agency.gov.uk/netregs t +44 (0)870 850 6506
Northern Ireland Environment Agency (NIEA)	NIEA is responsible for environmental protection in Northern Ireland. It provides a wide range of information on regulatory requirements (including pollution and waste controls) and on best practice (including resource efficiency). It also is responsible for protection natural heritage and the built environment, eg listed buildings and monuments.	www.doeni.gov.uk/niea t +44 (0)28 9054 0540
Quality Assurance Scheme for Carbon Offsetting (QAS)	A UK government-led initiative aimed at increasing consumers' understanding of the role of offsetting in tackling climate change and helping them to make informed purchases of good quality offsets. QAS provides a list of approved offset providers.	http://offsetting.decc.gov.uk Approved providers list: http://offsetting.decc.gov.uk/cms/approved-offsets/
Scottish Environment Protection Agency (SEPA)	SEPA is responsible for environmental protection in Scotland. It provides a wide range of information on regulatory requirements (including pollution and waste controls) and on best practice (including resource efficiency).	www.sepa.org.uk t +44 (0)1786 457700
Scottish Natural Heritage (SNH)	SNH works to care for Scotland's natural heritage, enabling people to enjoy it, helping people to understand and appreciate it, and supporting those who manage it. This includes important bidioversity and geodiversity sites. It has a wide range of publications and advice.	www.snh.gov.uk t +44 (0)1463 725000

Organisation	Description	Contact details
Society for the Environment (SocEnv)	A UK-based independent, not-for-profit organisation incorporated by Royal Charter and responsible for awarding the title Chartered Environmentalist (CEnv) to professional individuals through its licensed member bodies, eg IEMA, IES, EI.	www.socenv.org.uk t +44 (0)845 337 2951
Social Accountability International (SAI)	A US-based, non-profit organisation dedicated to the improvement of workplaces and communities by developing and implementing socially responsible standards and assisting improve social compliance of supply chains. It developed Social Accountability 8000 (SA 8000), a voluntary standard for workplaces based on International Labour Organization (ILO) and other human rights conventions.	www.sa-intl.org t +1 212 684 1414 (USA)
The Stationery Office (TSO)	Originally Her Majesty's Stationery Office (HMSO), TSO is the largest publisher in the UK, providing information in print, online and in electronic formats. It is a source of official publications (including policy papers, UK Acts of Parliament, UK Statutory Instruments) and a range of professional and business books on the environment and other topics.	Variety of agents and bookshops around the UK, including an online bookshop (visit website for details) www.tso.co.uk t +44 (0)1603 622211
UK Accreditation Service (UKAS)	UKAS is the sole national accreditation body recognised by the UK government to assess, against internationally agreed standards, organisations that provide certification, testing, inspection and calibration services. This includes accrediting the certifiers of standards such as ISO 14001 and BS OHSAS 18001. UKAS maintains a list (and contact details) of accredited certification bodies for environmental management systems, quality systems and greenhouse gas accounting.	www.ukas.com t +44 (0)20 8917 8400

Organisation	Description	Contact details
United Nations Environmental Programme (UNEP)	The UN body responsible for co-ordinating sustainability efforts. Conducts a range of initiatives, including environmental monitoring and assessment, information and research, and co-ordination of international policy development (eg climate change, ozone depletion, biodiversity). It has a range of publications relevant to business and others, eg 'Cleaner production', 'Energy' and 'Persistent organic chemicals'	**www.unep.org** UNEP Division of Technology, Industry and Economics: t +33 1 4437 1450 (France)
United Nations Framework Convention on Climate Change (UNFCCC)	The international treaty under which action is being formulated to reduce global warming and to cope with whatever temperature increases there are. It is supported by the UNFCCC secretariat. Under this treaty is the Kyoto Protocol, which set targets and mechanisms to combat climate change. The UNFCCC website provides a wealth of information on the treaty, the Kyoto Protocol and supporting initiatives.	**http://unfccc.int** Secretariat: t +49 228 815 1000 (Germany)
World Business Council for Sustainable Development (WBCSD)	A global association of some 200 companies that deals exclusively with business and sustainable development. It has a range of publications and case studies to help business understand the facts and trends concerning their areas of operation and their role, recasting the issues in a business light and helping to move towards action. Project areas include: water, energy efficiency, forest products, cement, and mobility.	**www.wbcsd.org** t +41 22 839 3100 (Switzerland)

Organisation	Description	Contact details
Worldwatch Institute	An independent research organisation that provides accessible, fact-based analysis of critical global issues. Worldwatch focuses on the 21st-century challenges of climate change, resource degradation, population growth and poverty by developing and disseminating solid data and innovative strategies for achieving a sustainable society. It has a wide range of publications, including 'Vital signs', which maps out key global trends.	www.worldwatch.org t +1 877 539 9946/ +1 202 452 1999 (USA)
WRAP	A UK-based organisation that helps businesses, local authorities, individuals and others reap the benefits of reducing waste, develop sustainable products and use resources in an efficient way. In 2010, Envirowise was incorporated into WRAP.	www.wrap.org.uk t +44 (0)1295 819900 Helpline: t +44 (0)808 100 2040

Selected publications

In addition to published standards such as ISO 14001, ISO 14004 and others listed in Appendix 3, the following publications may be particularly useful for those with environmental management responsibilities. Note that many of these publications are priced. Also, circumstances might change so that previously free publications become priced, publications go out of print, or new editions are published.

Title	Topic	Reference	Available from
Dictionary of environmental science and technology (4th edition) by Andrew Porteous (Open University, 2008)	A comprehensive explanation of environmental science, environmental management, environmental technology and related terms	ISBN 978 0 470 06195 4	General bookstores (published by Wiley http://eu.wiley.com) t +44 (0)1243 843294
The ENDS Report	Journal of environmental policy and legislation, including coverage of key issues, company news, UK and international developments in policy, legislation and best practice		Environmental Data Services www.endsreport.com t +44 (0)20 8267 8100 post@ends.co.uk
Environmental compliance manual	Practical advice and information on environmental legislation and regulations in the UK. Regularly updated in loose-leaf format		Croner Publications www.croner.co.uk t +44 (0)20 8247 1175

Title	Topic	Reference	Available from
The Environmentalist	A leading UK environmental publication (20 issues per year). It is sent free of charge to all IEMA members, but is also available on subscription. It contains a wide range of up-to-date information, best practice, policy changes and news on environmental issues		Institute of Environmental Management and Assessment www.iema.net/ shop
Factor four: doubling wealth – halving resource use by Ernst U von Weizsäcker (1998)	Outlines how it is possible to achieve a quadrupling of resource productivity	ISBN 978 1 853 83406 6	Earthscan www.earthscan. co.uk t +44 (0)20 7841 1930 earthinfo@ earthscan.co.uk
Guidance on how to measure and report your greenhouse gas emissions	Detailed guidance to UK businesses on measuring and reporting greenhouse gas emissions, including scoping and emission factors	PB13309 September 2009	Defra ww2.defra.gov.uk t +44 (0)20 7238 6000 www.defra.gov. uk/environment/ business/ reporting/pdf/ ghg-guidance.pdf
Green futures	Regular magazine highlighting developments in policy and best practice in environmental management and sustainability for a wide readership		Forum for the future www.forumfor thefuture.org/ greenfutures t +44 (0)20 7324 3660 post@green futures.org.uk t +44 (0)1223 564334

Title	Topic	Reference	Available from
Making a difference	A good practice guide to health, safety and environmental management, corporate responsibility and sustainable development		IOSH www.iosh.co.uk/ guidance t +44 (0)116 257 3100 www.iosh.co.uk
Practitioner	A series of best practice guides – each covering a particular environmental topic in detail, eg CSR or climate change. Normally free of charge to IEMA members, but is also available to non-members		Institute of Environmental Management and Assessment www.iema.net/ shop
State of the world 2010 – transforming cultures: from consumerism to sustainability	An authoritative assessment of global issues ranging from population, energy, and agriculture to materials use, health, and trade policy. Topics are covered from a strategic perspective, with an emphasis on innovation and problem-solving	ISBN 978 0 393 33726 6	Worldwatch Institute www.worldwatch. org t +1 877 539 9946 wwpub@ worldwatch.org
Vital signs 2010	The publication documents 24 trends that are shaping humanity's future and includes concise analyses and clear graphs	ISBN 978 1 878 07194 1	Worldwatch Institute www.worldwatch. org t +1 877 539 9946 wwpub@ worldwatch.org

Title	Topic	Reference	Available from
Waste minimisation for managers	The guide provides a self-help approach for managers to influence others. It contains suggestions for group exercises, tips to help develop a waste minimisation plan and support materials to help introduce waste minimisation into an organisation	GG367	Envirowise/WRAP http://envirowise. wrap.org.uk t +44 (0)800 585 794

Index

residual risk 62, 128
resource
  depletion 25, 32, 49, 89, 152
  efficiency 105, 179, 193, 232,
    234, 249
  productivity 13, 25, 193, 232,
    246, 250
reuse 32, 83, 85, 101, 106, 114,
    118, 121, 156, 158, 173,
    188–190, 196, 199, 205, 214,
    217, 246, 276, 279, 283
  and recovery 106, 114, 121, 158,
    199, 246, 283
reviews 64–65, 79, 81, 84, 97,
    182, 211, 214, 216, 233, 262
  management review 64–66,
    76–79, 82, 96–97, 106, 123,
    125, 215, 219, 221, 226, 233,
    243, 261
risk assessment 58, 61–63,
    127–128, 141, 180
risk management 7, 128–129, 159,
    167, 273

Sankey diagram 176, 187, 199
scattergram 197–198
scenario-building 234, 243–245
  -planning 244, 276, 280
scoring matrix 60–61
significant environmental aspects
    12, 43, 48, 54–56, 70, 84, 97,
    102, 104, 110, 114–115, 185,
    210, 233, 257–258, 261–262
site plans 71–74, 188
SMART 112–113, 117, 250, 261,
    281
source–pathway–receptor
    relationship 25
staff 34, 68–69, 77, 106–107,
    130–131, 145, 149, 181
stakeholders 7–8, 12–13, 34–37,
    39, 41, 45, 50, 56, 58–62, 65, 76,
    79, 87, 91, 101, 104–108, 115,
    123, 125, 137, 139, 143,
    151–153, 156, 158–159, 166,
    169, 184, 187, 204, 218, 226,
    235, 240, 243, 247, 250–251,
    253–256, 258–263, 265, 267,
    269, 280–281
SWOT analysis 234, 241–243,
    276, 281
suppliers 11, 35, 51–52, 73, 76,
    81, 89, 91, 106, 108–109, 118,
    123, 125, 132, 136, 147, 149,
    152–153, 194, 196, 203,
    204–215, 220, 224, 228, 240,
    246–247, 250, 253–254, 281
  assessment 81, 208–210
sustainability 8, 13, 22–23, 27, 79,
    83, 166, 211, 219, 229–230,
    232–236, 243, 245–247,
    249–251, 263, 274, 276
sustainable development 7, 104,
    229–230, 232–234, 243, 249,
    253, 269

targets 8, 12, 39, 42, 65, 72,
    74–77, 81, 96–97, 102–104, 106,
    109–121, 124–125, 128, 136,
    140, 145, 147–148, 150–152,
    166, 168, 191, 197, 201,
    206–207, 209–210, 214–215,
    218, 221, 231, 238–239, 244,
    250, 258, 270, 272, 275–276,
    281
tiered response 129–131
tradeable permit 39–41, 219, 222,
    238–239, 282
training 73–74, 96, 108–109,
    118–119, 123, 125, 127,
    132–142, 151, 165, 176–177,
    181, 184, 190–192, 198, 201,
    210–211, 220, 247, 278

unplanned events 12, 159, 164,
    169
urgency/importance matrix 116